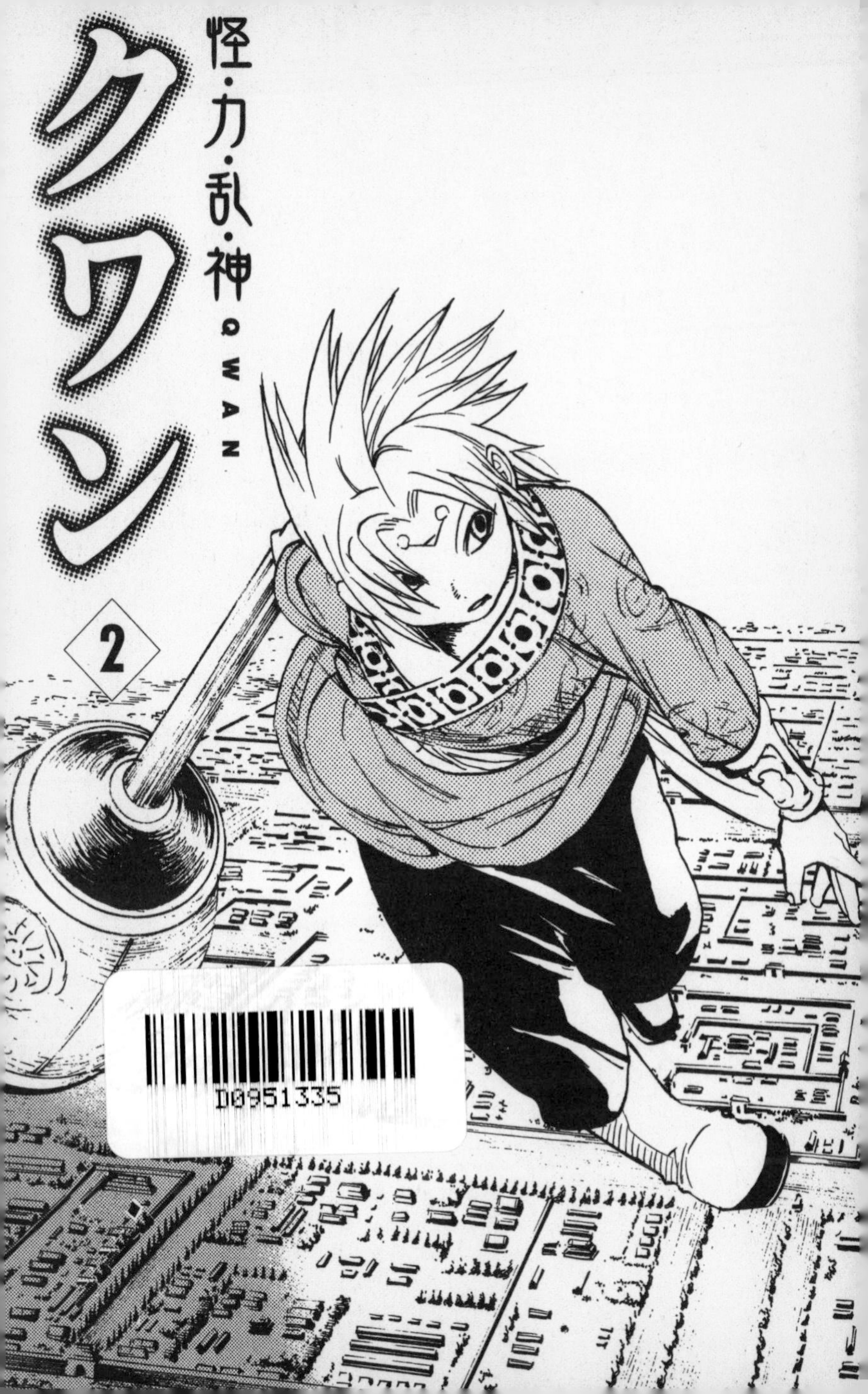
怪・力・乱・神
クワン
QWAN
2

Qwan Vol. 2
Created by Aki Shimizu

Translation - Mike Kiefl
English Adaptation - David Mirsky
Retouch and Lettering - Eric Pineda
Production Artist - James Dashiell
Cover Design - Gary Shum

Editor - Carol Fox
Digital Imaging Manager - Chris Buford
Pre-Press Manager - Antonio DePietro
Production Managers - Jennifer Miller and Mutsumi Miyazaki
Art Director - Matt Alford
Managing Editor - Jill Freshney
VP of Production - Ron Klamert
Editor-in-Chief - Mike Kiley
President and C.O.O. - John Parker
Publisher and C.E.O. - Stuart Levy

A 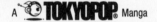 Manga

TOKYOPOP Inc.
5900 Wilshire Blvd. Suite 2000
Los Angeles, CA 90036

E-mail: info@TOKYOPOP.com
Come visit us online at www.TOKYOPOP.com

ISBN: 1-59532-535-2

First TOKYOPOP printing: July 2005
10 9 8 7 6 5 4 3 2 1
Printed in Canada

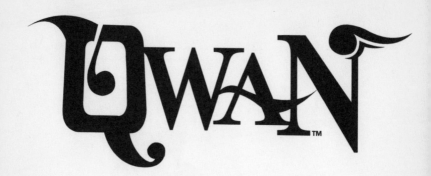

Volume 2

By
Aki Shimizu

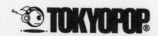

HAMBURG // LONDON // LOS ANGELES // TOKYO

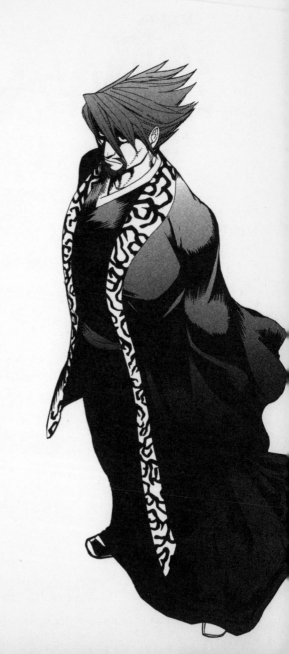

The Journey Thus Far...

Chikei is your average wandering ne'er-do-well... until he crosses paths with Qwan, a mysterious amnesiac kid who swallows demons whole and claims to be from heaven.

Never one to miss an opportunity to mooch off others, Chikei takes up with Qwan to earn a few bucks by ridding towns of evil spirits. In their travels they meet Daki, a young girl with the power to control insects. She has the scent of a demon all over her, but try as he might, Qwan cannot eat her. Then in the next town they meet Daki's father, a frightening man named Yuushi who also smells of demons, and Shaga, a mysterious prostitute who seems to know a little too much about Qwan.

After Chikei narrowly escapes an attack by Yuushi, Shaga tells Qwan to seek the Essential Arts of Peace-- a scroll that, according to Shaga, will reveal Qwan's true identity and purpose. It is said to be hidden deep within the walls of the Imperial Palace, so Qwan leaves Chikei in the brothel and sets off to find the Emperor's chief eunuch, Cao Jie--reputedly the only man who could get him past the guards.

As fate would have it, he runs into Aman, Cao Jie's grandson. Aman had just led Qwan to the chief eunuch...and Yuushi, who also seeks the scroll, is hot on his heels.

Table of Contents

Chapter The Sixth

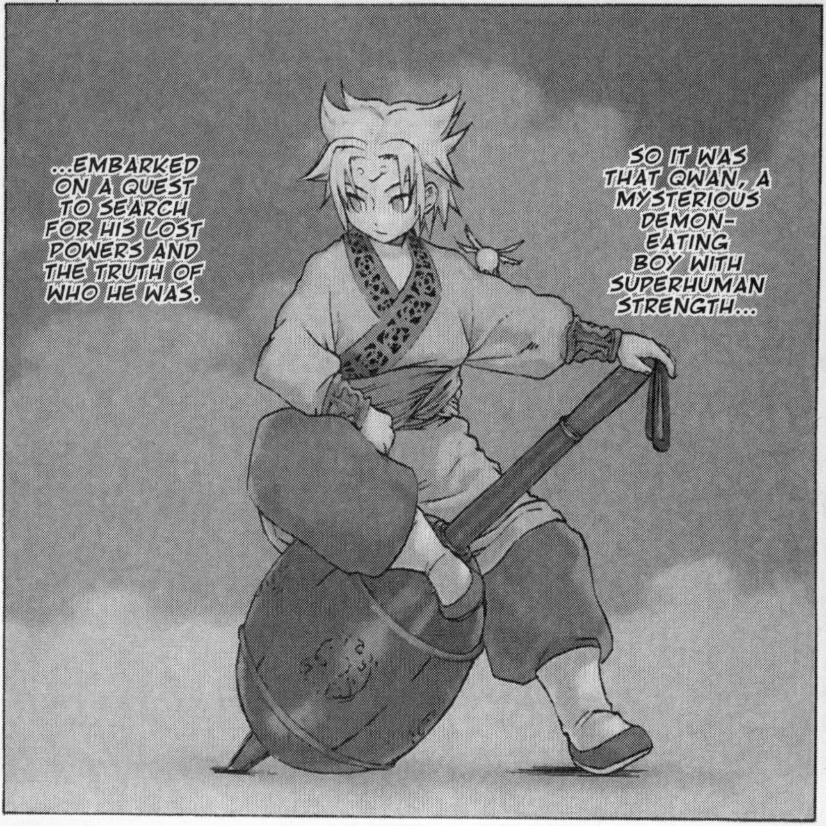
SO IT WAS THAT QWAN, A MYSTERIOUS DEMON-EATING BOY WITH SUPERHUMAN STRENGTH...
...EMBARKED ON A QUEST TO SEARCH FOR HIS LOST POWERS AND THE TRUTH OF WHO HE WAS.

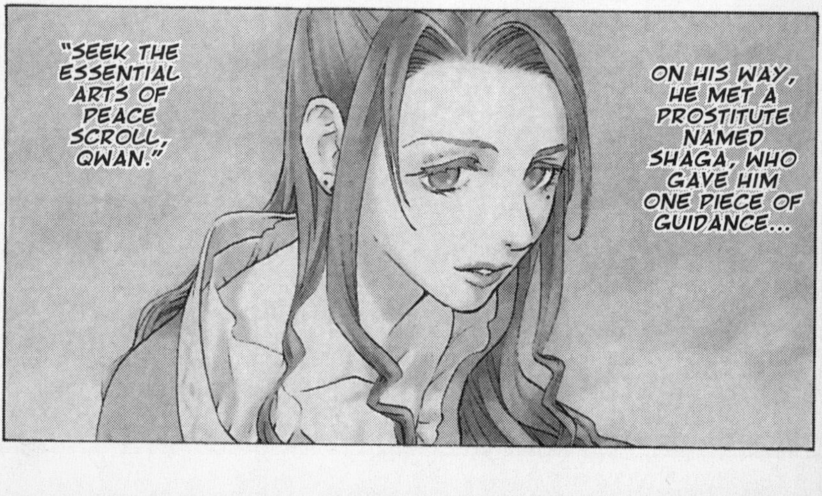
ON HIS WAY, HE MET A PROSTITUTE NAMED SHAGA, WHO GAVE HIM ONE PIECE OF GUIDANCE...
"SEEK THE ESSENTIAL ARTS OF PEACE SCROLL, QWAN."

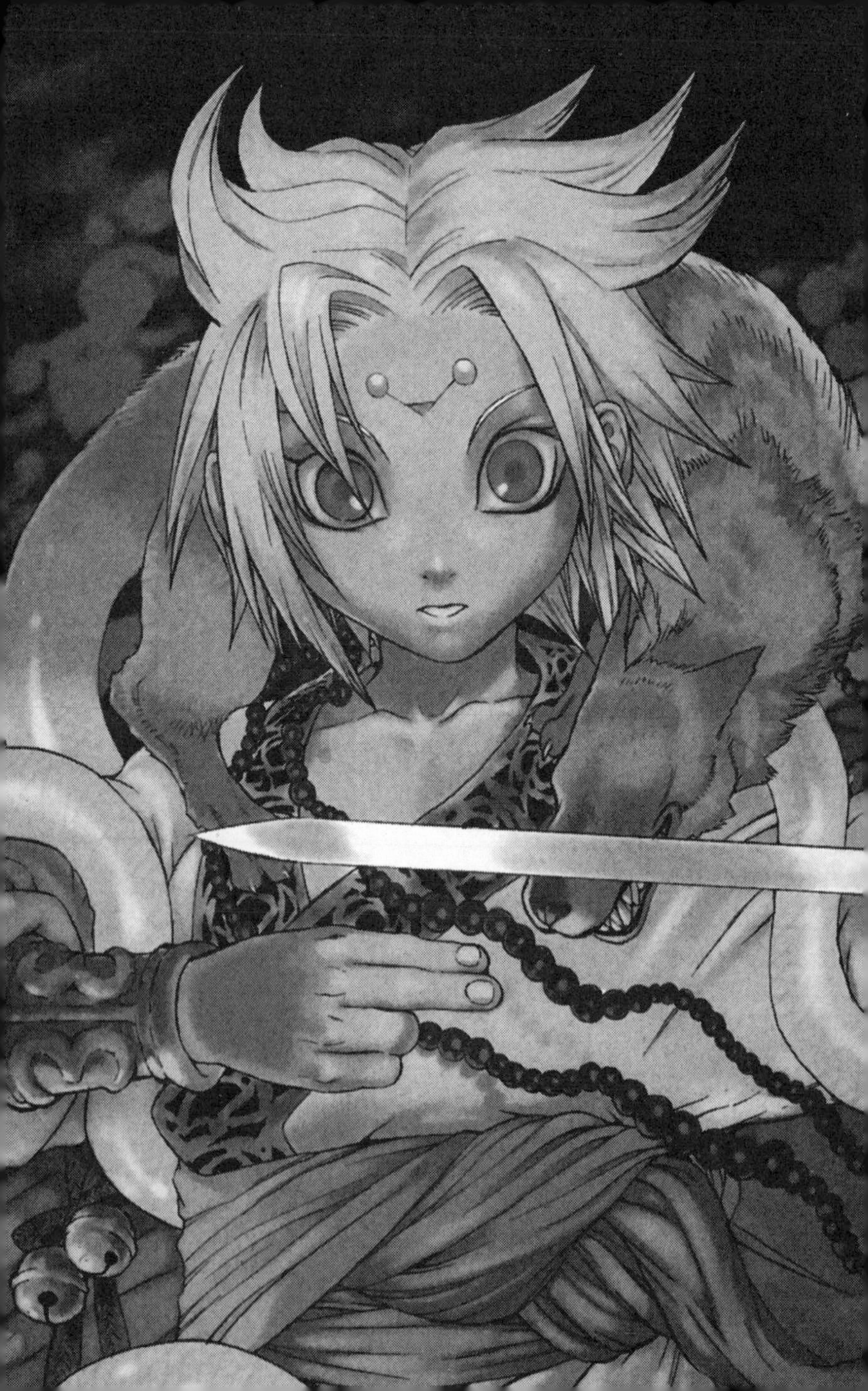

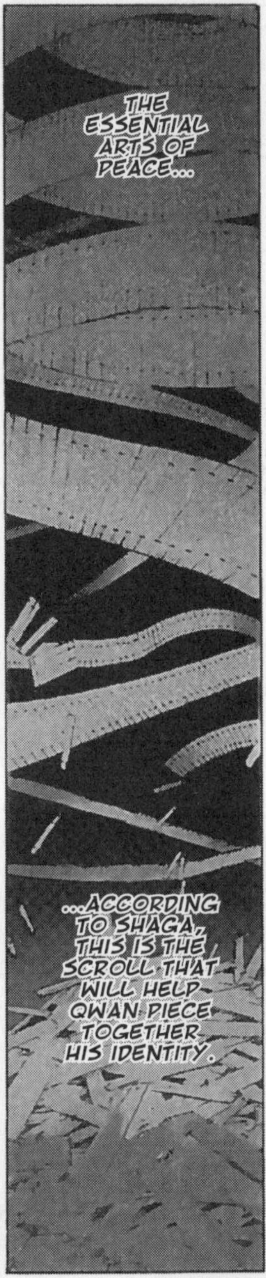
THE ESSENTIAL ARTS OF PEACE...
...ACCORDING TO SHAGA, THIS IS THE SCROLL THAT WILL HELP QWAN PIECE TOGETHER HIS IDENTITY.

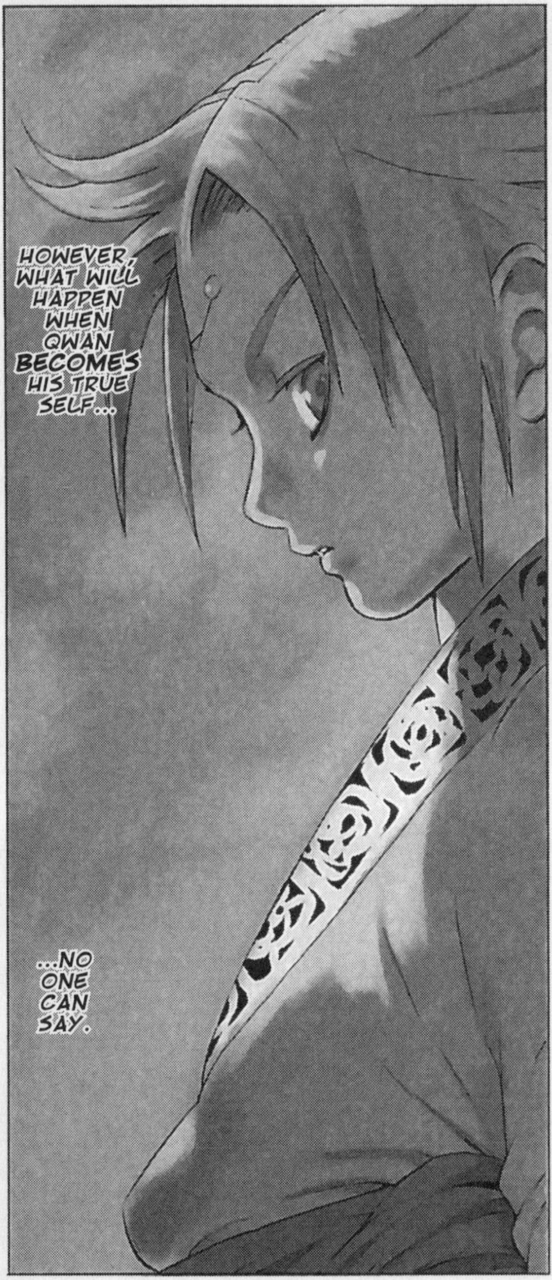
HOWEVER, WHAT WILL HAPPEN WHEN QWAN BECOMES HIS TRUE SELF...
...NO ONE CAN SAY.

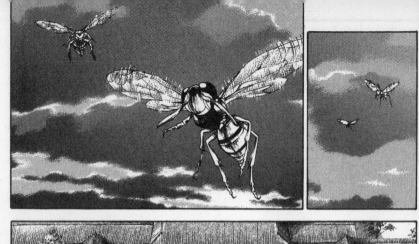

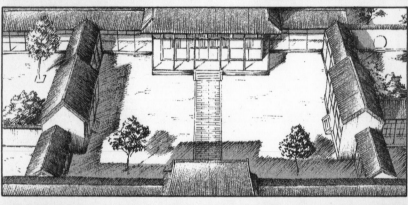

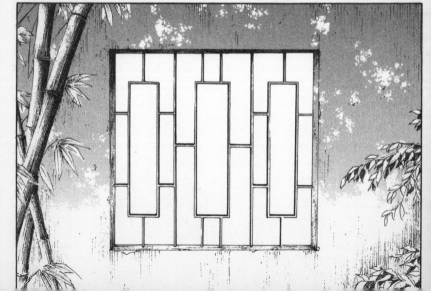

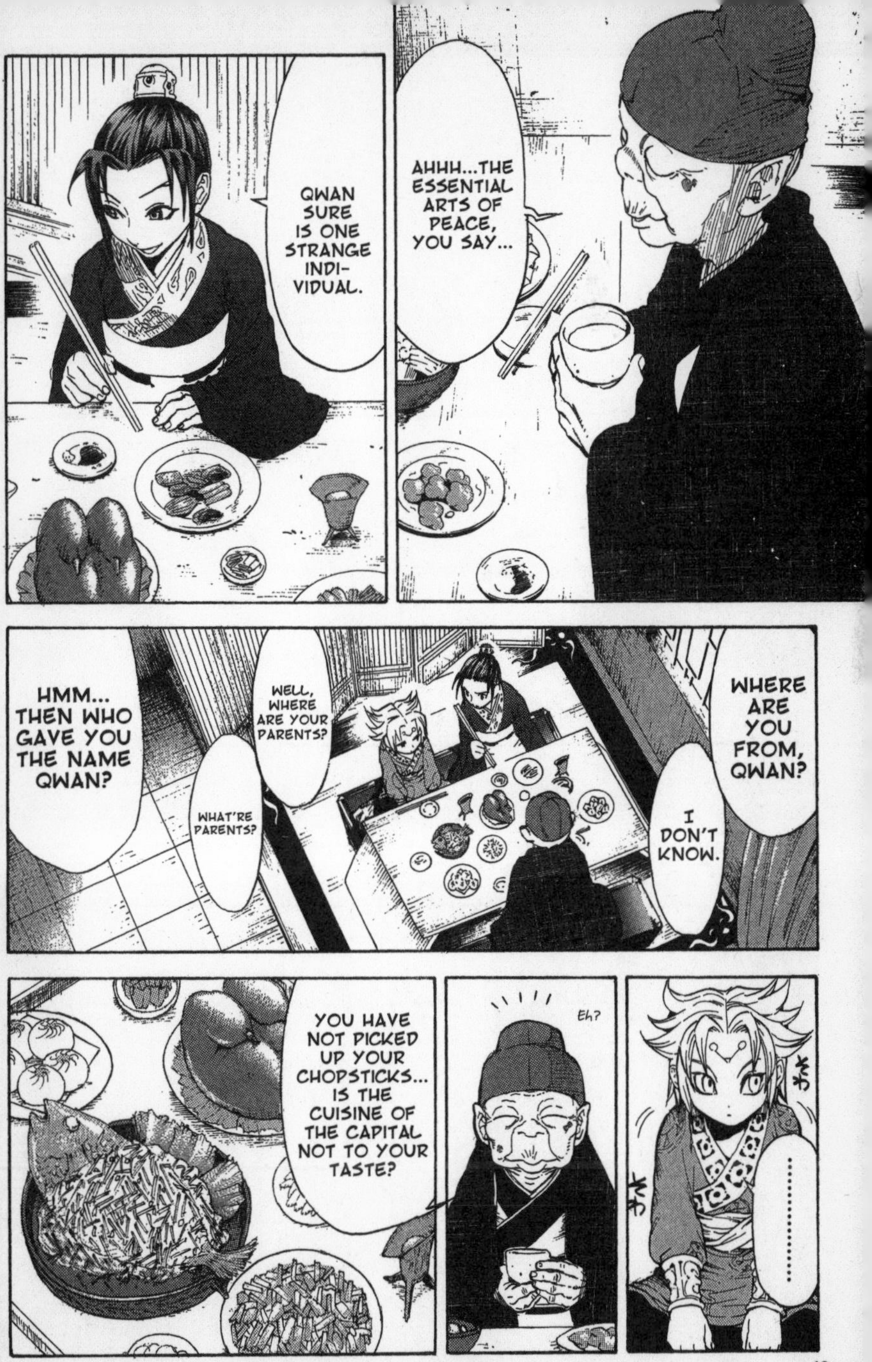
AHHH...THE ESSENTIAL ARTS OF PEACE, YOU SAY...
QWAN SURE IS ONE STRANGE INDI-VIDUAL.
WHERE ARE YOU FROM, QWAN?
I DON'T KNOW.
WELL, WHERE ARE YOUR PARENTS?
WHAT'RE PARENTS?
HMM... THEN WHO GAVE YOU THE NAME QWAN?
....
Eh?
YOU HAVE NOT PICKED UP YOUR CHOPSTICKS... IS THE CUISINE OF THE CAPITAL NOT TO YOUR TASTE?

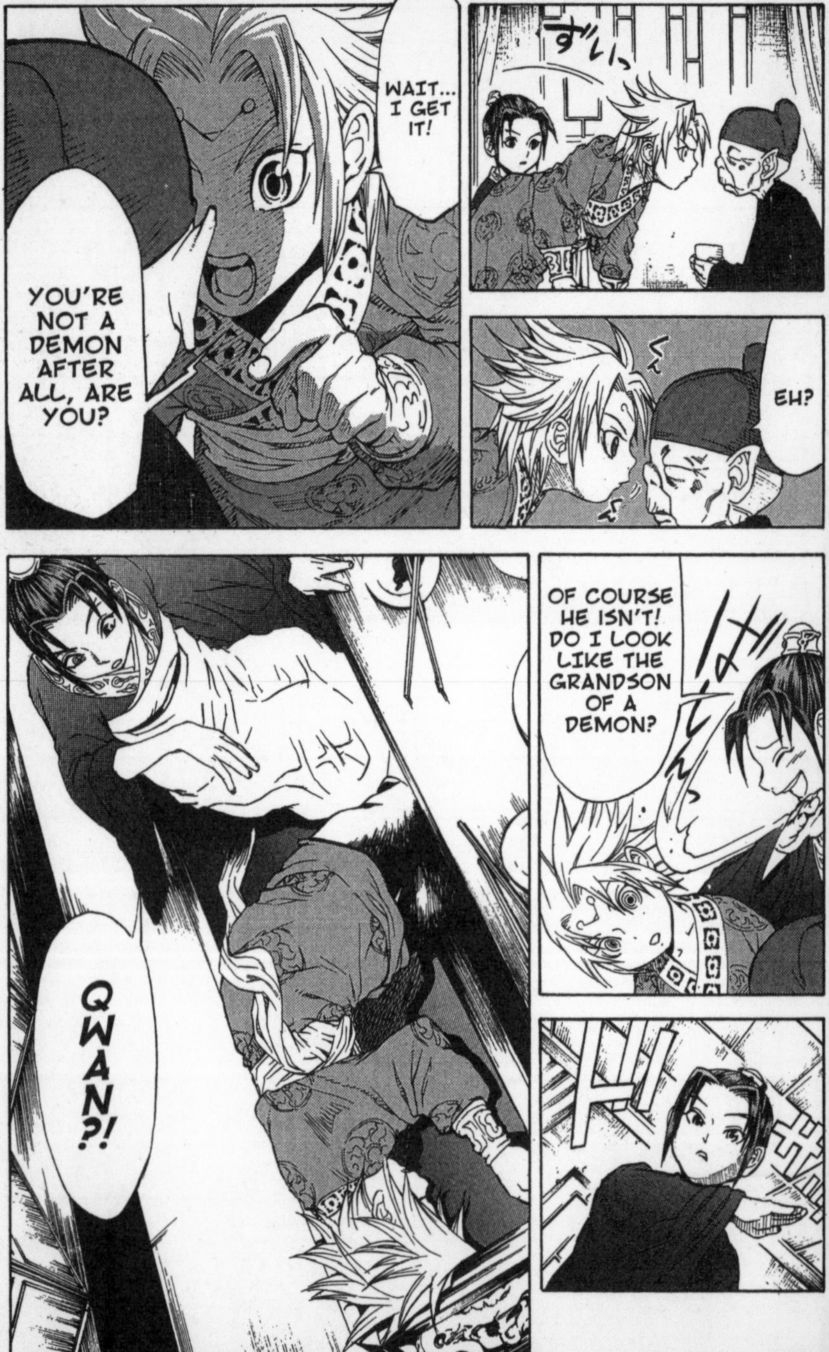
ずいっ
EH?
WAIT... I GET IT!
YOU'RE NOT A DEMON AFTER ALL, ARE YOU?
OF COURSE HE ISN'T! DO I LOOK LIKE THE GRANDSON OF A DEMON?
QWAN?!

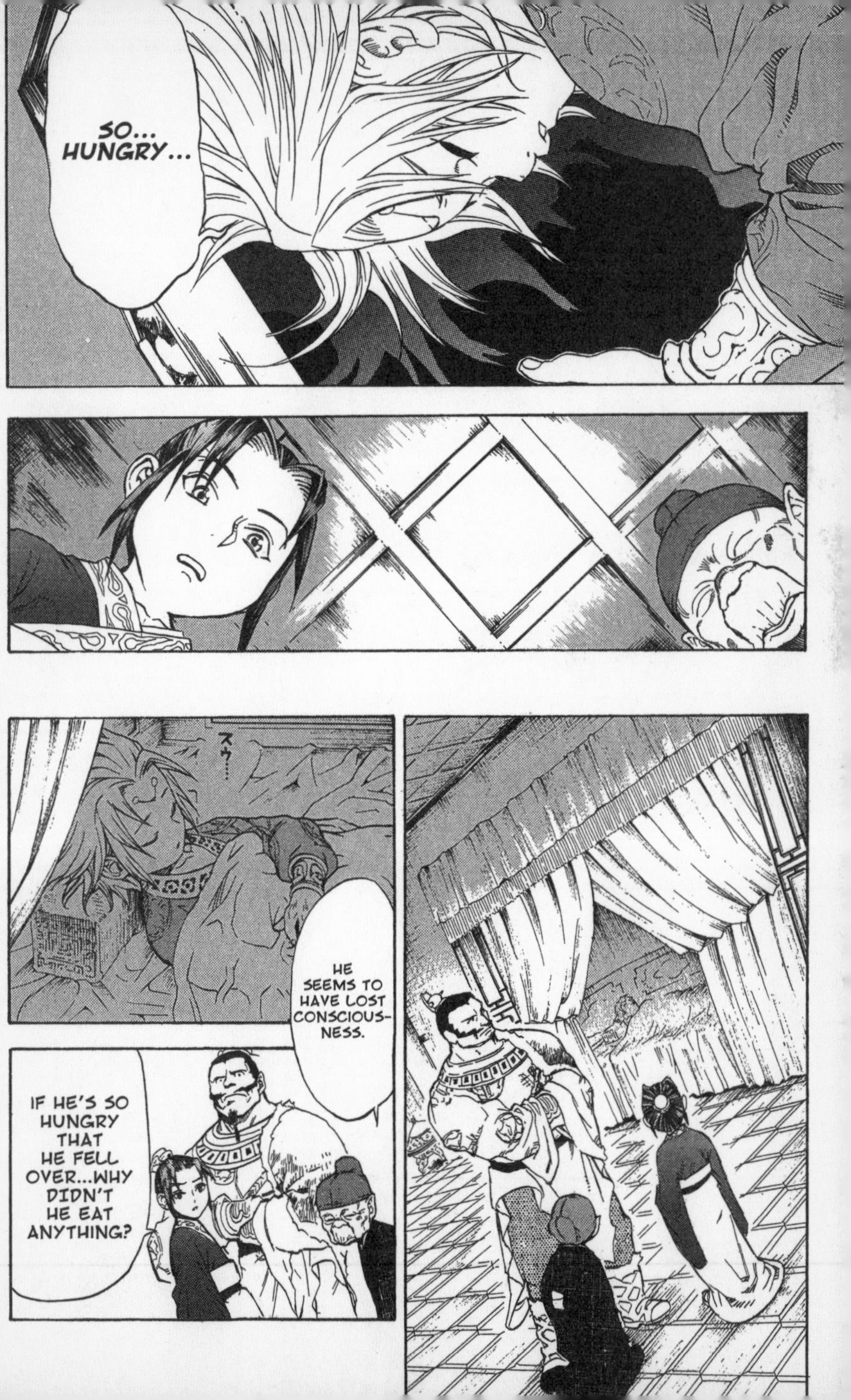
SO... HUNGRY...
スゥ…
HE SEEMS TO HAVE LOST CONSCIOUSNESS.
IF HE'S SO HUNGRY THAT HE FELL OVER...WHY DIDN'T HE EAT ANYTHING?

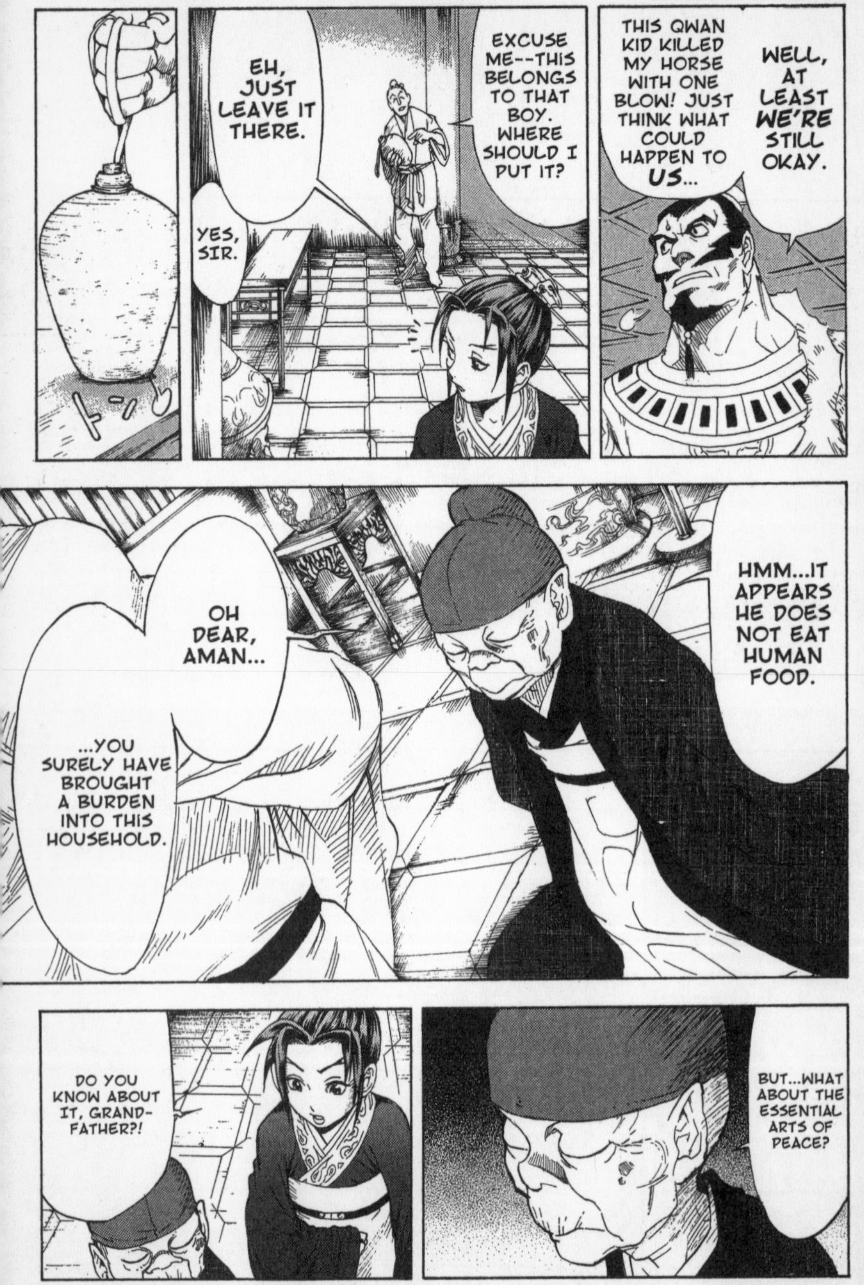
WELL, AT LEAST WE'RE STILL OKAY.
THIS QWAN KID KILLED MY HORSE WITH ONE BLOW! JUST THINK WHAT COULD HAPPEN TO US...
EXCUSE ME--THIS BELONGS TO THAT BOY. WHERE SHOULD I PUT IT?
EH, JUST LEAVE IT THERE.
YES, SIR.
HMM...IT APPEARS HE DOES NOT EAT HUMAN FOOD.
OH DEAR, AMAN...
...YOU SURELY HAVE BROUGHT A BURDEN INTO THIS HOUSEHOLD.
BUT...WHAT ABOUT THE ESSENTIAL ARTS OF PEACE?
DO YOU KNOW ABOUT IT, GRAND-FATHER?!

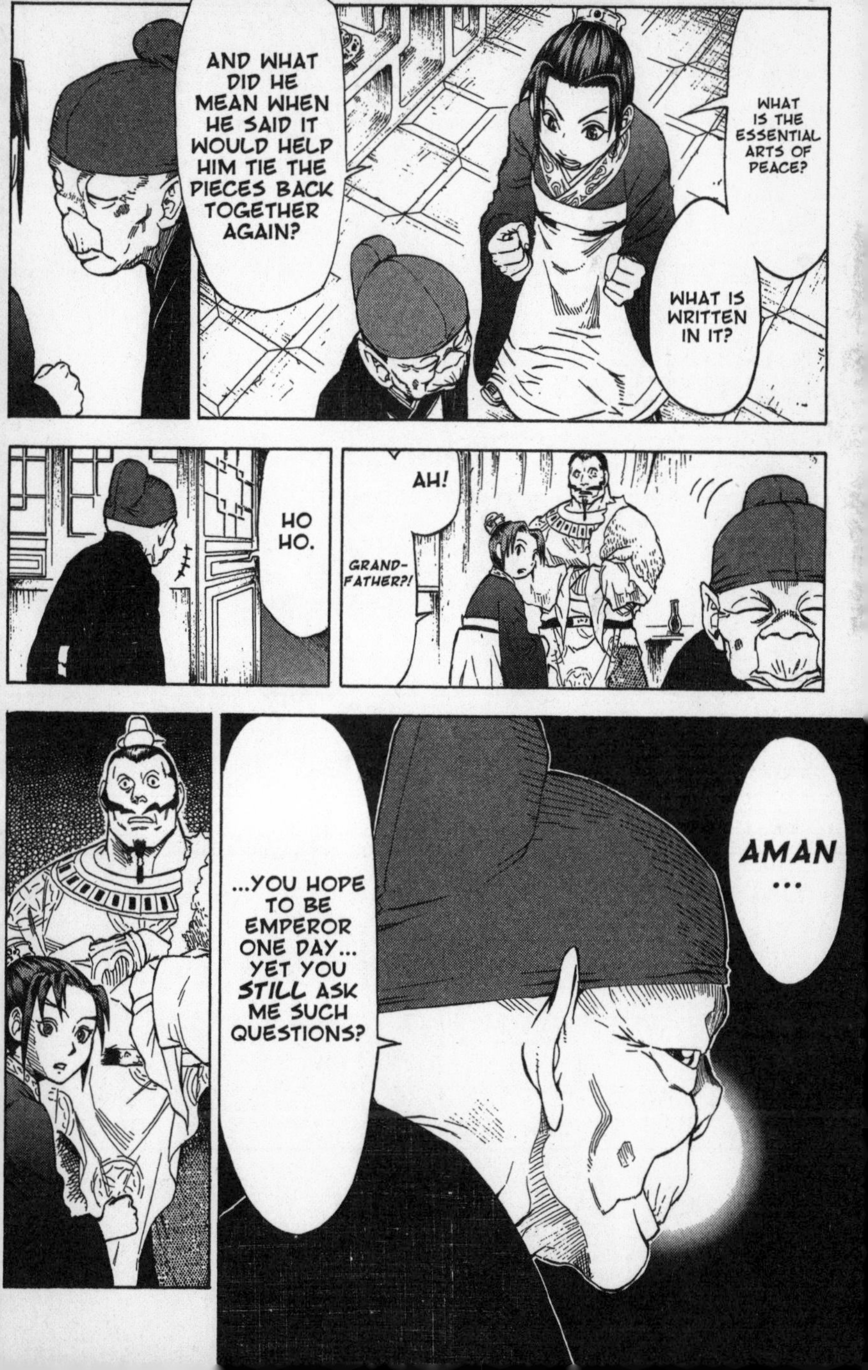
WHAT IS THE ESSENTIAL ARTS OF PEACE?
WHAT IS WRITTEN IN IT?
AND WHAT DID HE MEAN WHEN HE SAID IT WOULD HELP HIM TIE THE PIECES BACK TOGETHER AGAIN?
AH!
GRAND-FATHER?!
HO HO.
AMAN ...
...YOU HOPE TO BE EMPEROR ONE DAY... YET YOU STILL ASK ME SUCH QUESTIONS?

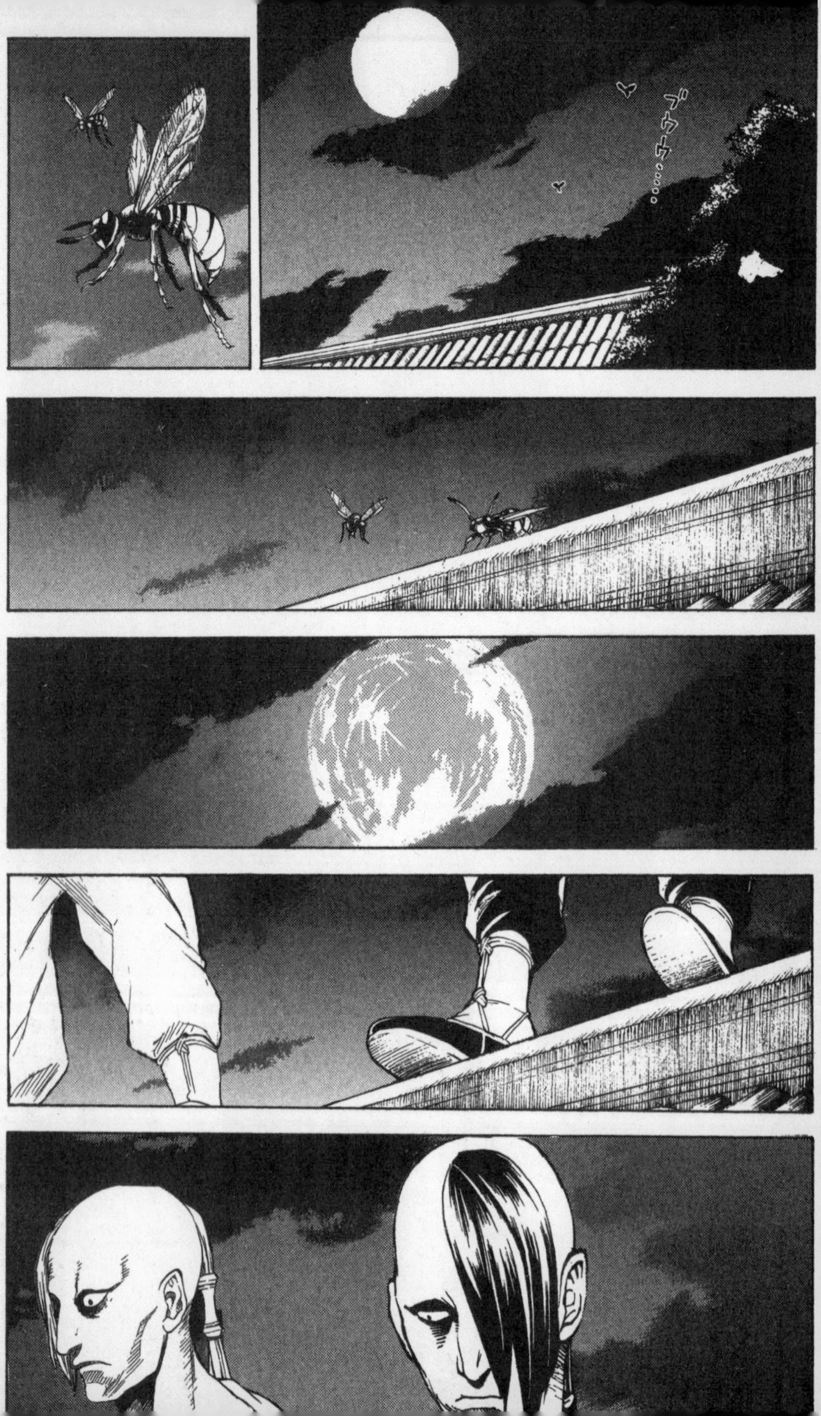
ブウウ。。。。。

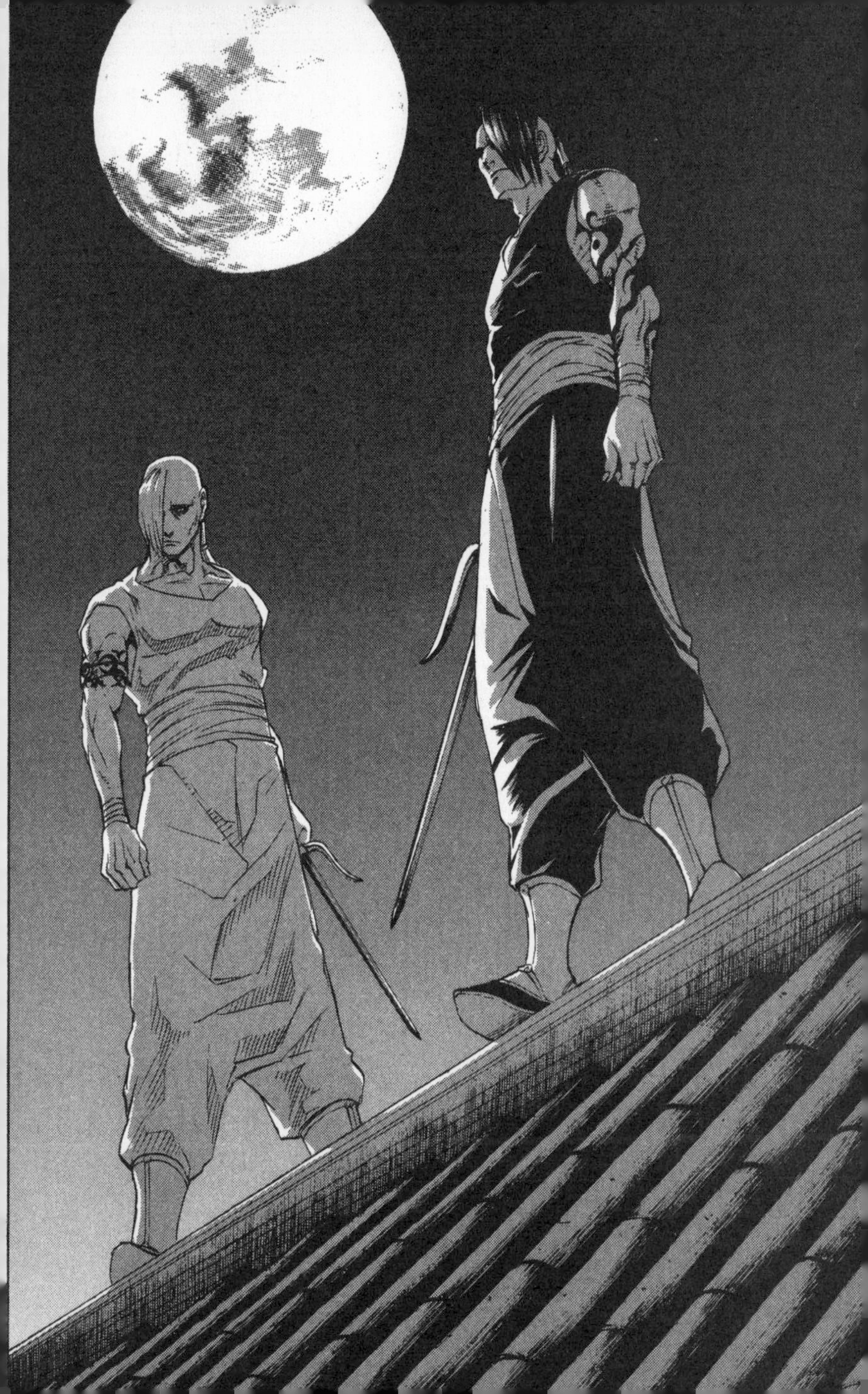

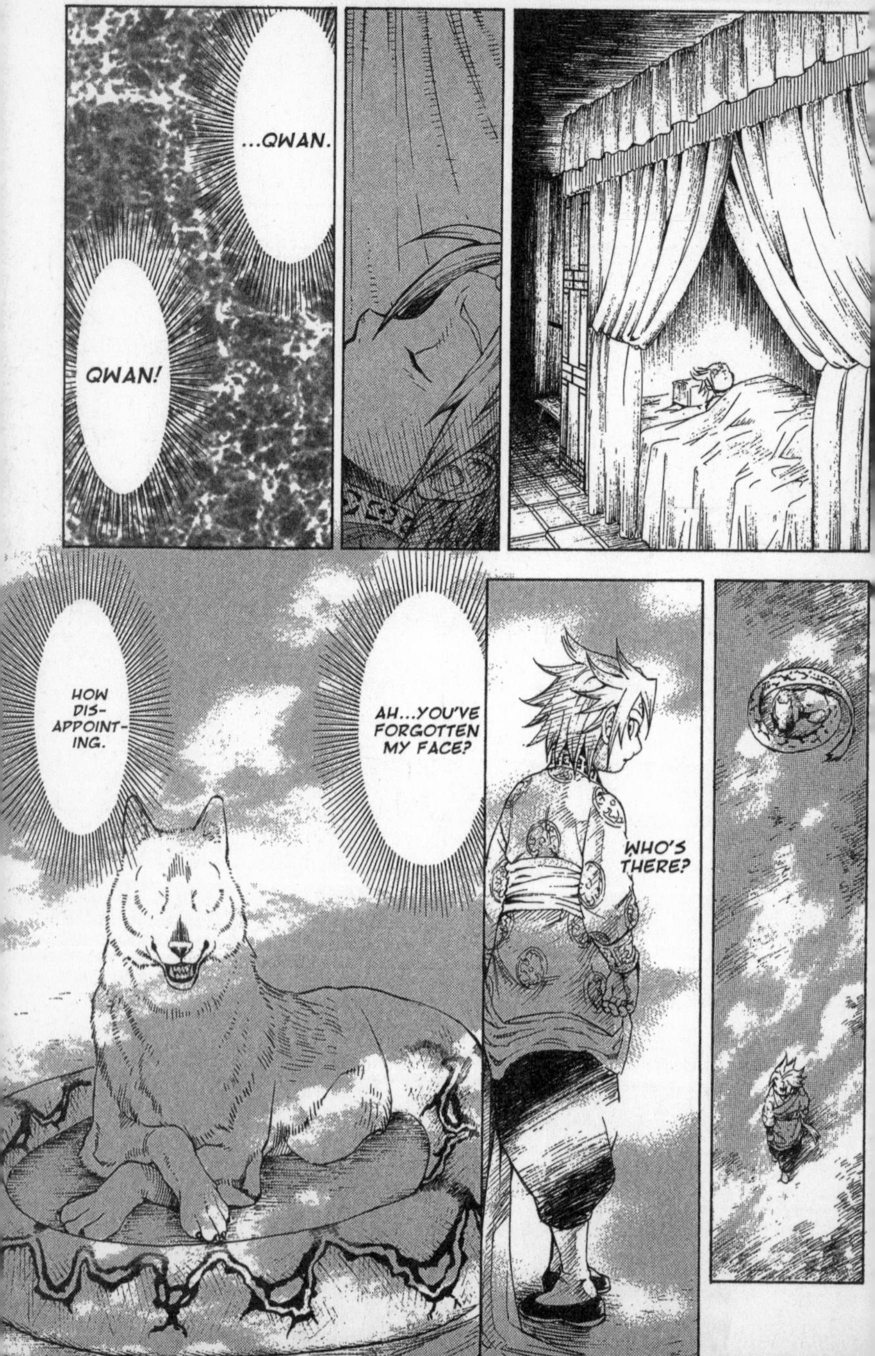
...QWAN.
QWAN!
WHO'S THERE?
AH...YOU'VE FORGOTTEN MY FACE?
HOW DISAPPOINTING.

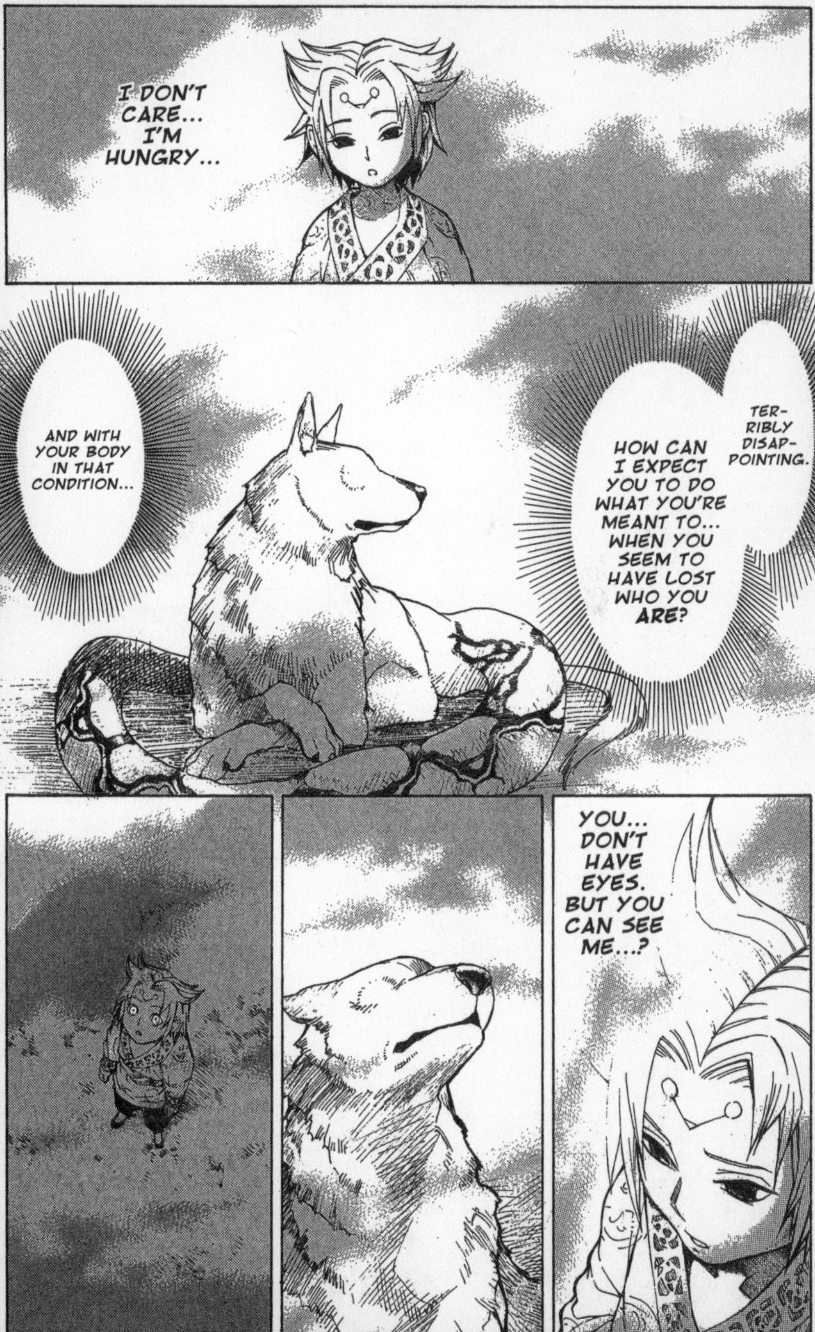
I DON'T CARE... I'M HUNGRY...
TER-RIBLY DISAP-POINTING.
HOW CAN I EXPECT YOU TO DO WHAT YOU'RE MEANT TO... WHEN YOU SEEM TO HAVE LOST WHO YOU ARE?
AND WITH YOUR BODY IN THAT CONDITION...
YOU... DON'T HAVE EYES. BUT YOU CAN SEE ME...?

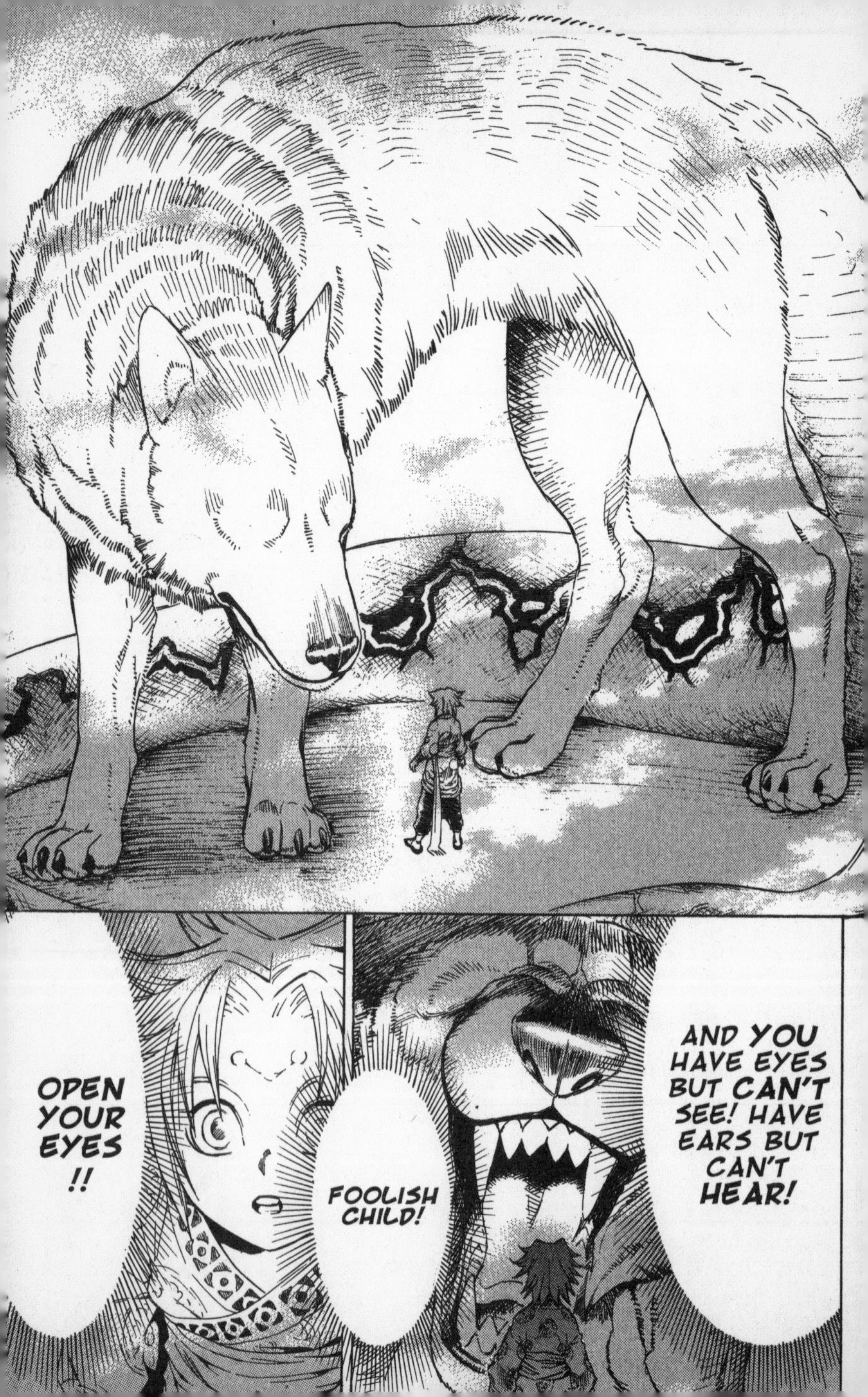
AND YOU HAVE EYES BUT CAN'T SEE! HAVE EARS BUT CAN'T HEAR!
FOOLISH CHILD!
OPEN YOUR EYES !!

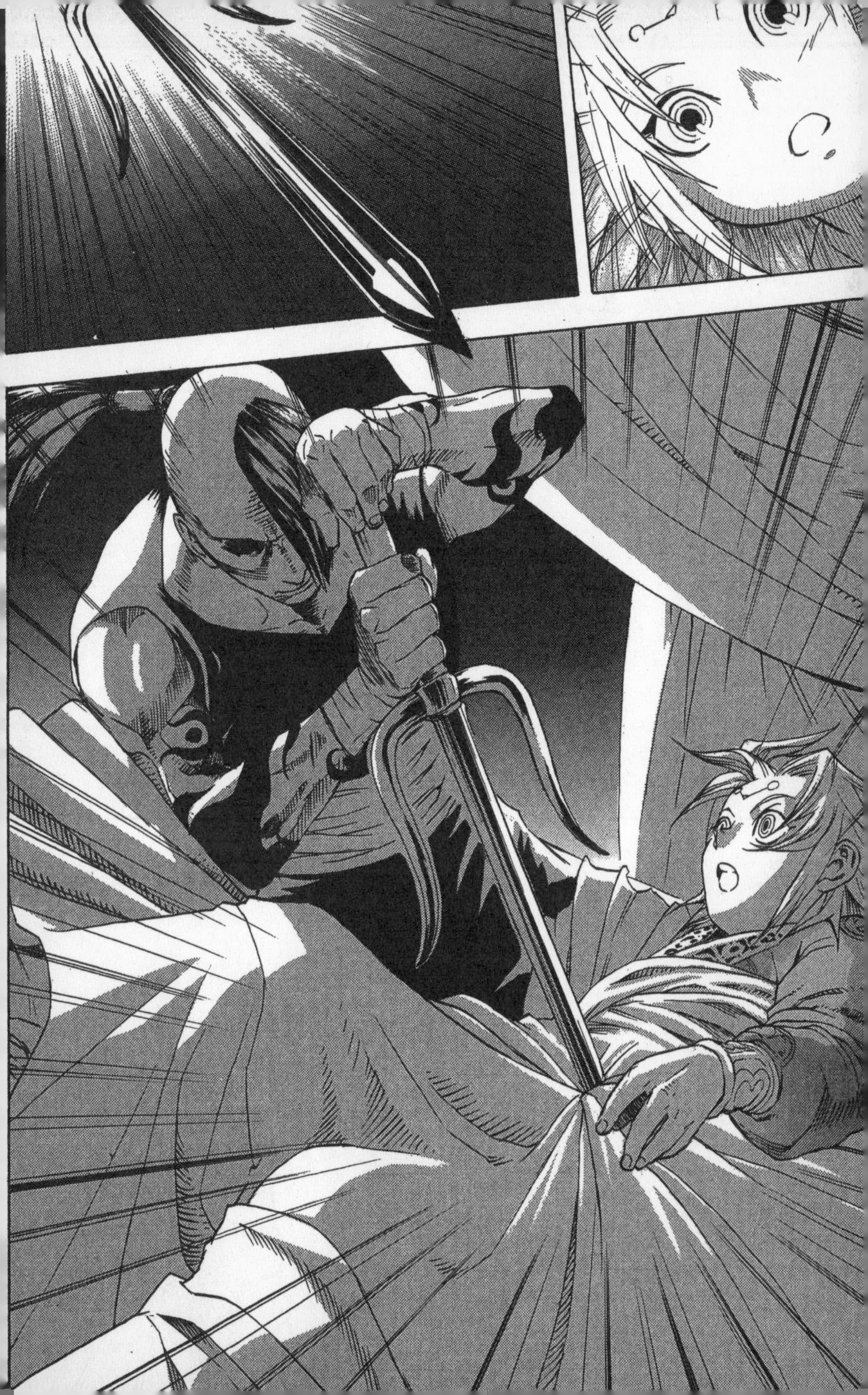

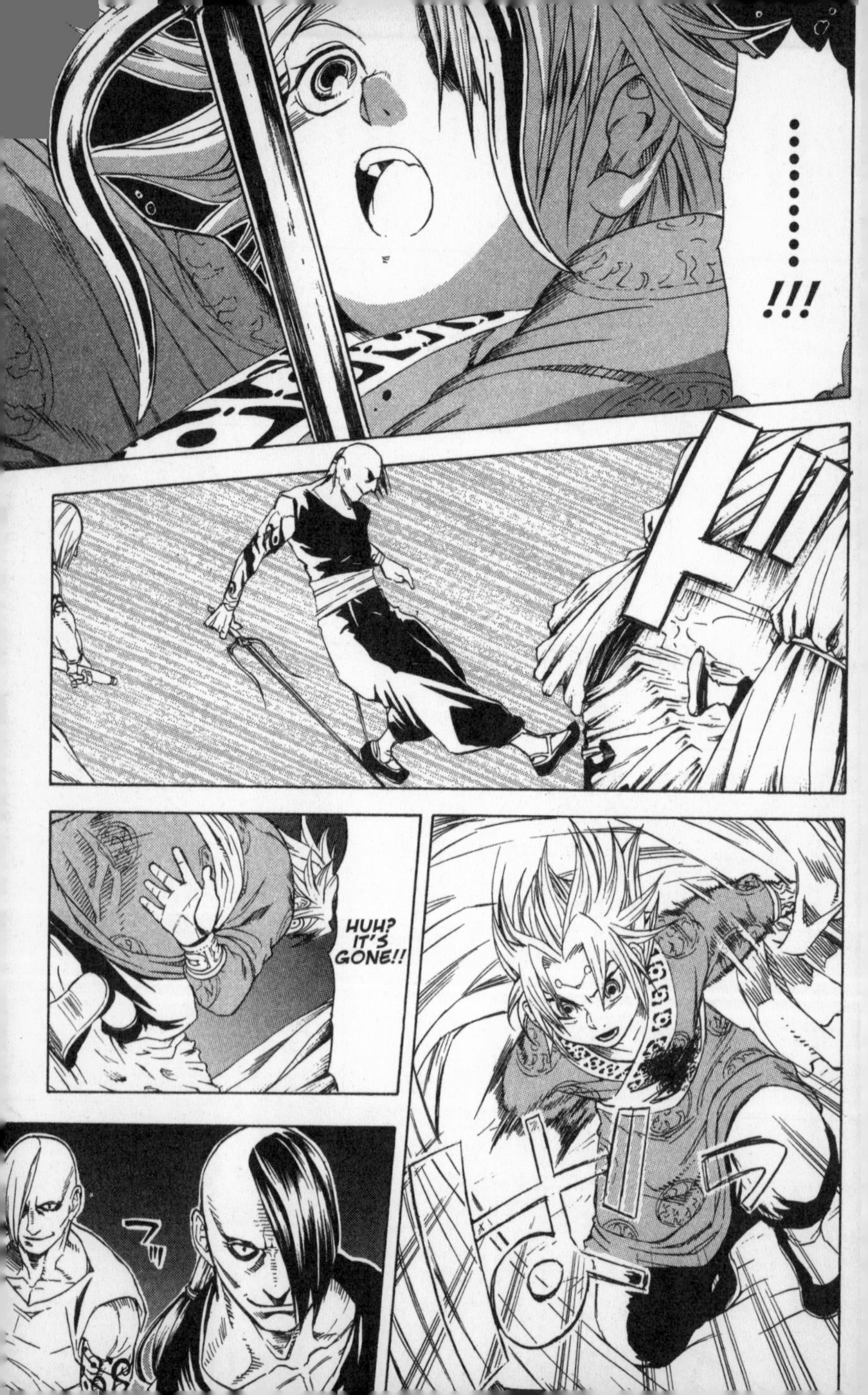
.........!!!
HUH? IT'S GONE!!

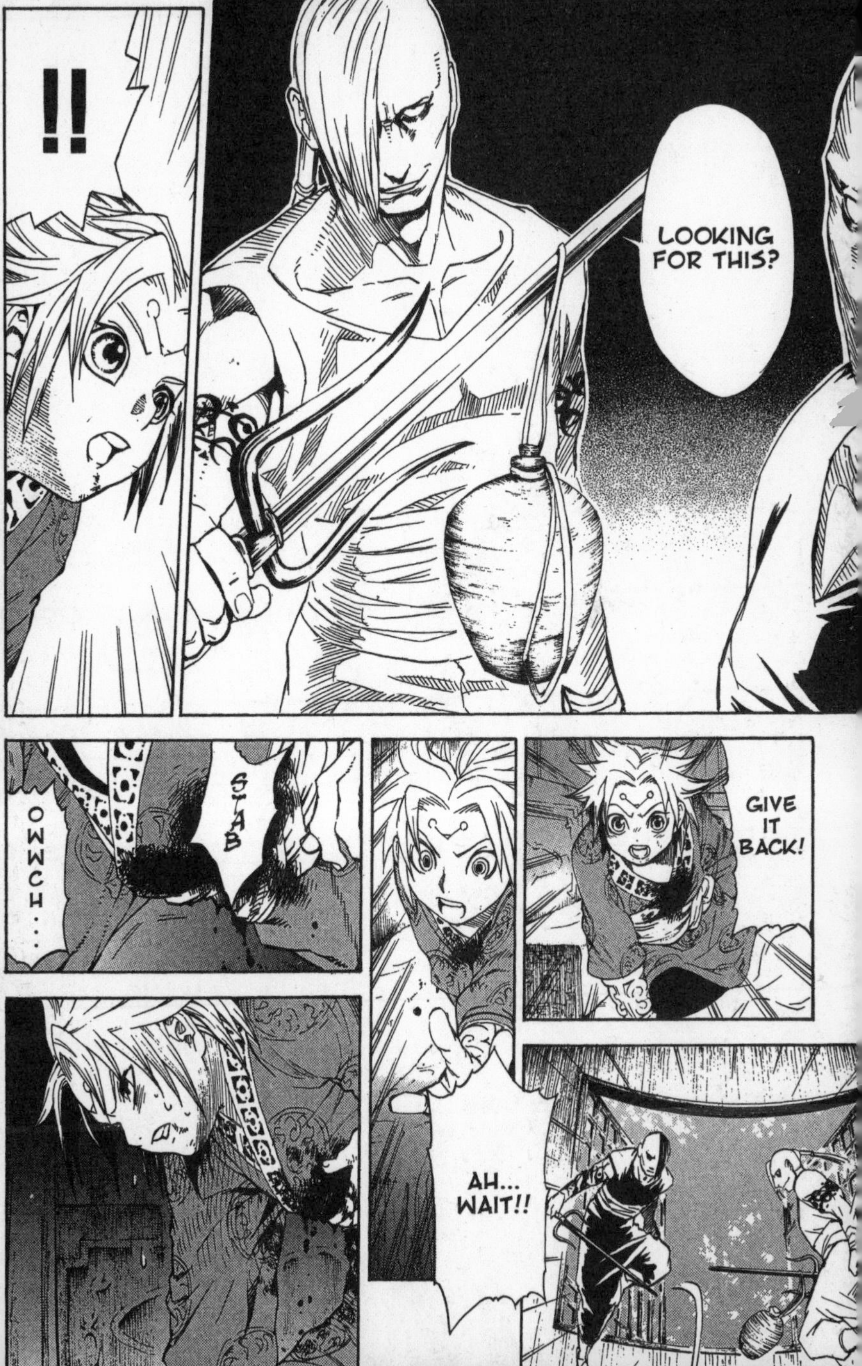
LOOKING FOR THIS?
!!
GIVE IT BACK!
AH... WAIT!!
STAB
OWWCH...

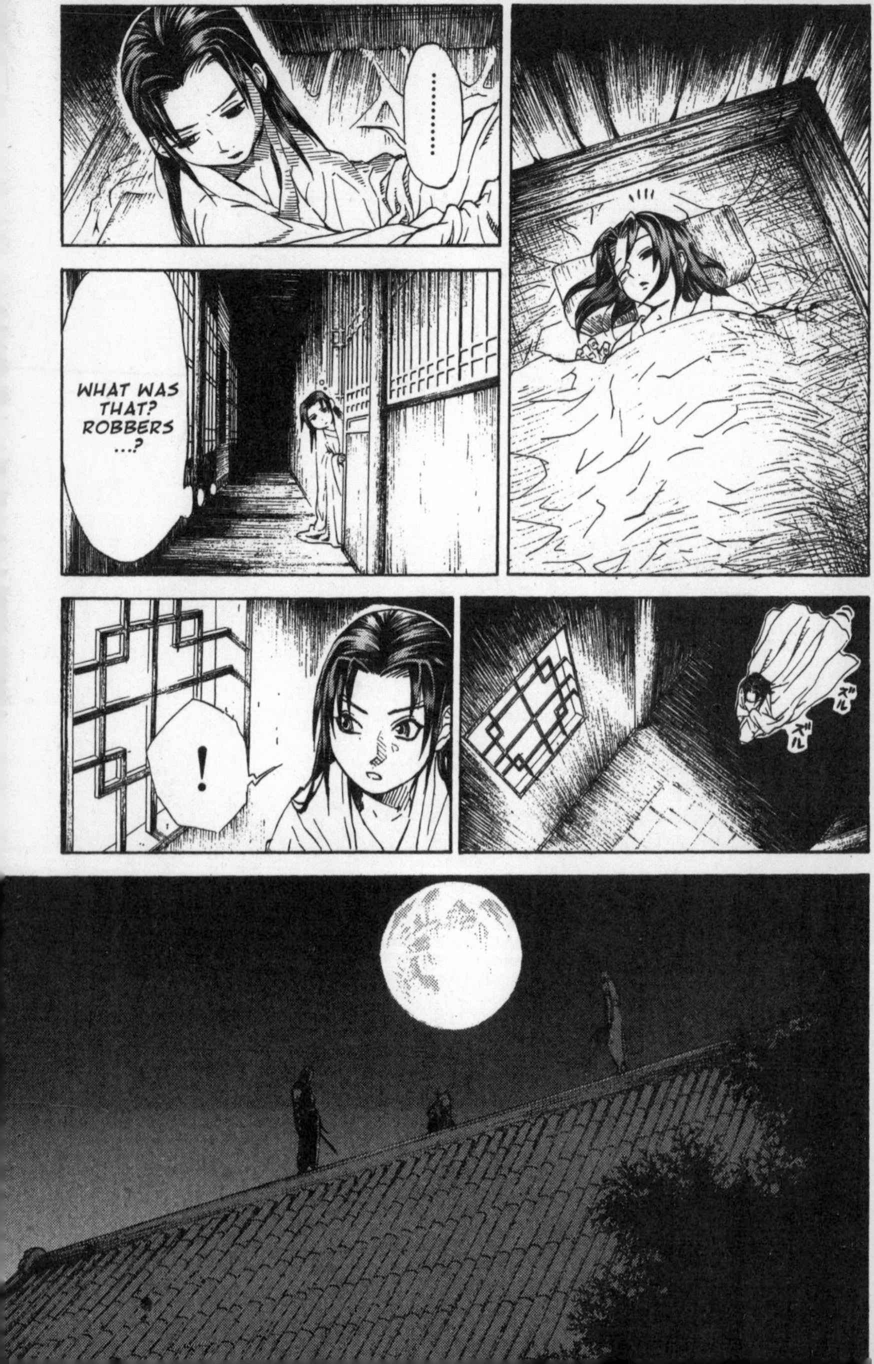

....
WHAT WAS THAT? ROBBERS ...?
ズル
ズル
!

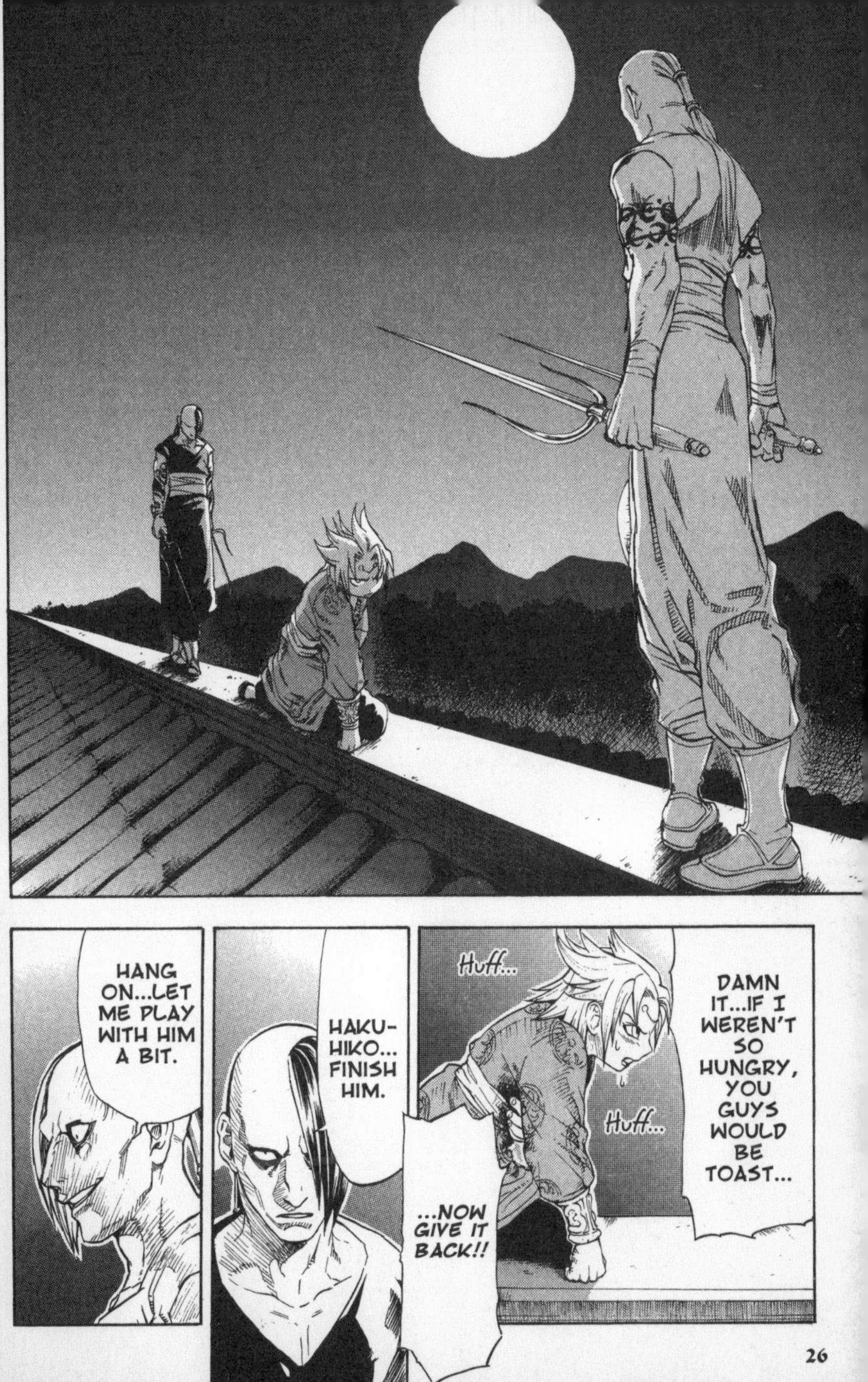
Huff...
DAMN IT...IF I WEREN'T SO HUNGRY, YOU GUYS WOULD BE TOAST...
Huff...
...NOW GIVE IT BACK!!
HAKU-HIKO... FINISH HIM.
HANG ON...LET ME PLAY WITH HIM A BIT.

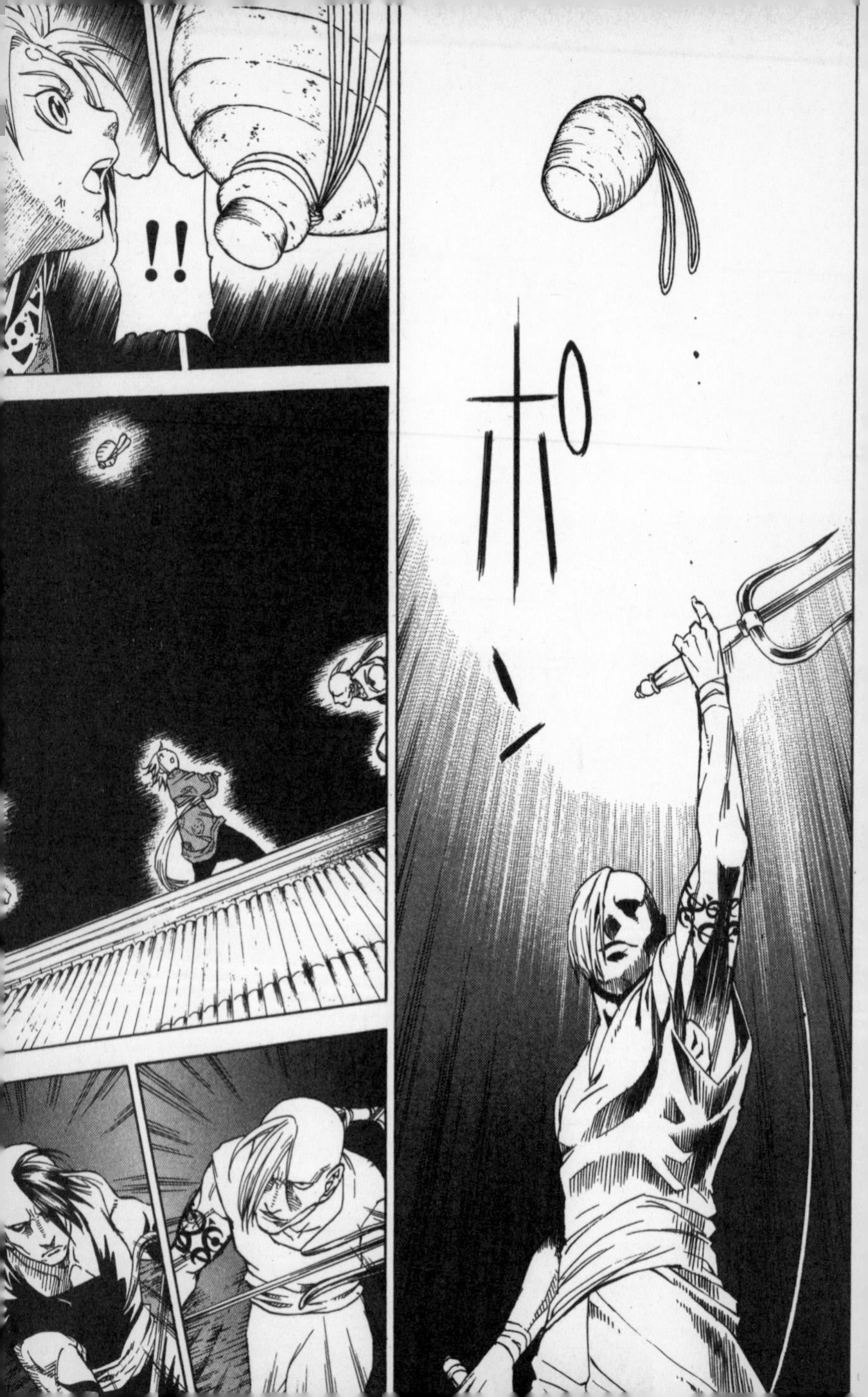
ポーン
!!

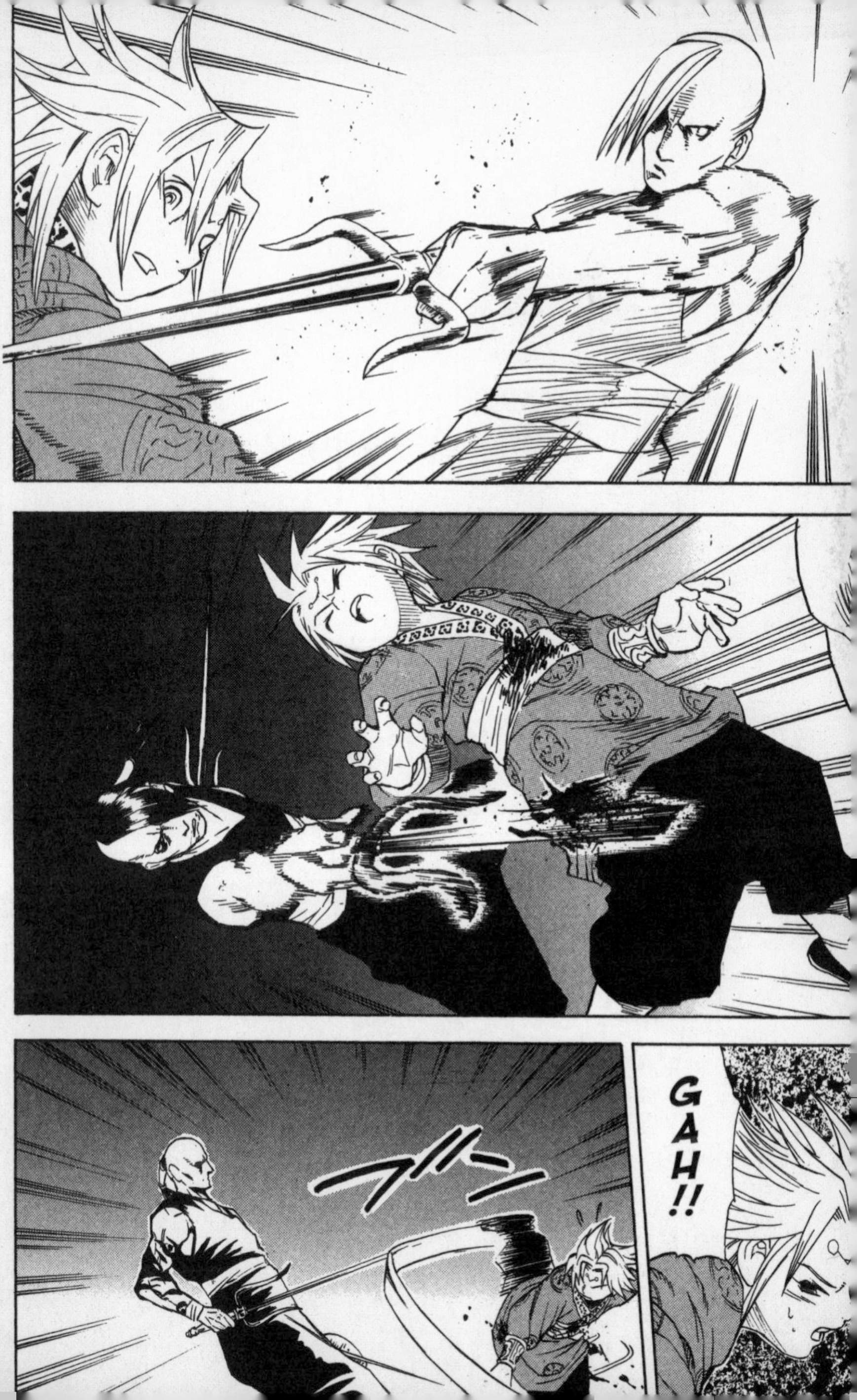
GAH!!

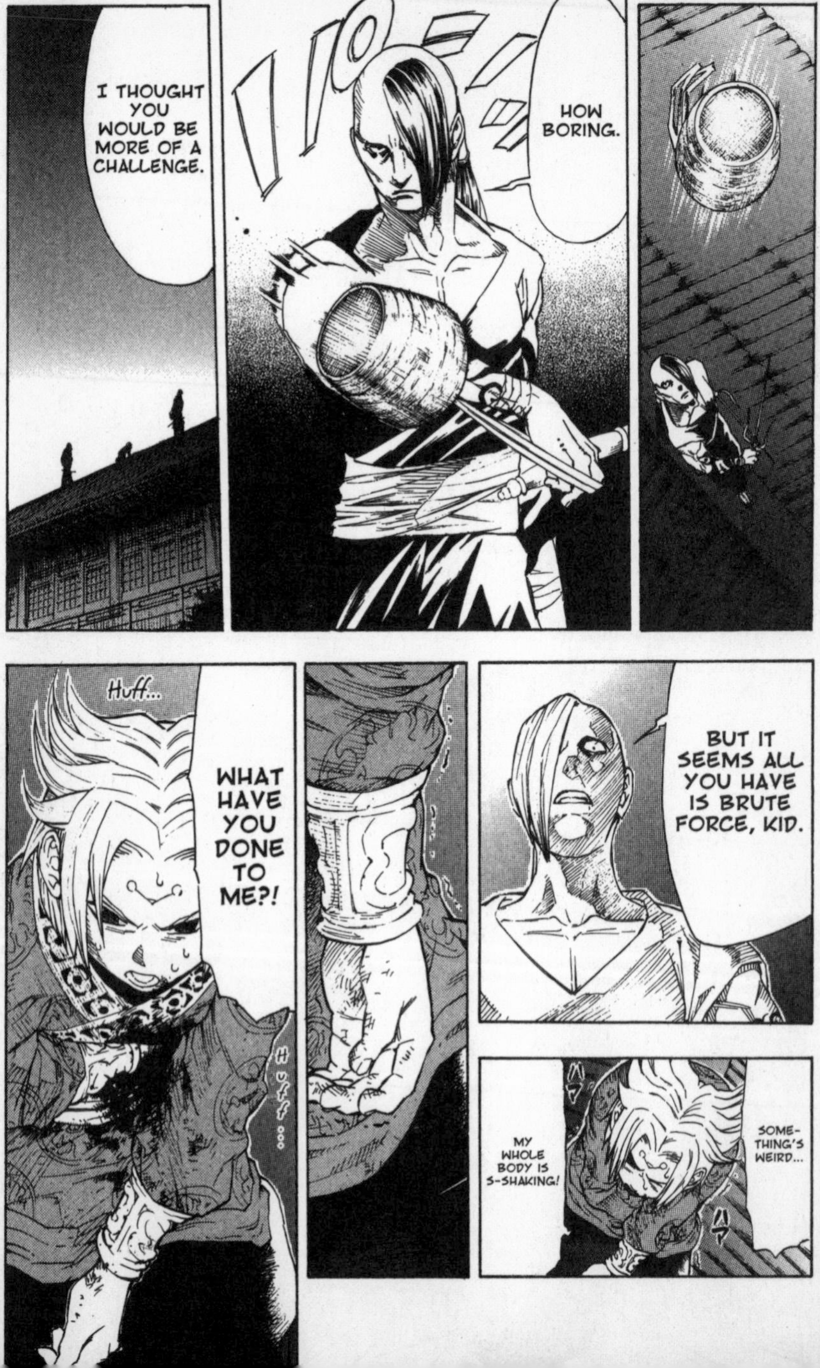
HOW BORING.
I THOUGHT YOU WOULD BE MORE OF A CHALLENGE.
BUT IT SEEMS ALL YOU HAVE IS BRUTE FORCE, KID.
SOME-THING'S WEIRD...
MY WHOLE BODY IS S-SHAKING!
Huff...
WHAT HAVE YOU DONE TO ME?!
Huff...

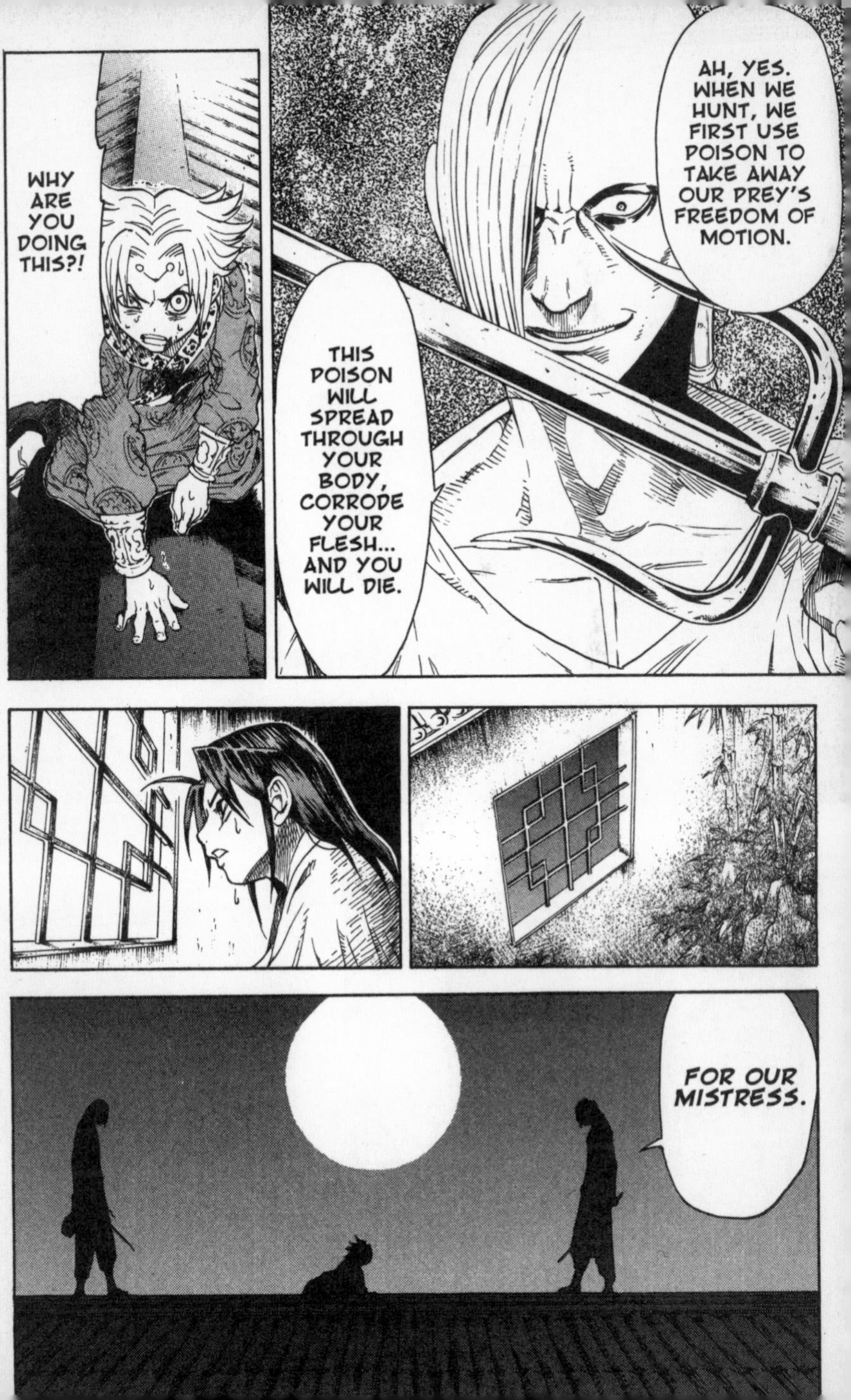
AH, YES. WHEN WE HUNT, WE FIRST USE POISON TO TAKE AWAY OUR PREY'S FREEDOM OF MOTION.
THIS POISON WILL SPREAD THROUGH YOUR BODY, CORRODE YOUR FLESH... AND YOU WILL DIE.
WHY ARE YOU DOING THIS?!
FOR OUR MISTRESS.

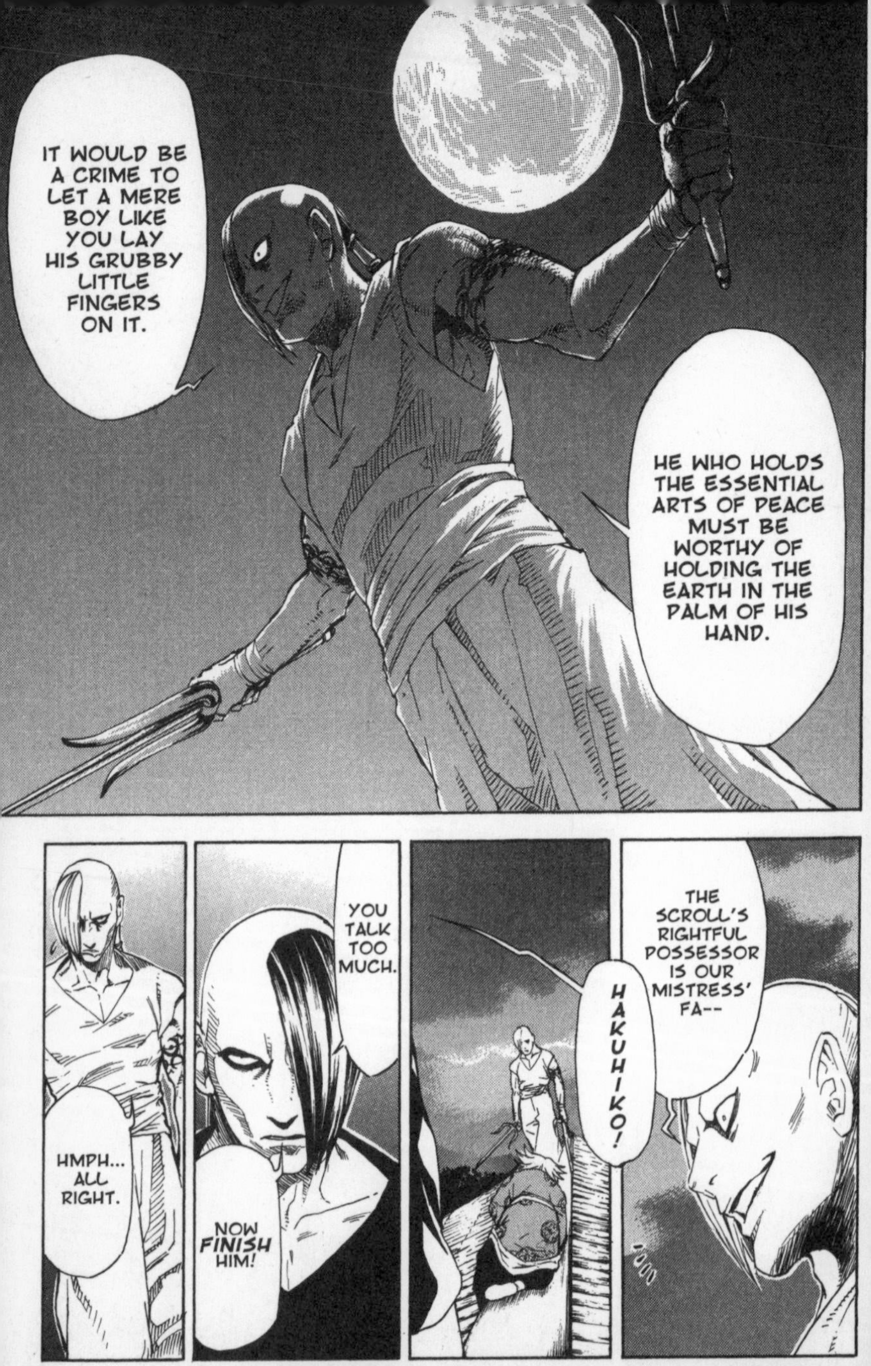
HE WHO HOLDS THE ESSENTIAL ARTS OF PEACE MUST BE WORTHY OF HOLDING THE EARTH IN THE PALM OF HIS HAND.
IT WOULD BE A CRIME TO LET A MERE BOY LIKE YOU LAY HIS GRUBBY LITTLE FINGERS ON IT.
THE SCROLL'S RIGHTFUL POSSESSOR IS OUR MISTRESS' FA--
HAKUHIKO!
YOU TALK TOO MUCH.
NOW *FINISH* HIM!
HMPH... ALL RIGHT.

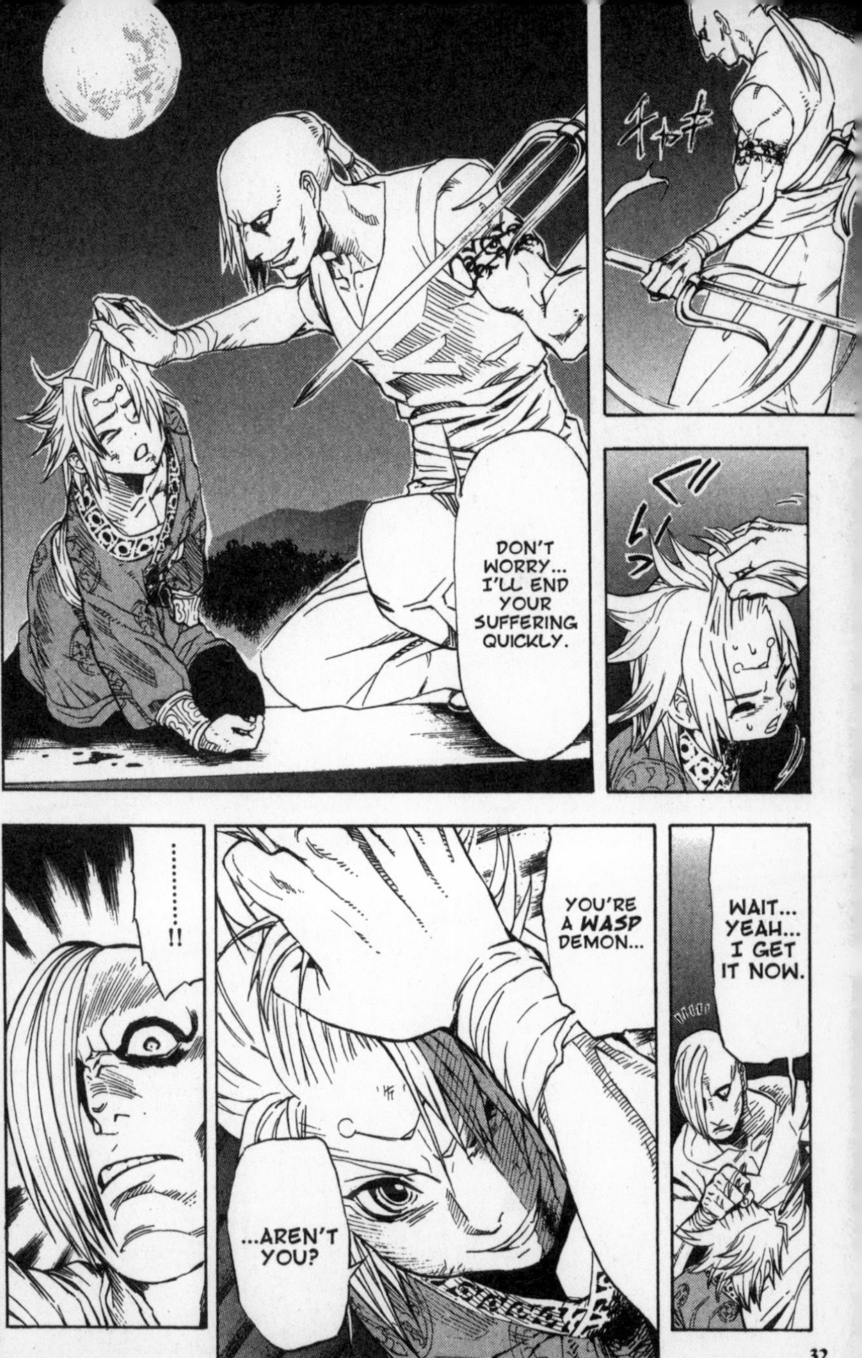
DON'T WORRY... I'LL END YOUR SUFFERING QUICKLY.
WAIT... YEAH... I GET IT NOW.
YOU'RE A WASP DEMON...
...AREN'T YOU?
......!!

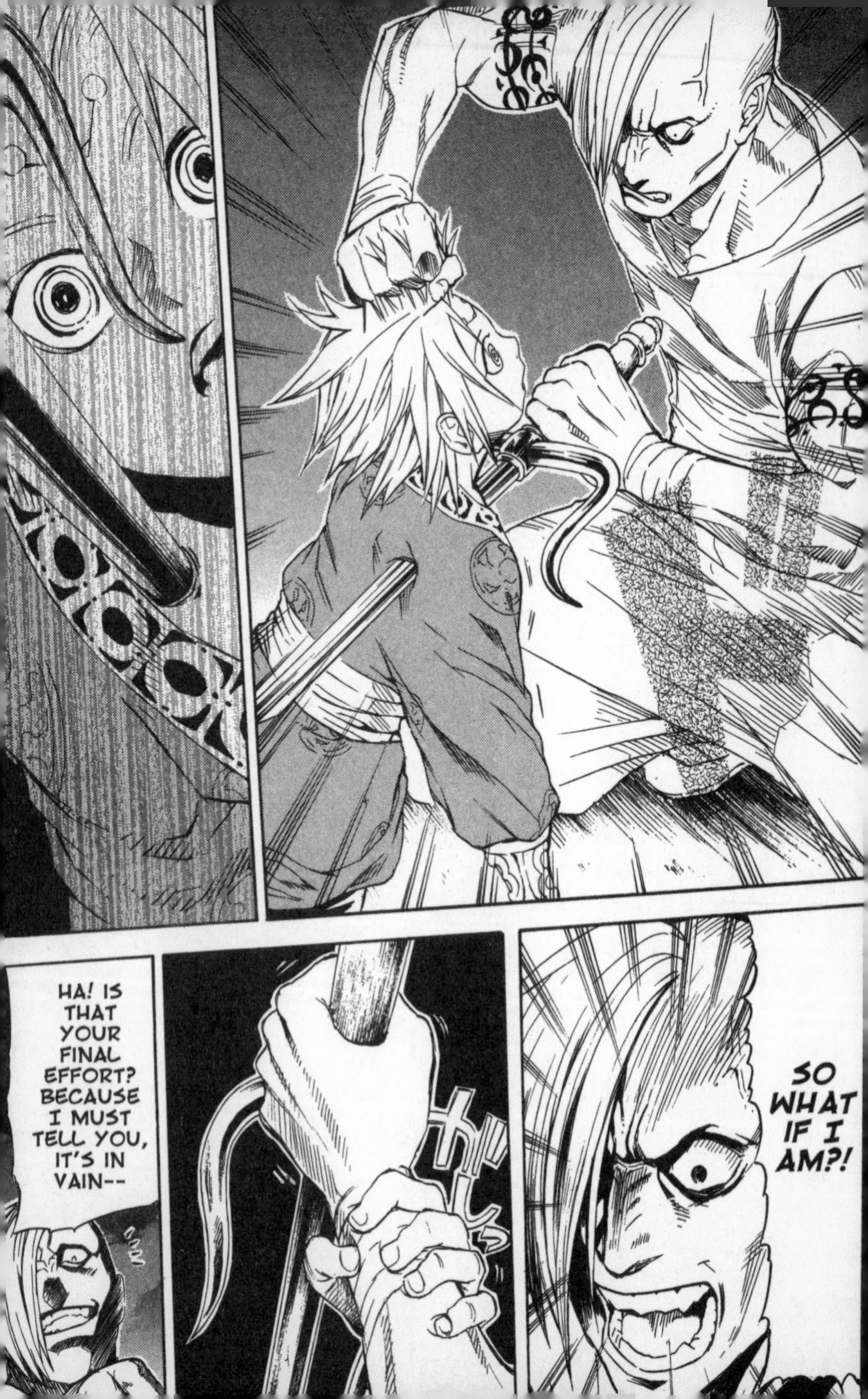
HA! IS THAT YOUR FINAL EFFORT? BECAUSE I MUST TELL YOU, IT'S IN VAIN--
SO WHAT IF I AM?!

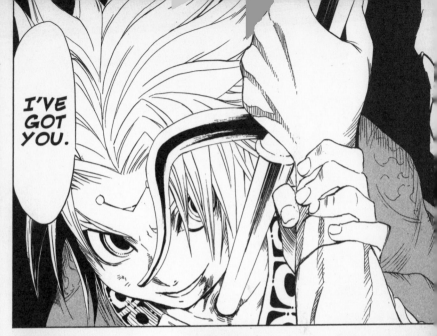

I'VE GOT YOU.

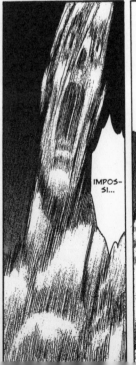

IMPOS-SI...

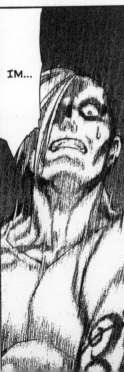

IM...

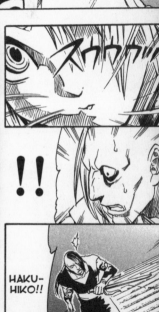

!!

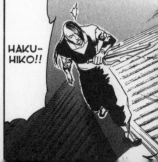

HAKU-HIKO!!

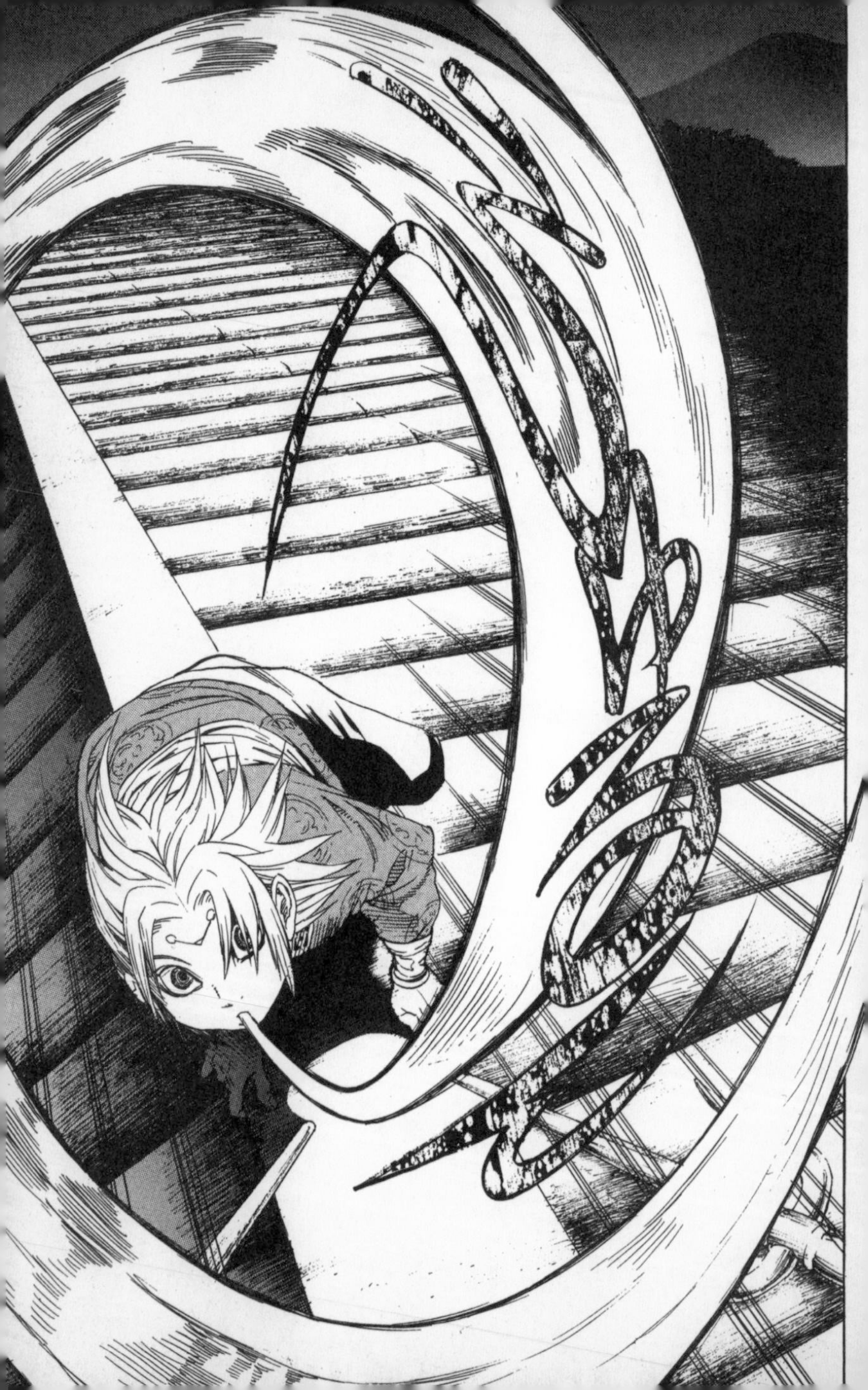

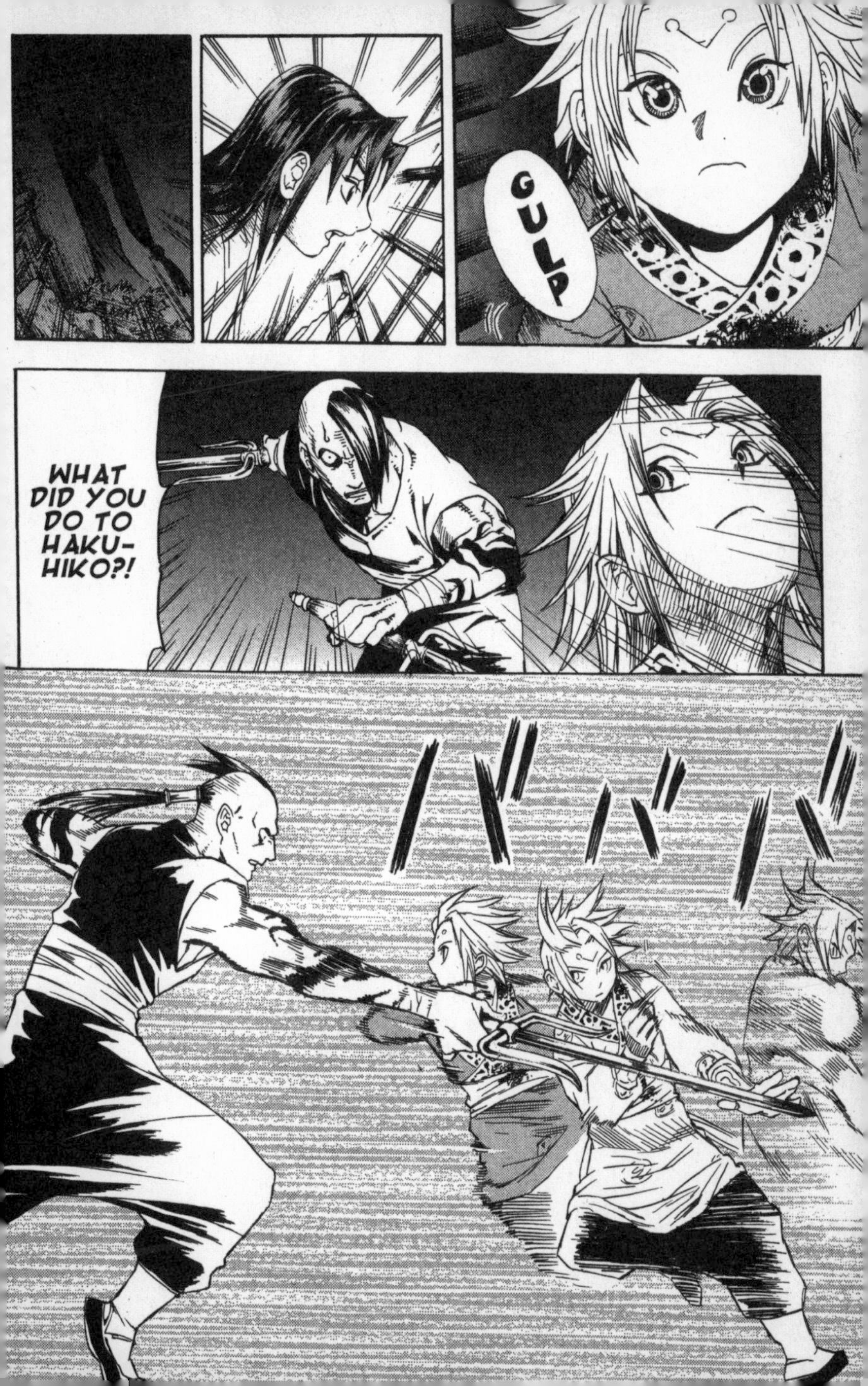
GULP
WHAT DID YOU DO TO HAKU-HIKO?!

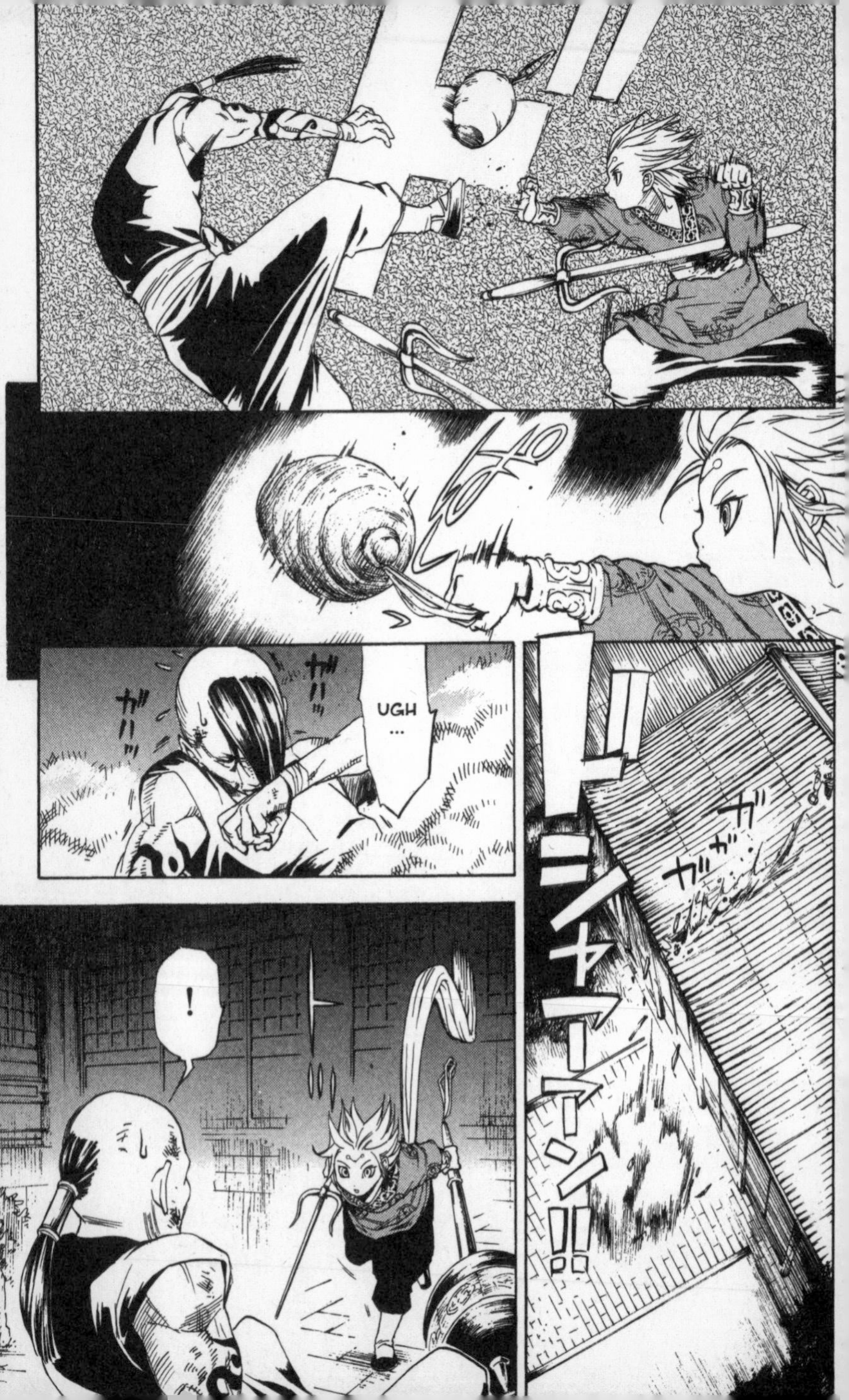
UGH ...
!

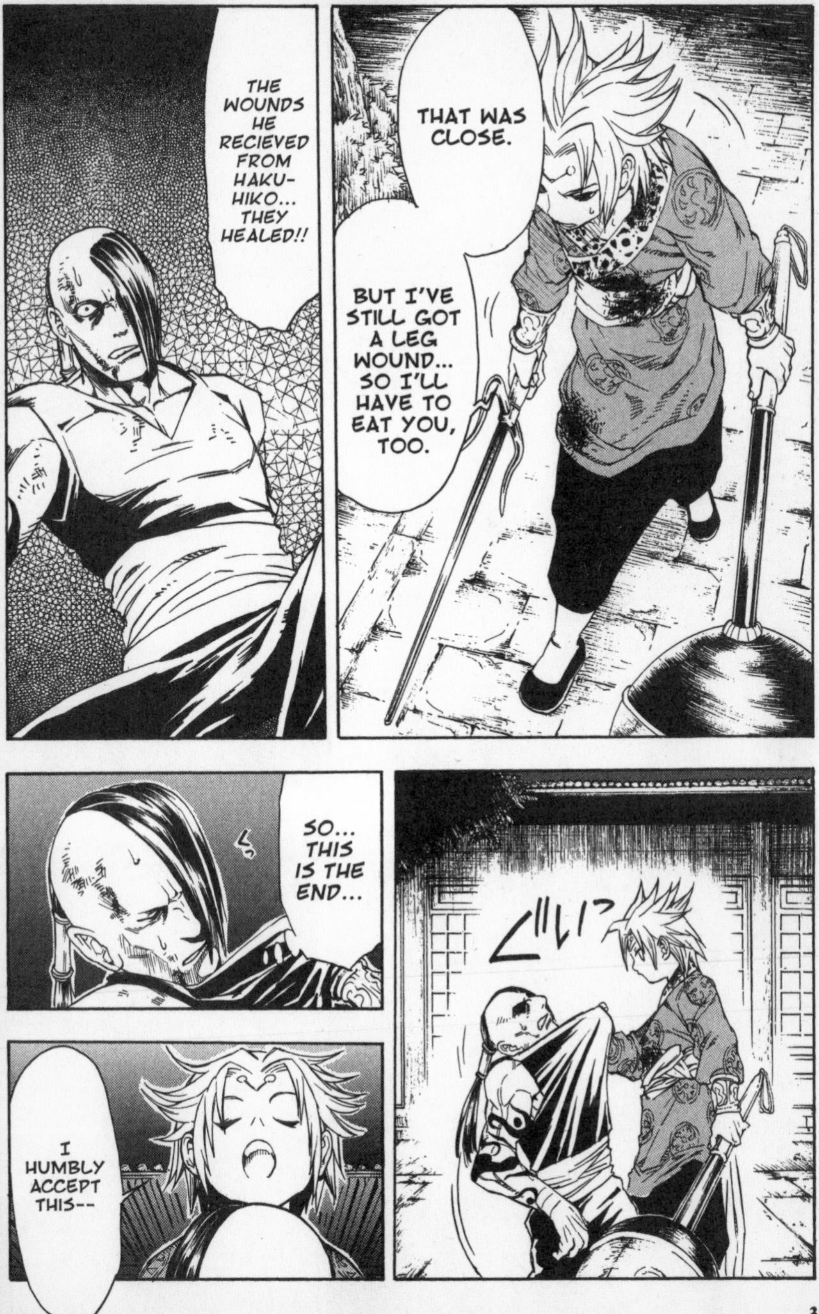
THAT WAS CLOSE.
BUT I'VE STILL GOT A LEG WOUND... SO I'LL HAVE TO EAT YOU, TOO.
THE WOUNDS HE RECIEVED FROM HAKU-HIKO... THEY HEALED!!
SO... THIS IS THE END...
I HUMBLY ACCEPT THIS--

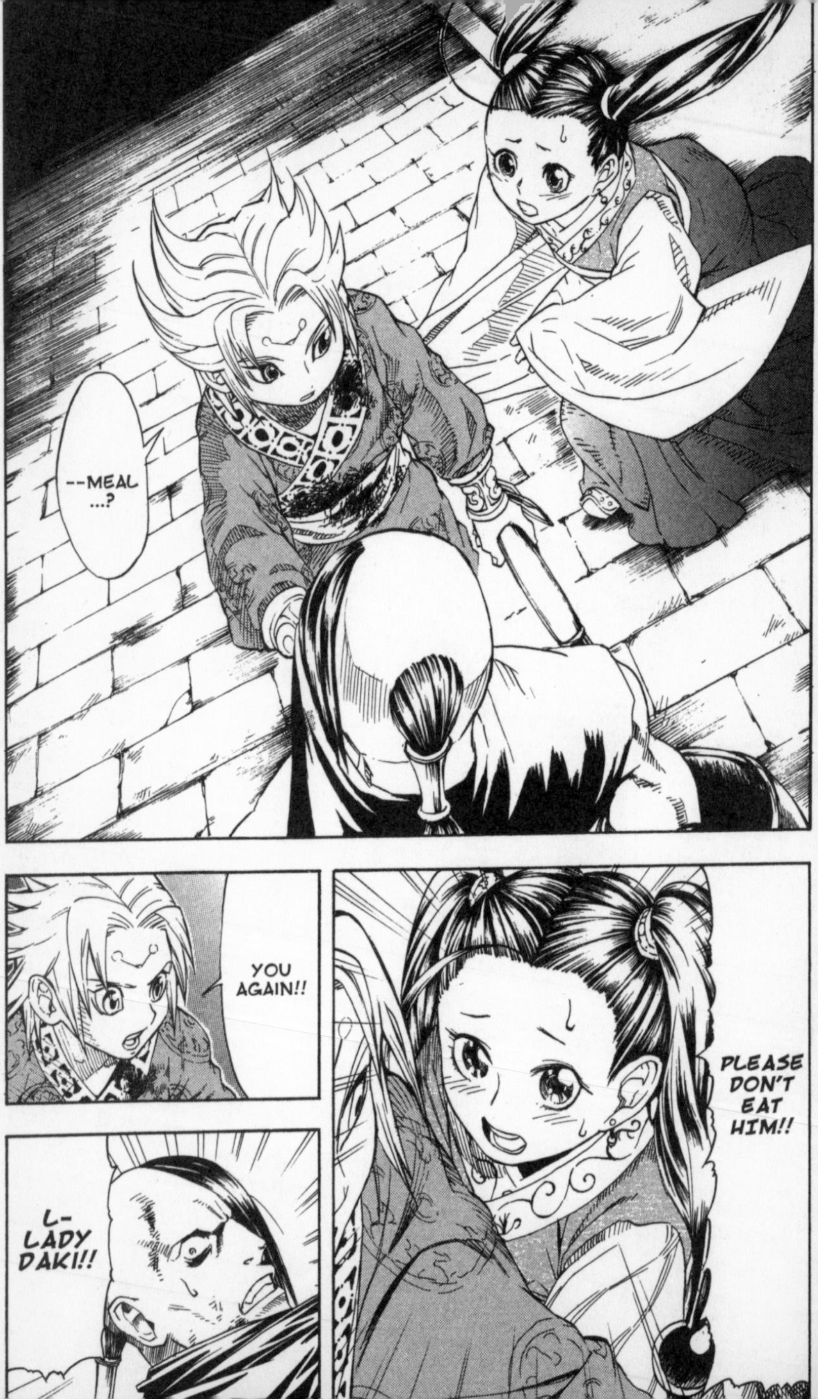
--MEAL ...?
PLEASE DON'T EAT HIM!!
YOU AGAIN!!
L-LADY DAKI!!

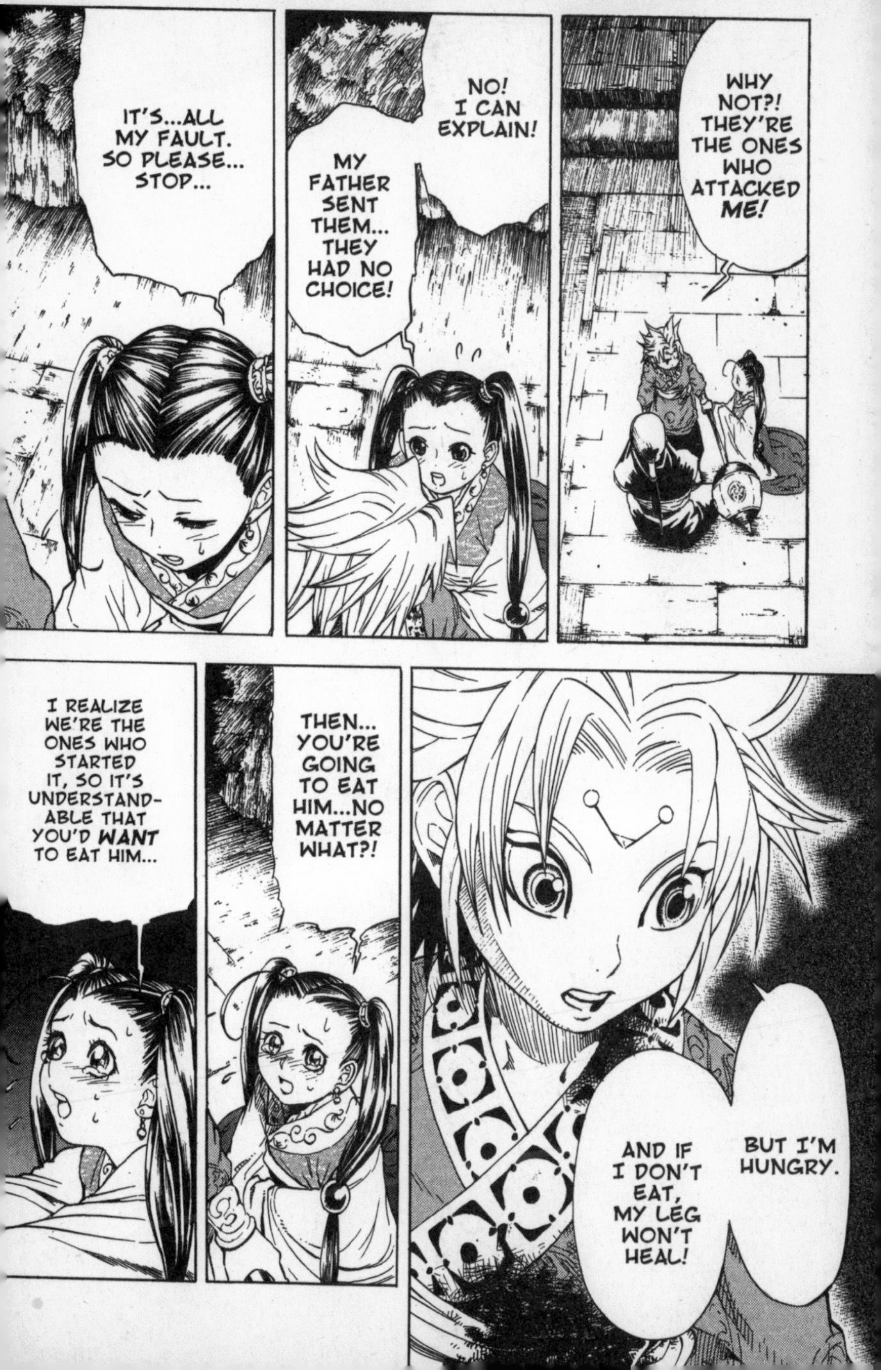
WHY NOT?! THEY'RE THE ONES WHO ATTACKED ME!
NO! I CAN EXPLAIN!
MY FATHER SENT THEM... THEY HAD NO CHOICE!
IT'S...ALL MY FAULT. SO PLEASE... STOP...
BUT I'M HUNGRY.
AND IF I DON'T EAT, MY LEG WON'T HEAL!
THEN... YOU'RE GOING TO EAT HIM...NO MATTER WHAT?!
I REALIZE WE'RE THE ONES WHO STARTED IT, SO IT'S UNDERSTANDABLE THAT YOU'D WANT TO EAT HIM...

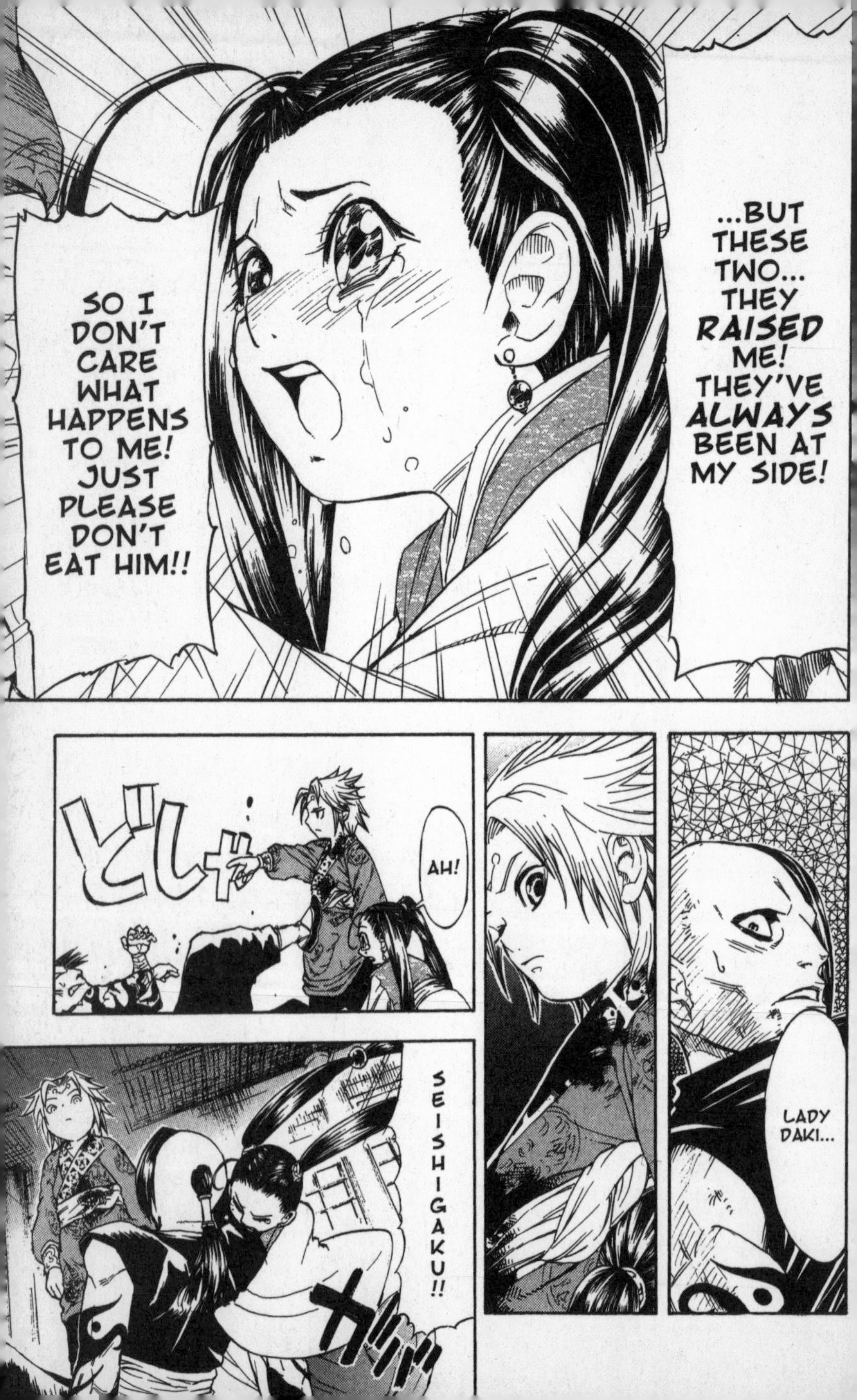
...BUT THESE TWO... THEY RAISED ME! THEY'VE ALWAYS BEEN AT MY SIDE!
SO I DON'T CARE WHAT HAPPENS TO ME! JUST PLEASE DON'T EAT HIM!!
LADY DAKI...
どしゃ
AH!
SEISHIGAKU!!

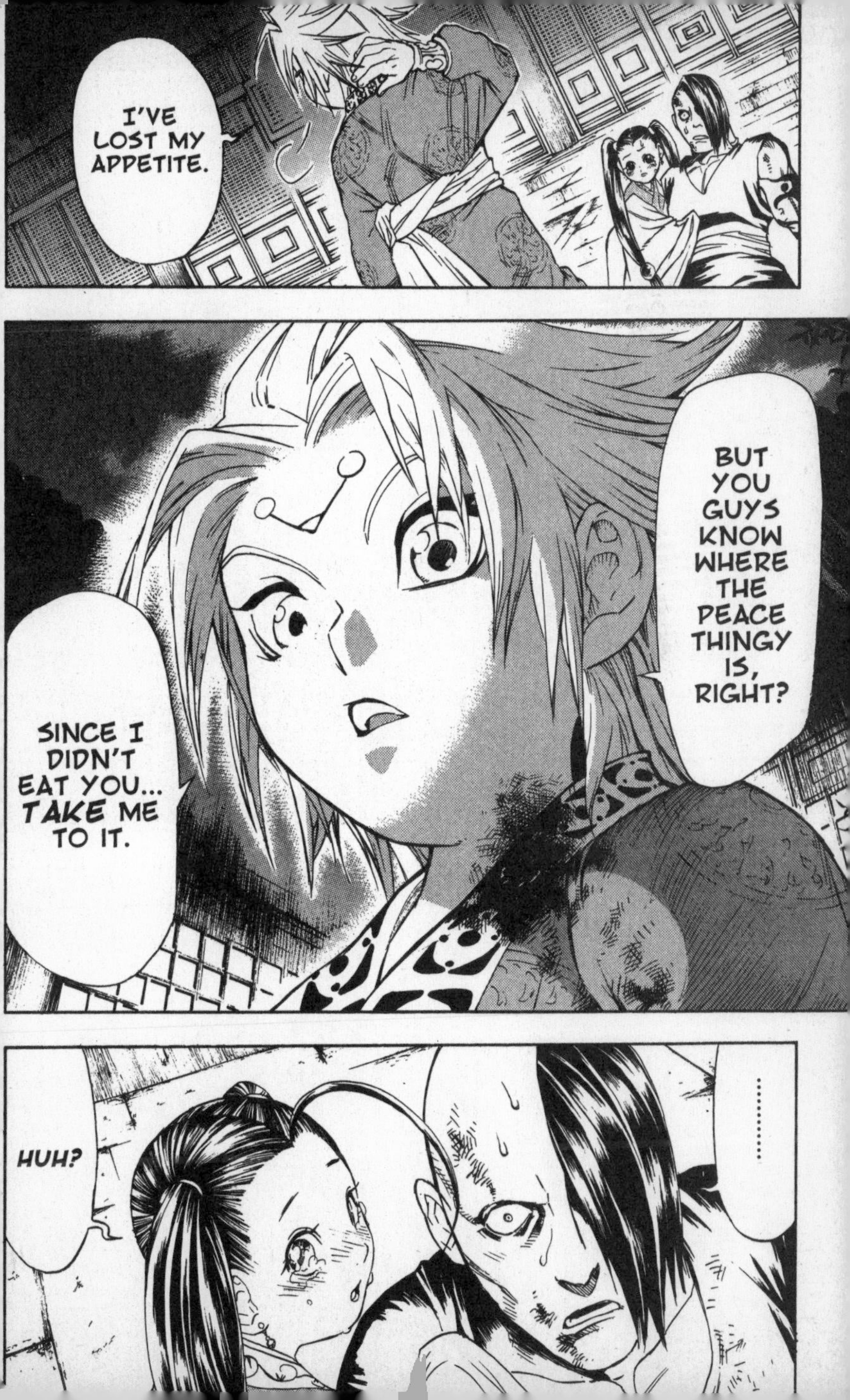
I'VE LOST MY APPETITE.
BUT YOU GUYS KNOW WHERE THE PEACE THINGY IS, RIGHT?
SINCE I DIDN'T EAT YOU... *TAKE* ME TO IT.
......
HUH?

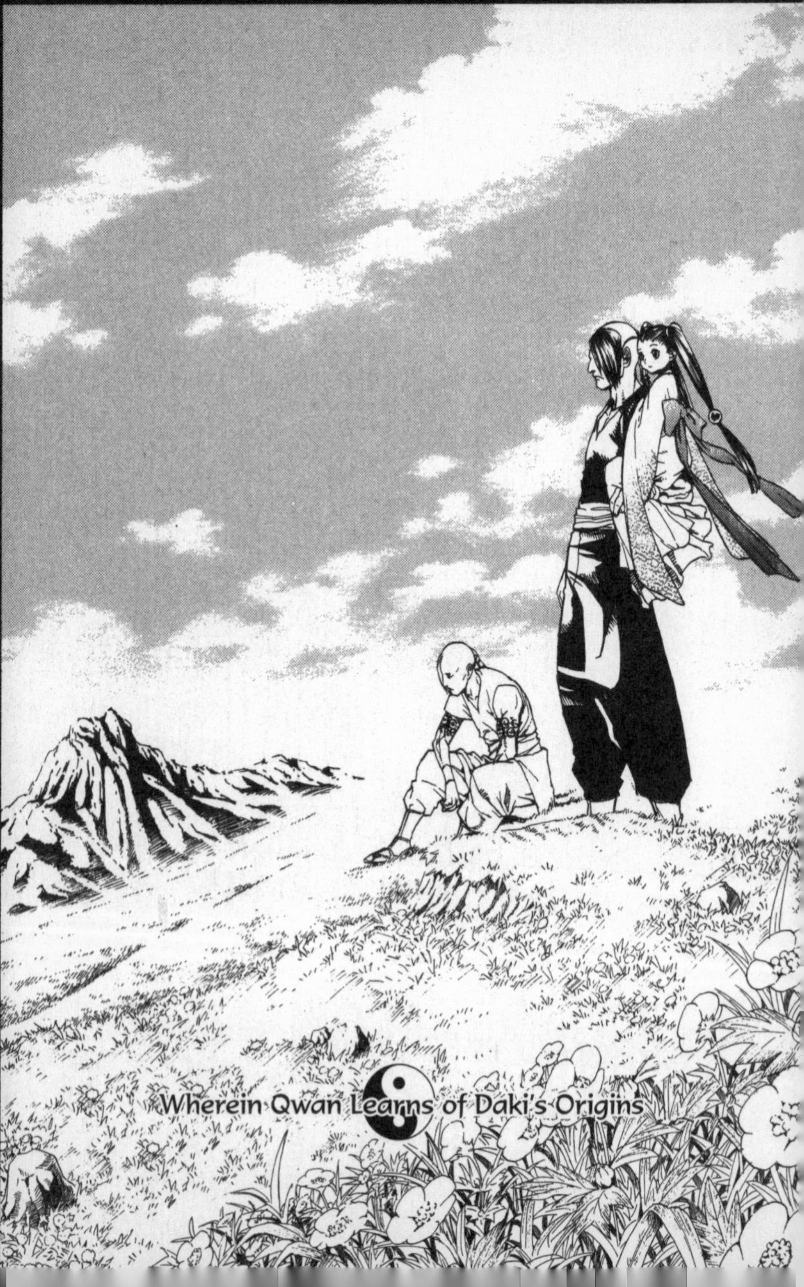
Wherein Qwan Learns of Daki's Origins

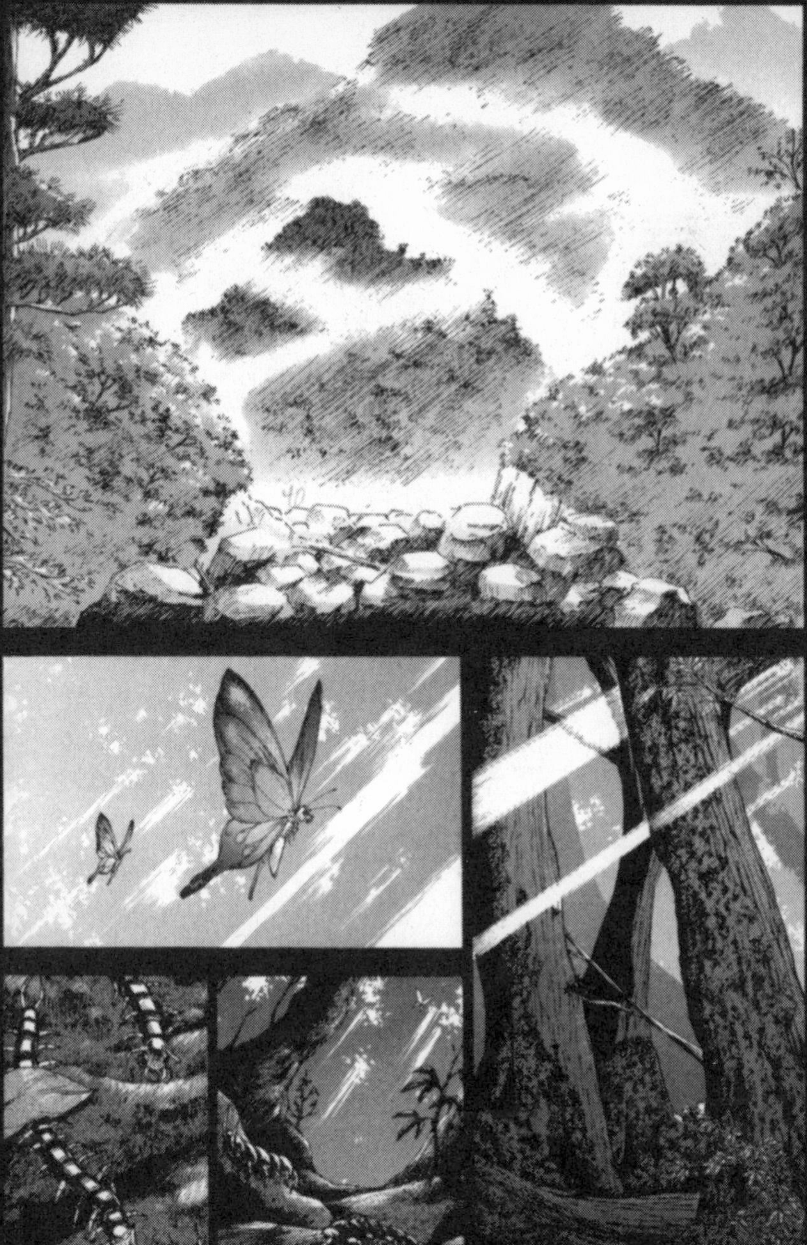

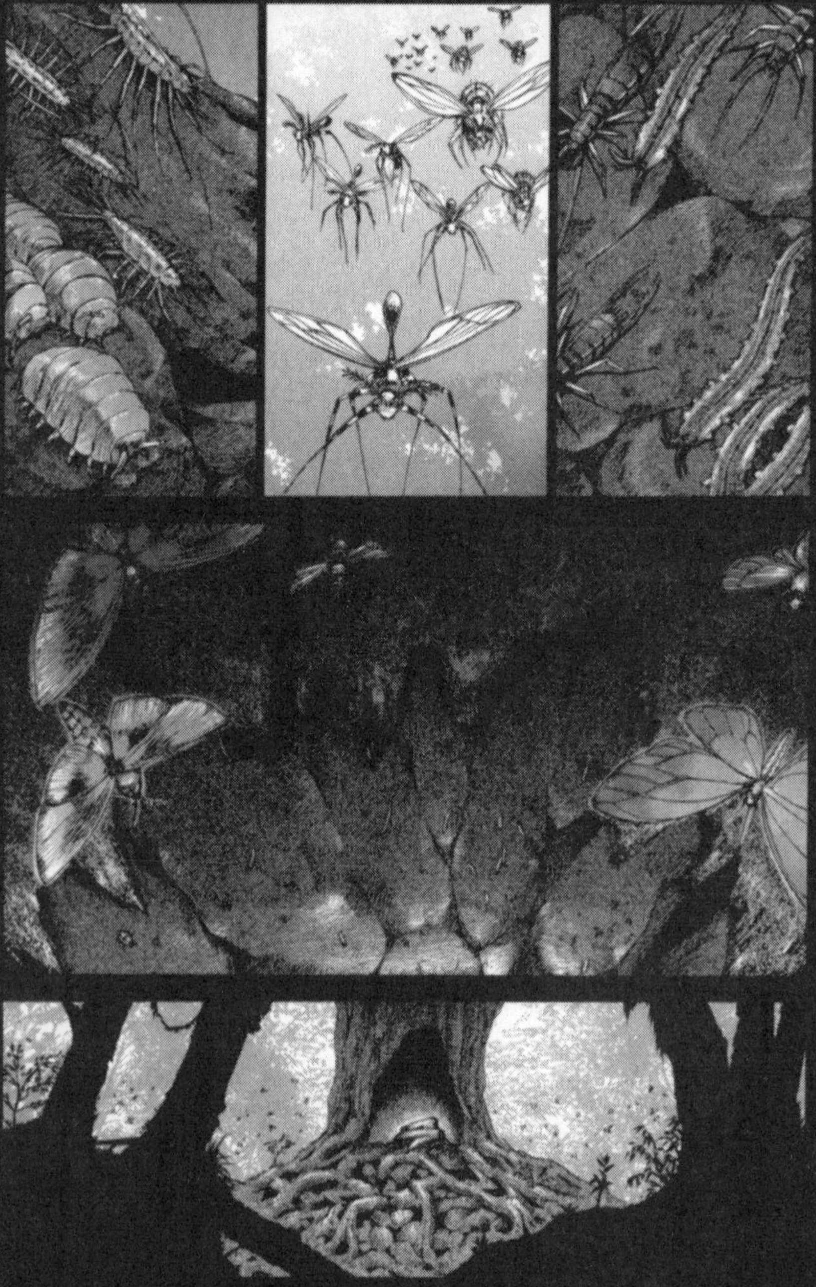

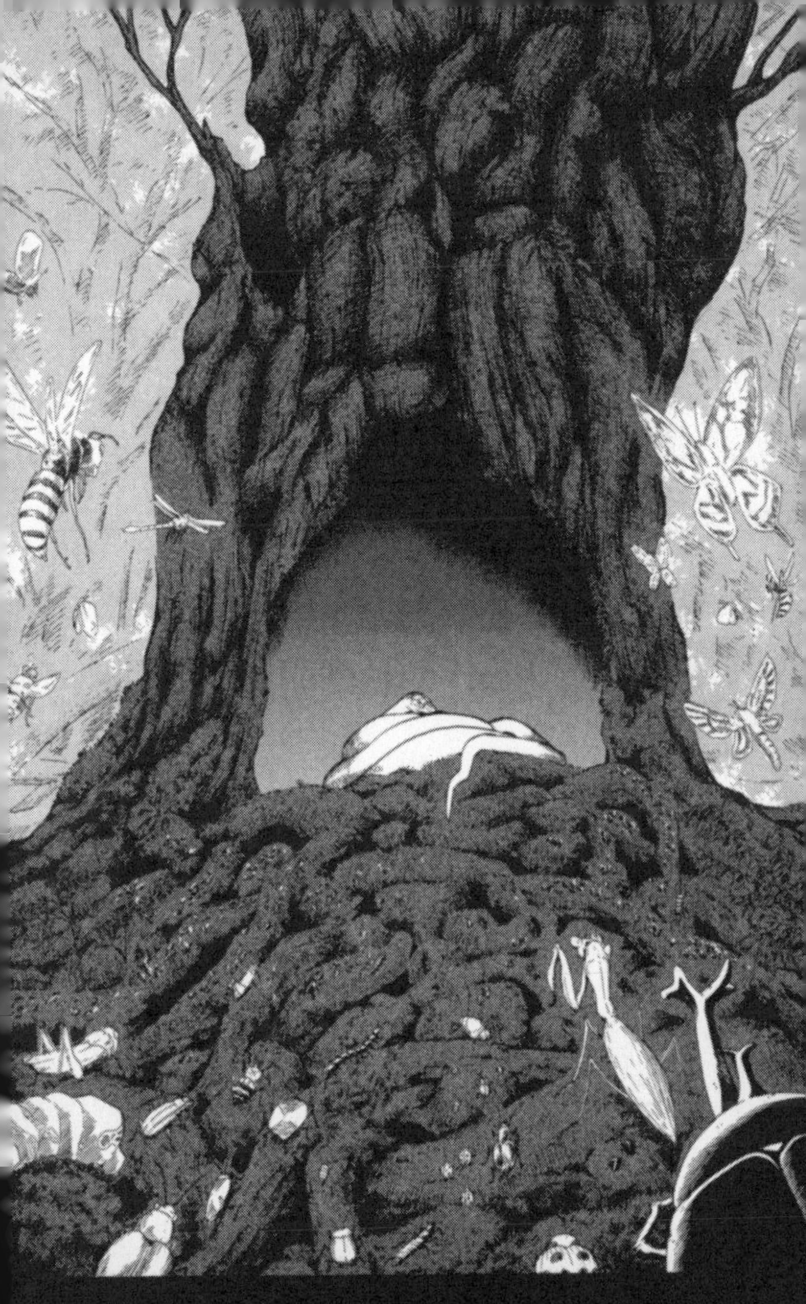

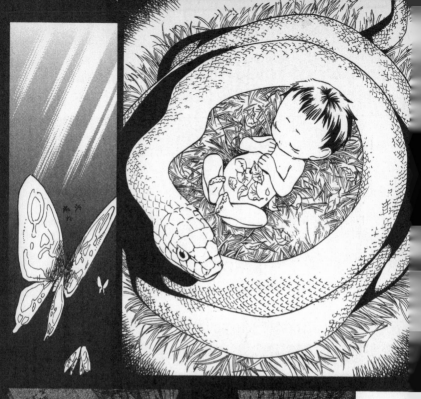

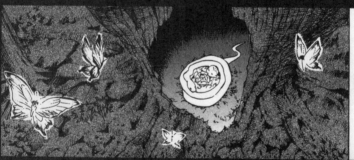

IT TRULY WAS A BIZARRE SIGHT...

...A LONE HUMAN BABY IN A FOREST OF BUGS.

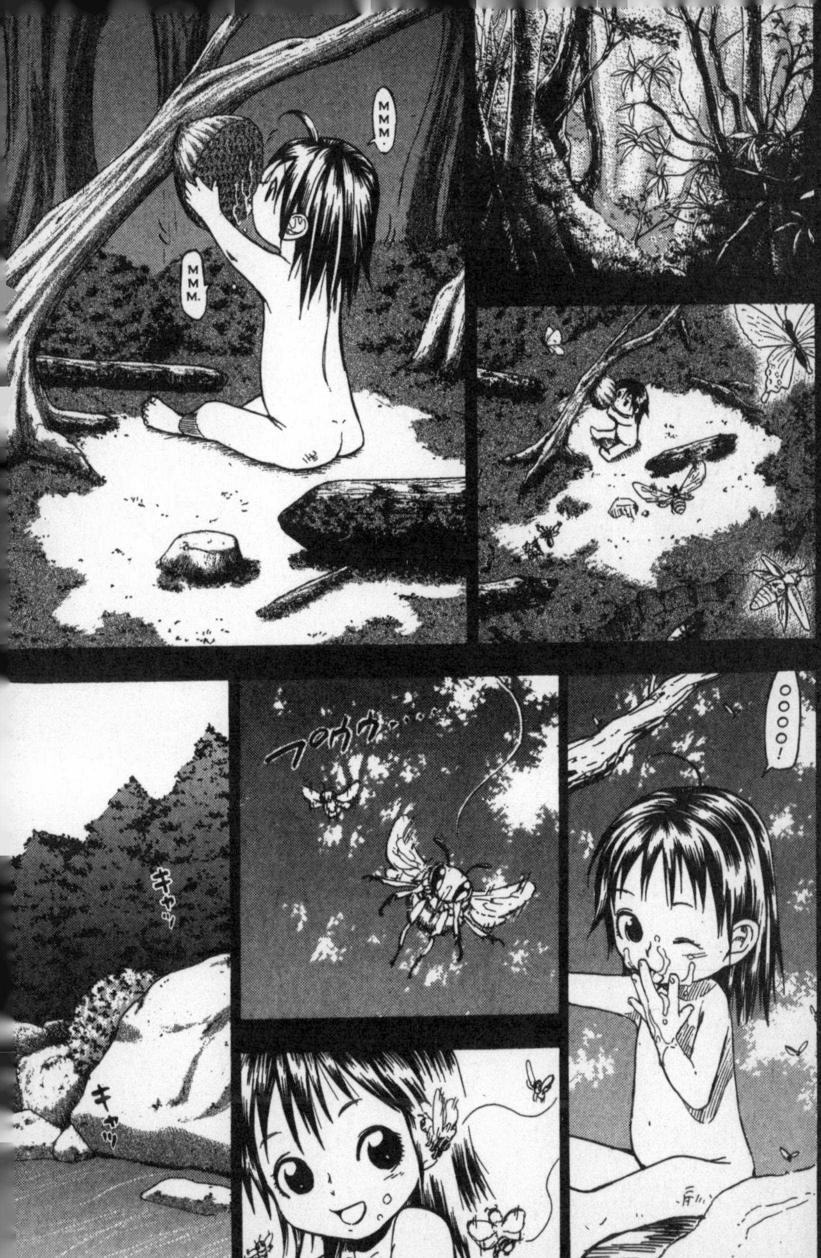
MMM.
MMM.
OOOO!
プウウ
キャッ
キャッ

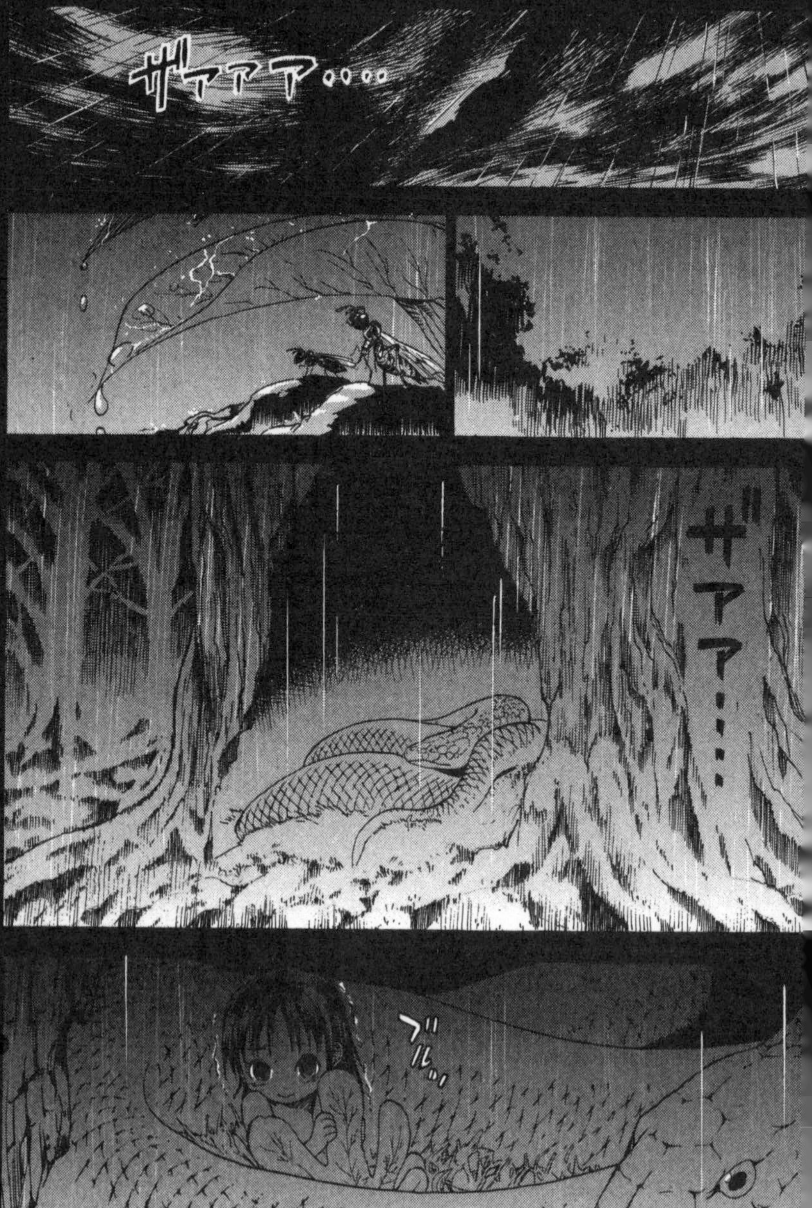
ザァァア……
ザアア…
ブルッ

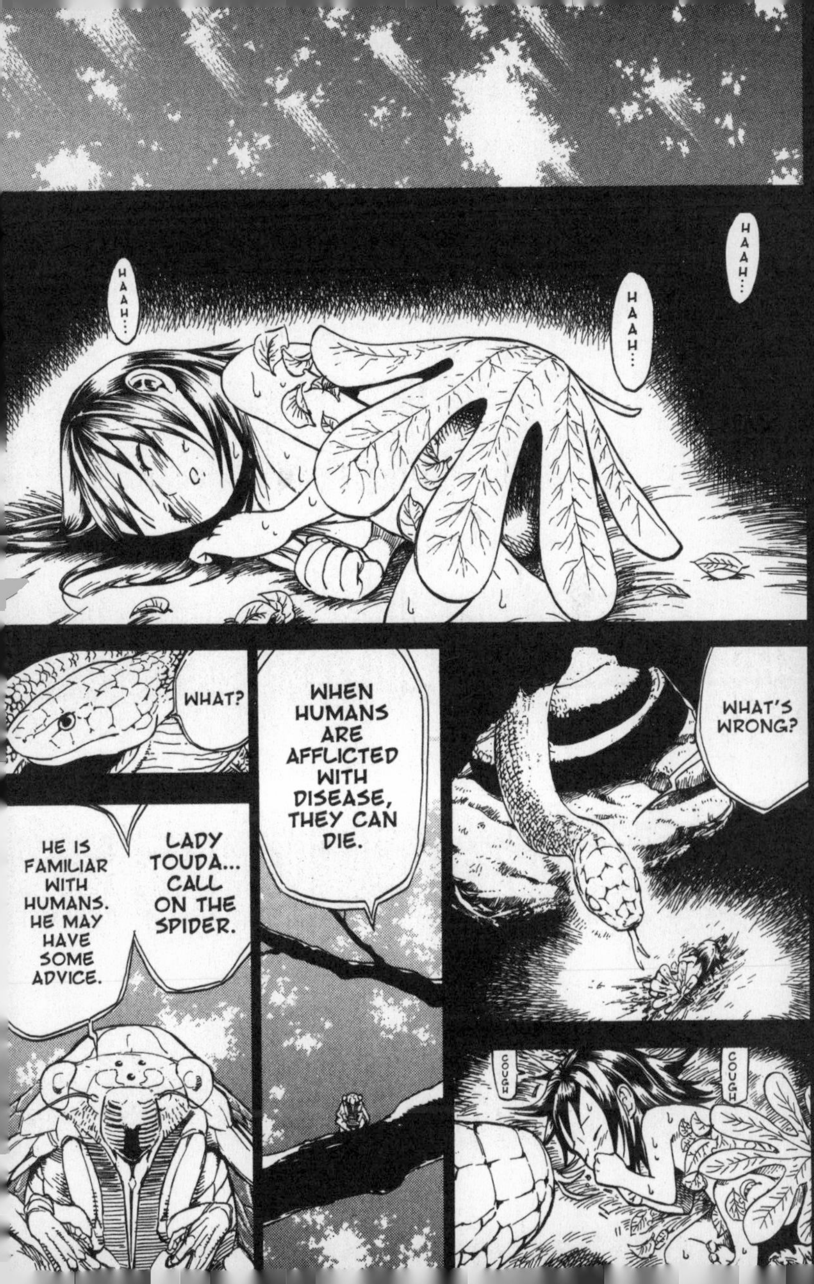
HAAH...
HAAH...
HAAH...
WHAT'S WRONG?
COUGH
COUGH
WHEN HUMANS ARE AFFLICTED WITH DISEASE, THEY CAN DIE.
WHAT?
LADY TOUDA... CALL ON THE SPIDER.
HE IS FAMILIAR WITH HUMANS. HE MAY HAVE SOME ADVICE.

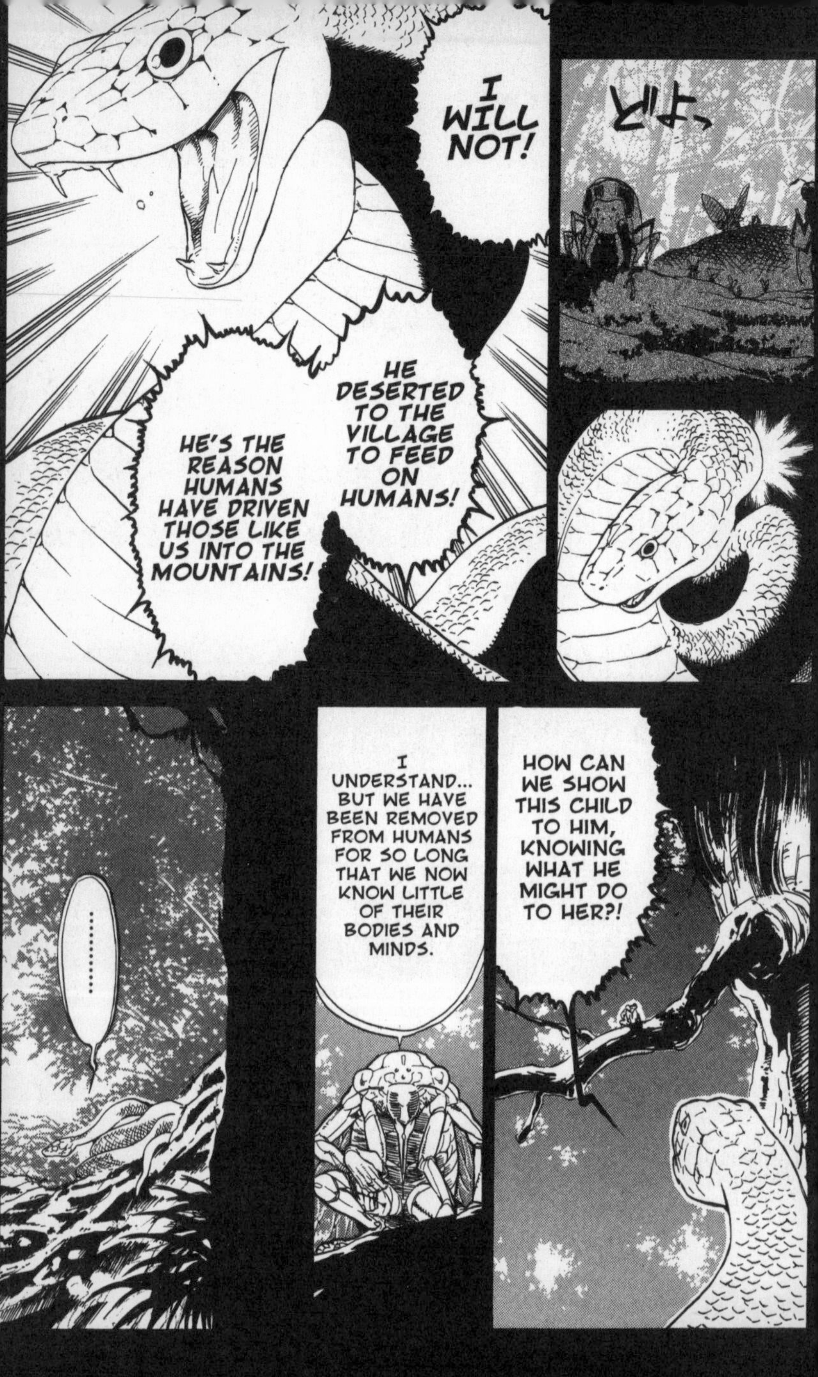

どよっ
I WILL NOT!
HE DESERTED TO THE VILLAGE TO FEED ON HUMANS!
HE'S THE REASON HUMANS HAVE DRIVEN THOSE LIKE US INTO THE MOUNTAINS!
HOW CAN WE SHOW THIS CHILD TO HIM, KNOWING WHAT HE MIGHT DO TO HER?!
I UNDERSTAND... BUT WE HAVE BEEN REMOVED FROM HUMANS FOR SO LONG THAT WE NOW KNOW LITTLE OF THEIR BODIES AND MINDS.
....

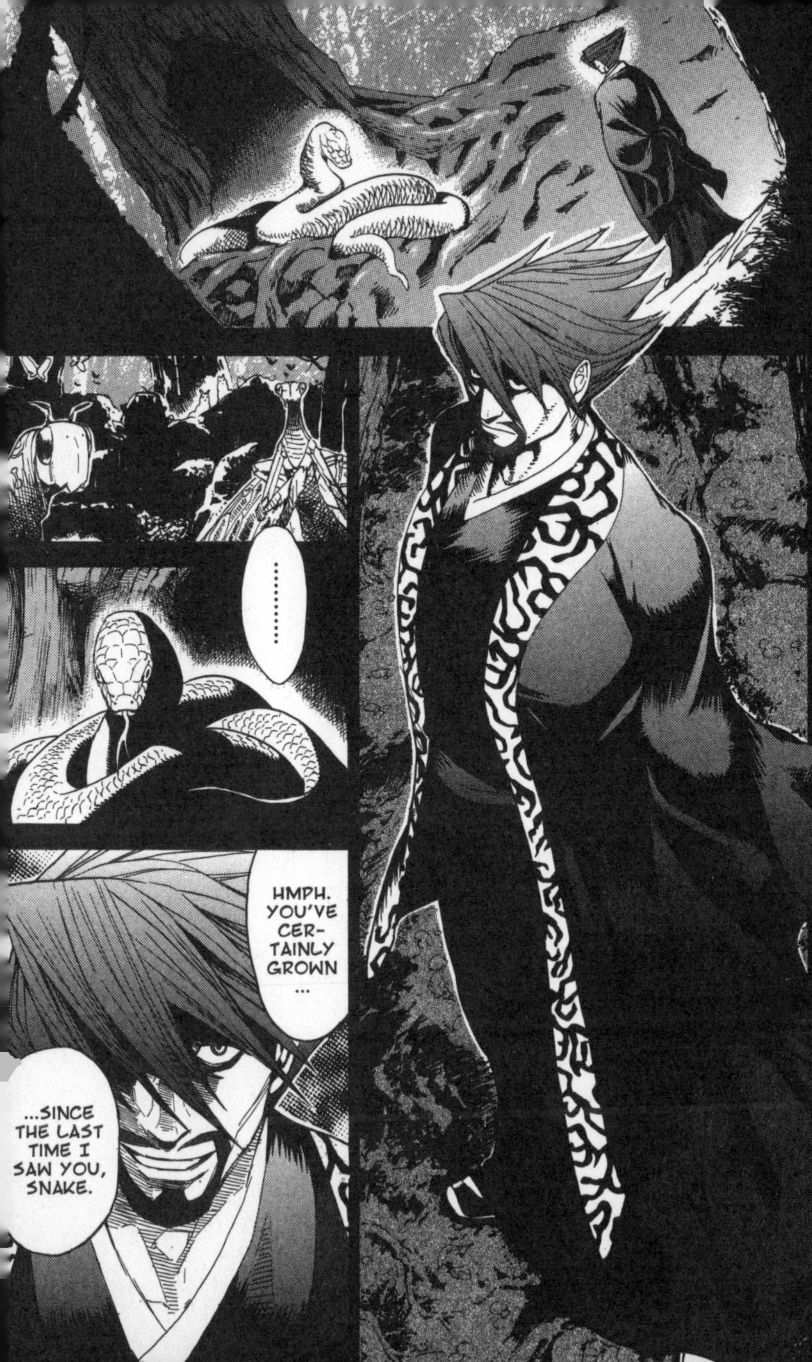

......
HMPH. YOU'VE CER-TAINLY GROWN ...
...SINCE THE LAST TIME I SAW YOU, SNAKE.

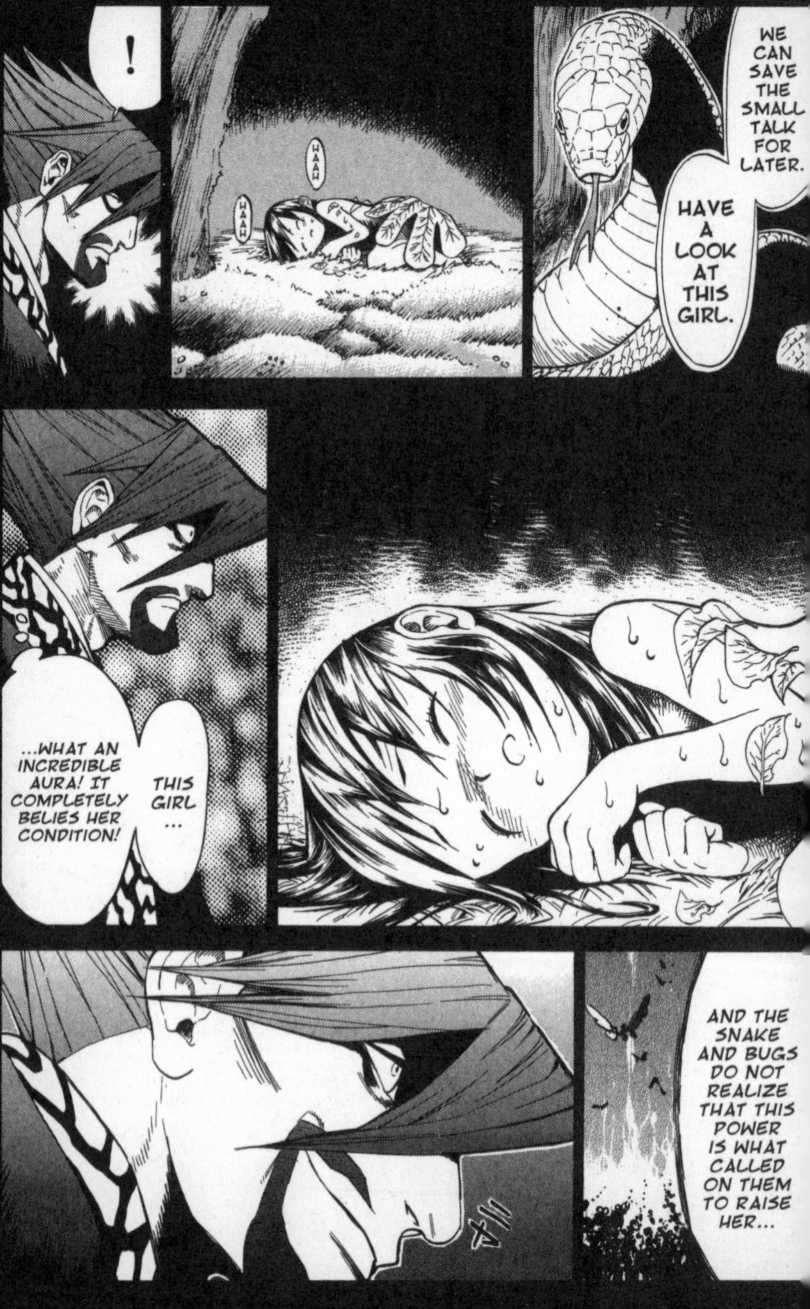
WE CAN SAVE THE SMALL TALK FOR LATER.
HAVE A LOOK AT THIS GIRL.
HAAH
HAAH
!
THIS GIRL ...
...WHAT AN INCREDIBLE AURA! IT COMPLETELY BELIES HER CONDITION!
AND THE SNAKE AND BUGS DO NOT REALIZE THAT THIS POWER IS WHAT CALLED ON THEM TO RAISE HER...

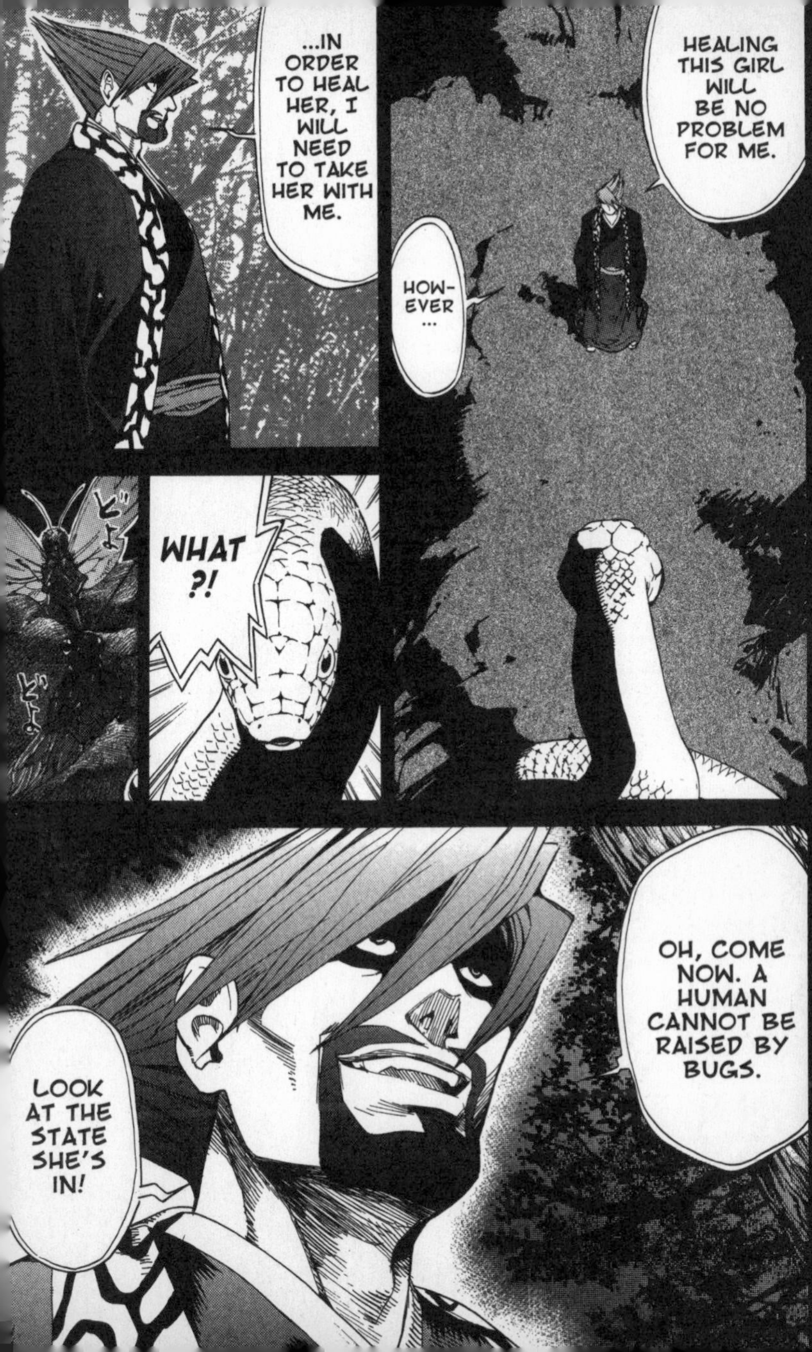
HEALING THIS GIRL WILL BE NO PROBLEM FOR ME.
HOW-EVER...
...IN ORDER TO HEAL HER, I WILL NEED TO TAKE HER WITH ME.
WHAT?!
OH, COME NOW. A HUMAN CANNOT BE RAISED BY BUGS.
LOOK AT THE STATE SHE'S IN!

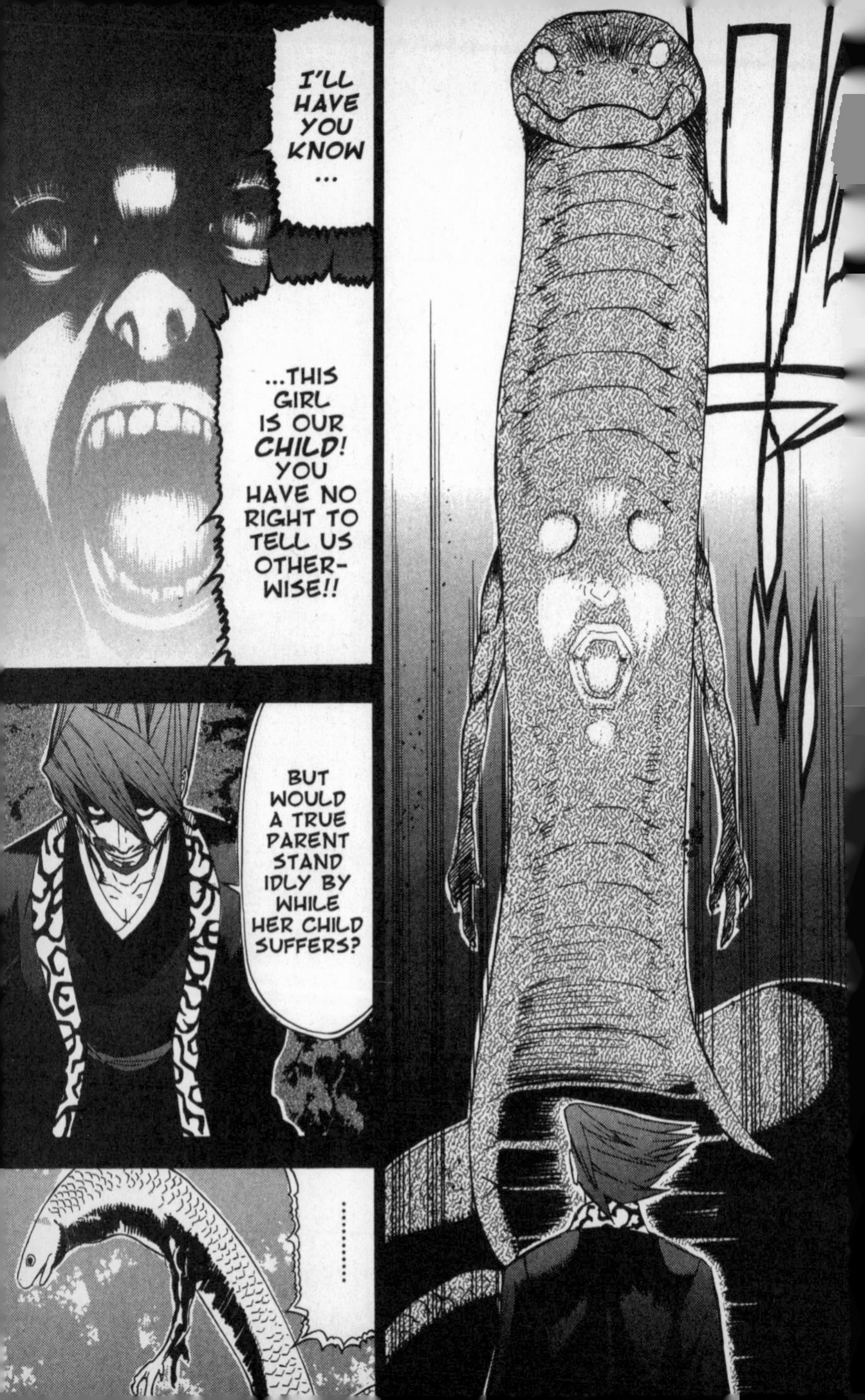
I'LL HAVE YOU KNOW ...
...THIS GIRL IS OUR CHILD! YOU HAVE NO RIGHT TO TELL US OTHER-WISE!!
BUT WOULD A TRUE PARENT STAND IDLY BY WHILE HER CHILD SUFFERS?
....

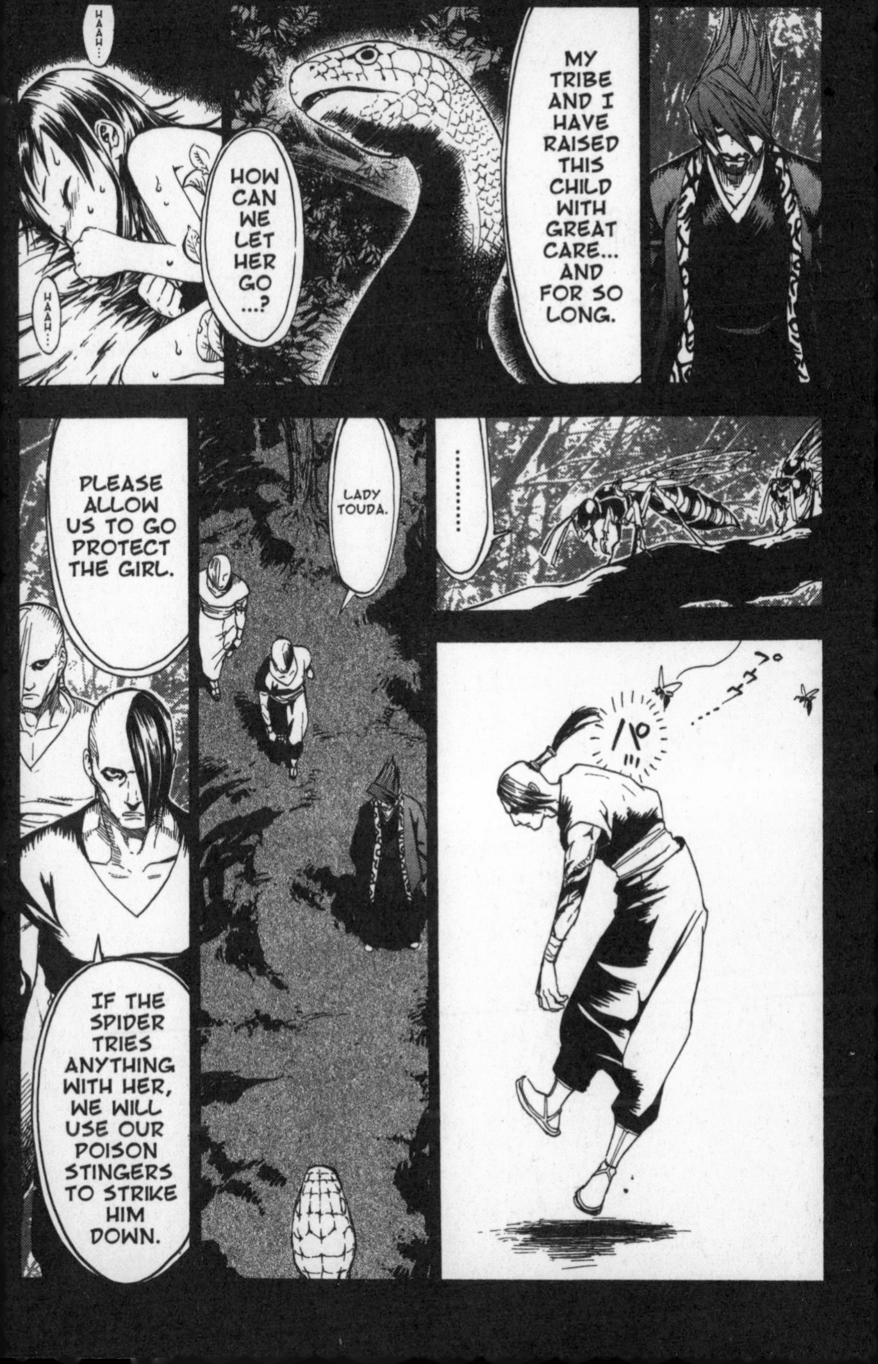

MY TRIBE AND I HAVE RAISED THIS CHILD WITH GREAT CARE... AND FOR SO LONG.
HOW CAN WE LET HER GO ...?
HAAH...
HAAH...
......
LADY TOUDA.
PLEASE ALLOW US TO GO PROTECT THE GIRL.
IF THE SPIDER TRIES ANYTHING WITH HER, WE WILL USE OUR POISON STINGERS TO STRIKE HIM DOWN.

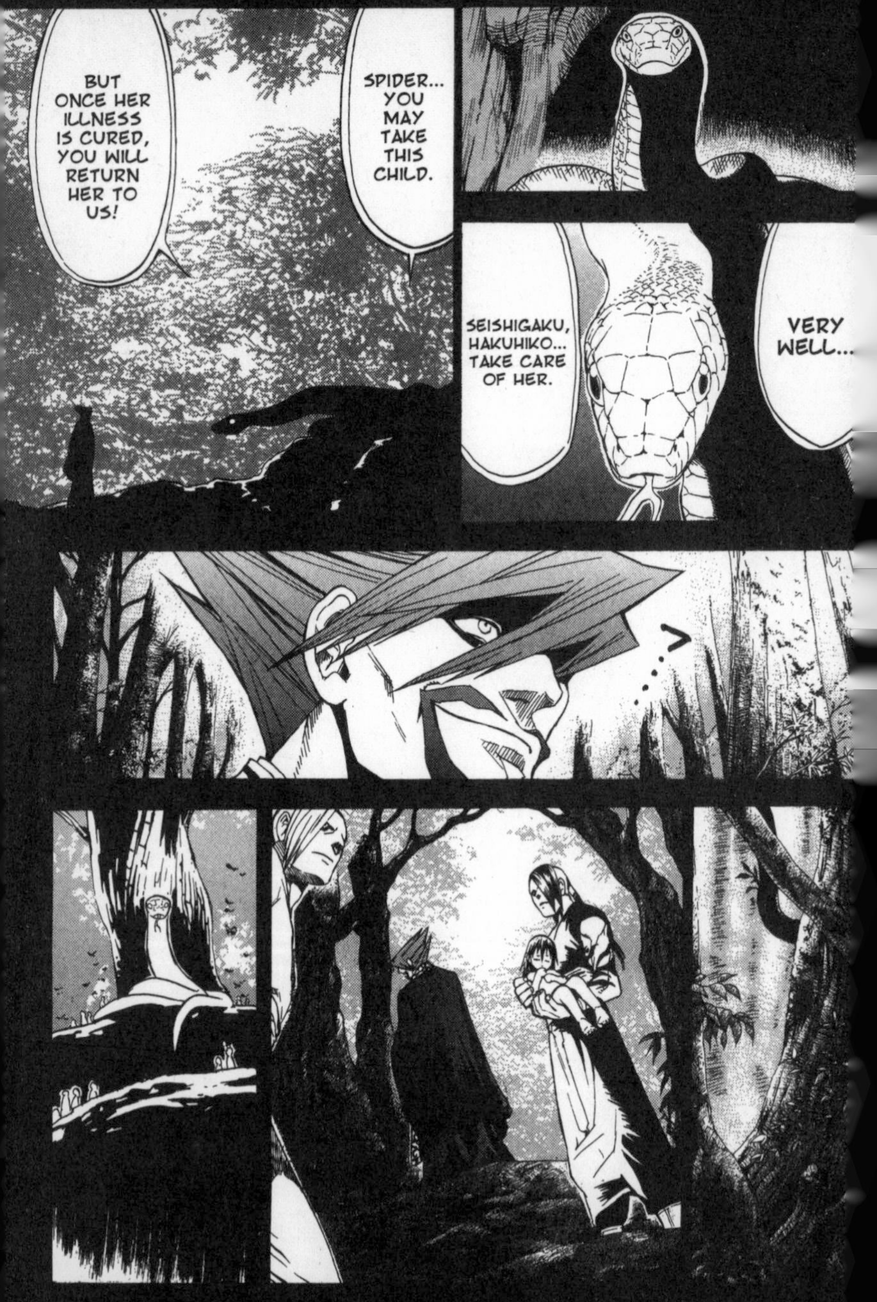
VERY WELL...
SEISHIGAKU, HAKUHIKO... TAKE CARE OF HER.
SPIDER... YOU MAY TAKE THIS CHILD.
BUT ONCE HER ILLNESS IS CURED, YOU WILL RETURN HER TO US!
...

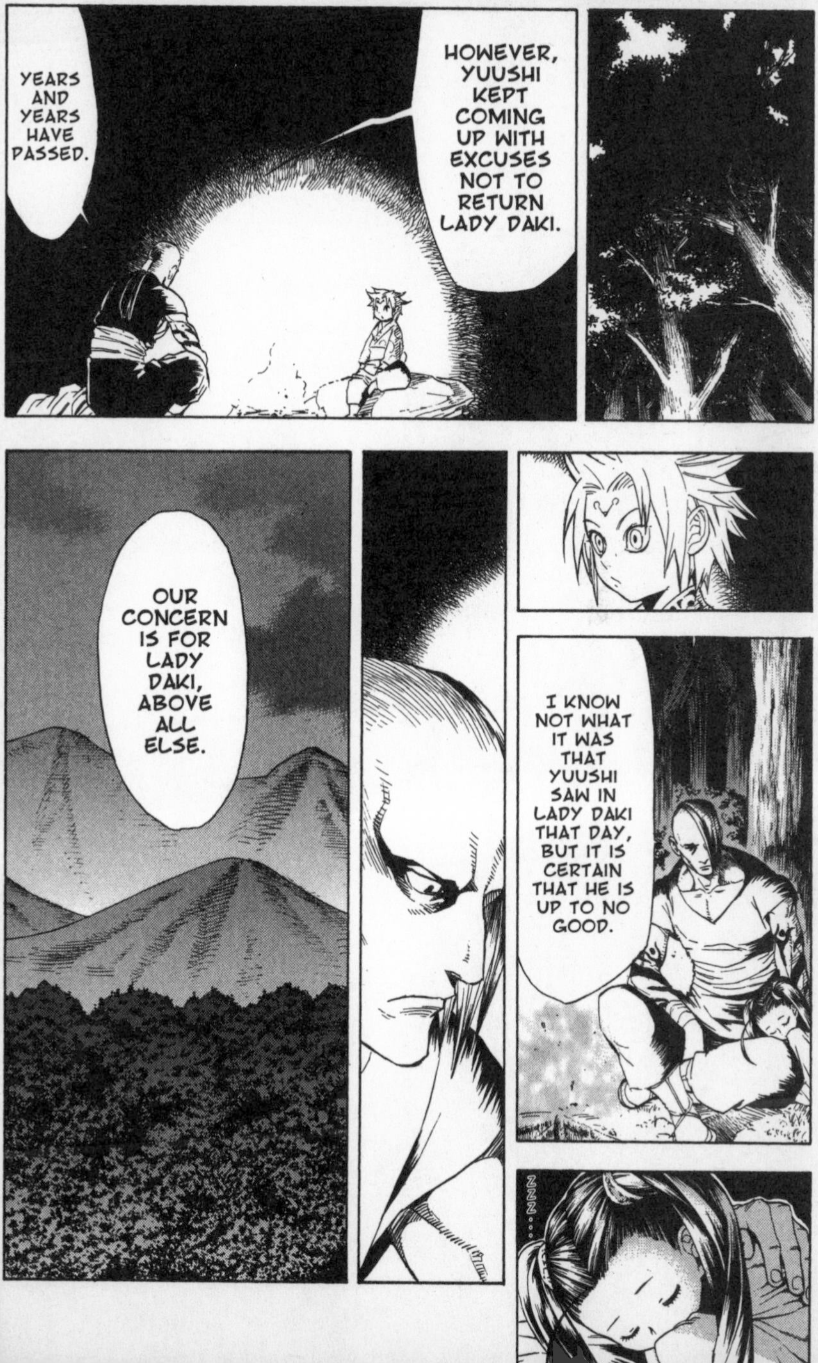
HOWEVER, YUUSHI KEPT COMING UP WITH EXCUSES NOT TO RETURN LADY DAKI.
YEARS AND YEARS HAVE PASSED.
I KNOW NOT WHAT IT WAS THAT YUUSHI SAW IN LADY DAKI THAT DAY, BUT IT IS CERTAIN THAT HE IS UP TO NO GOOD.
ZZZ...
OUR CONCERN IS FOR LADY DAKI, ABOVE ALL ELSE.

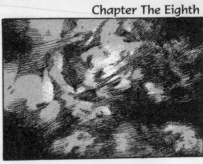

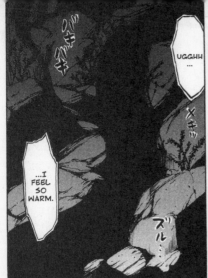

UGGHH ...

...I FEEL SO WARM.

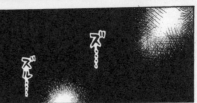

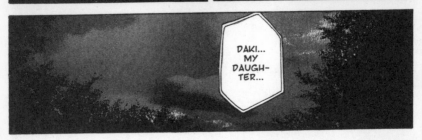

DAKI... MY DAUGH- TER...

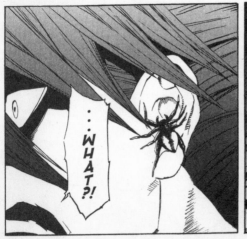

...WHAT?!

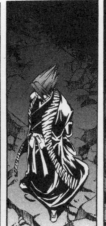

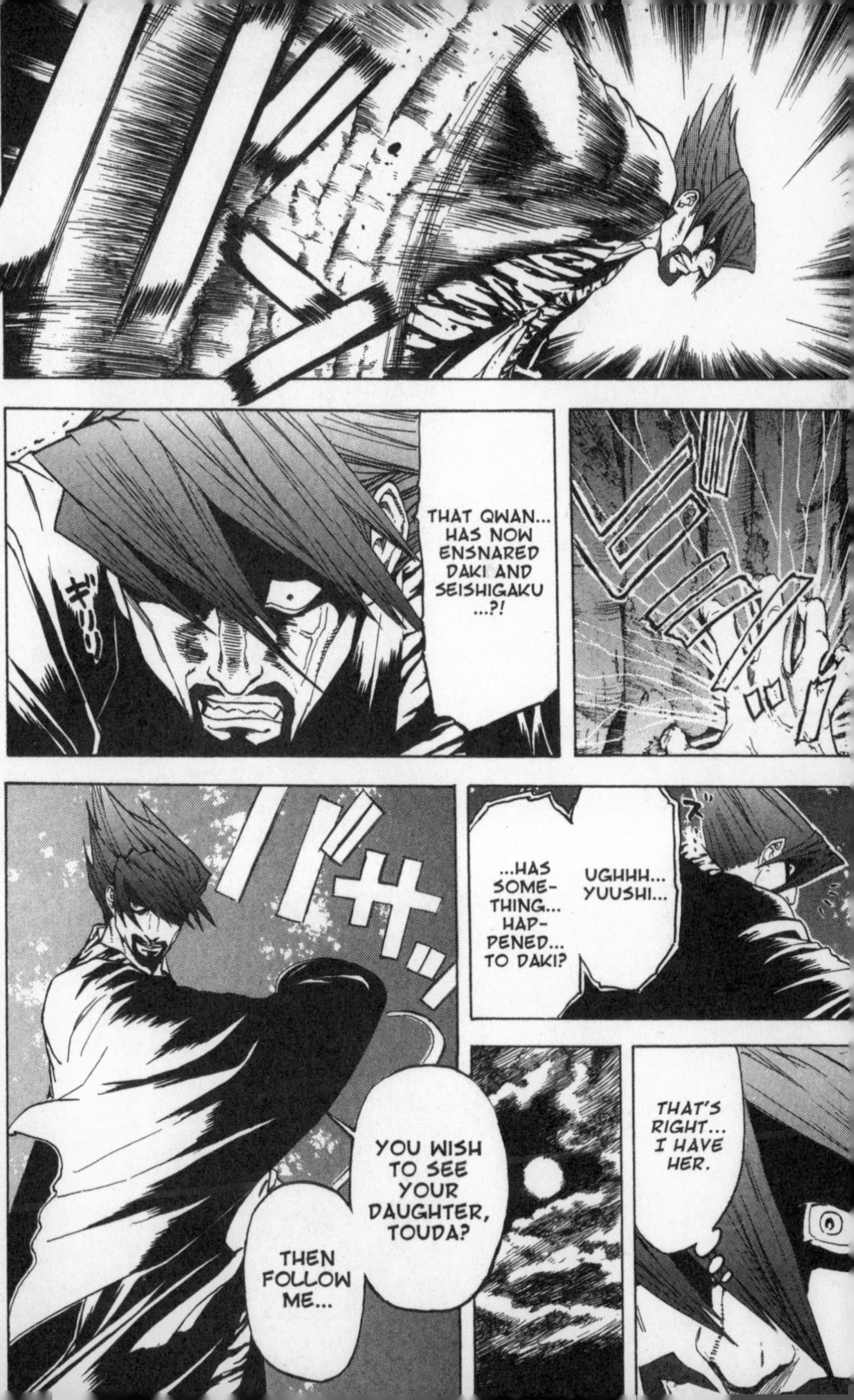
THAT QWAN... HAS NOW ENSNARED DAKI AND SEISHIGAKU ...?!
ギリ
UGHHH... YUUSHI...
...HAS SOME-THING... HAP-PENED... TO DAKI?
THAT'S RIGHT... I HAVE HER.
YOU WISH TO SEE YOUR DAUGHTER, TOUDA?
THEN FOLLOW ME...

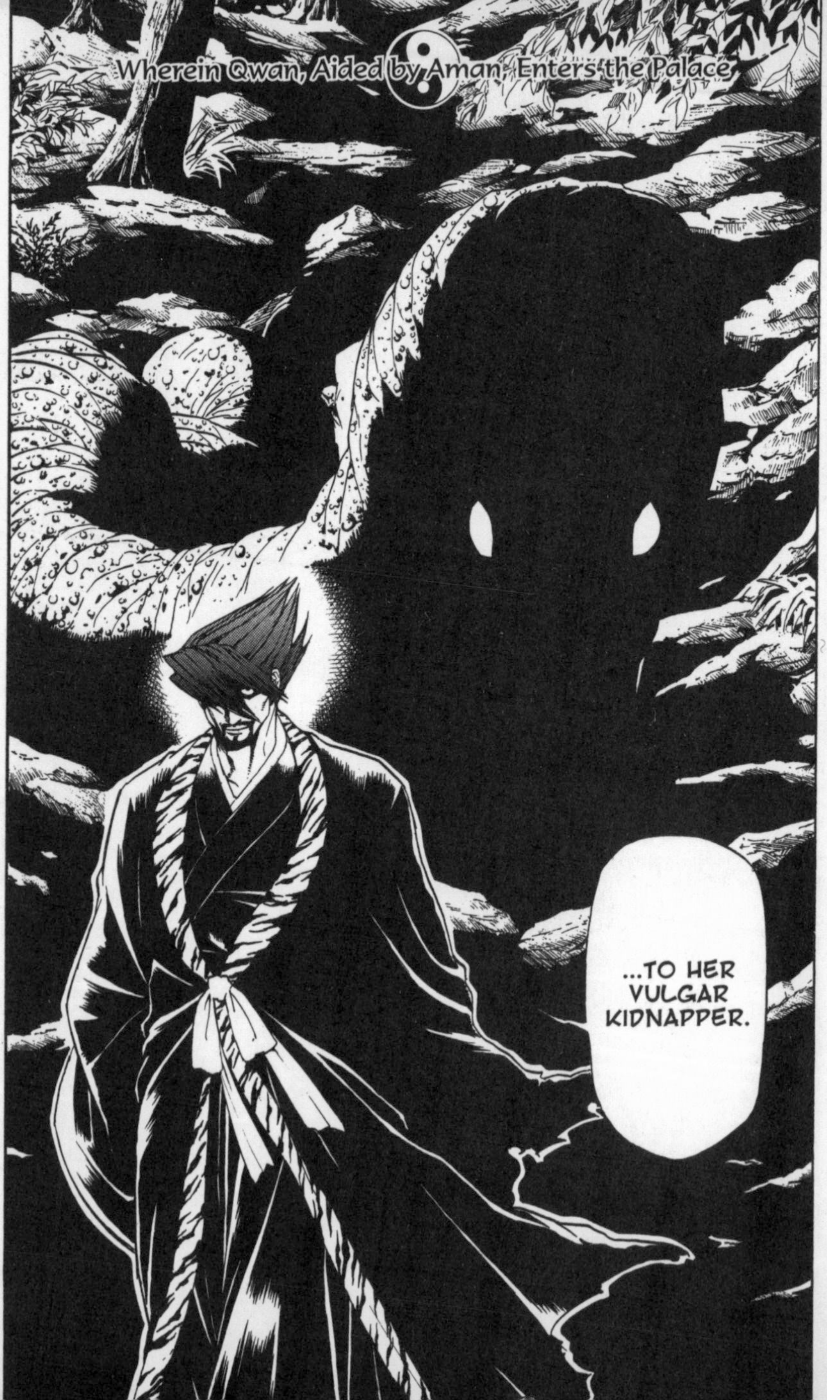

Wherein Qwan, Aided by Aman, Enters the Palace
...TO HER VULGAR KIDNAPPER.

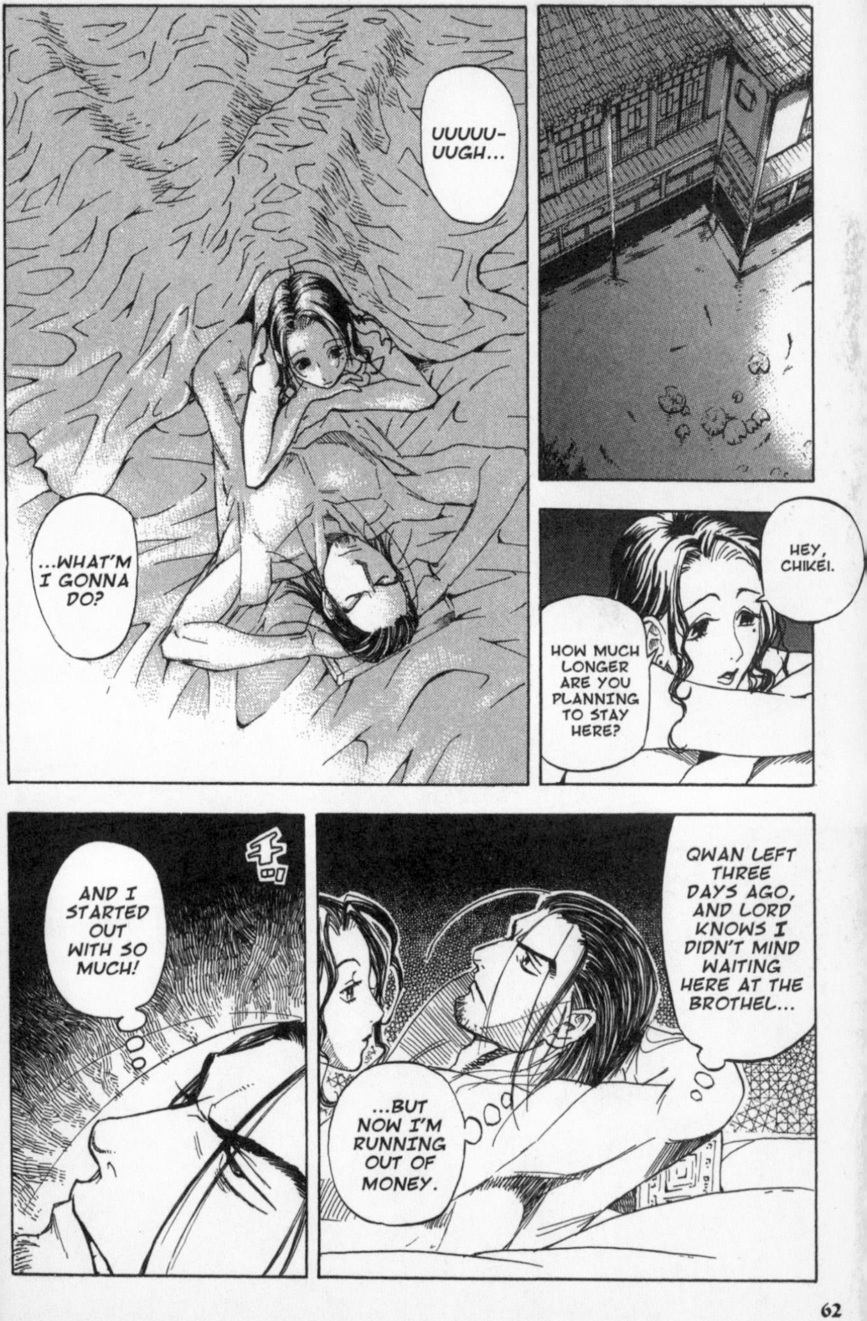
HEY, CHIKEI.
HOW MUCH LONGER ARE YOU PLANNING TO STAY HERE?
UUUUU-UUGH...
...WHAT'M I GONNA DO?
QWAN LEFT THREE DAYS AGO, AND LORD KNOWS I DIDN'T MIND WAITING HERE AT THE BROTHEL...
...BUT NOW I'M RUNNING OUT OF MONEY.
AND I STARTED OUT WITH SO MUCH!

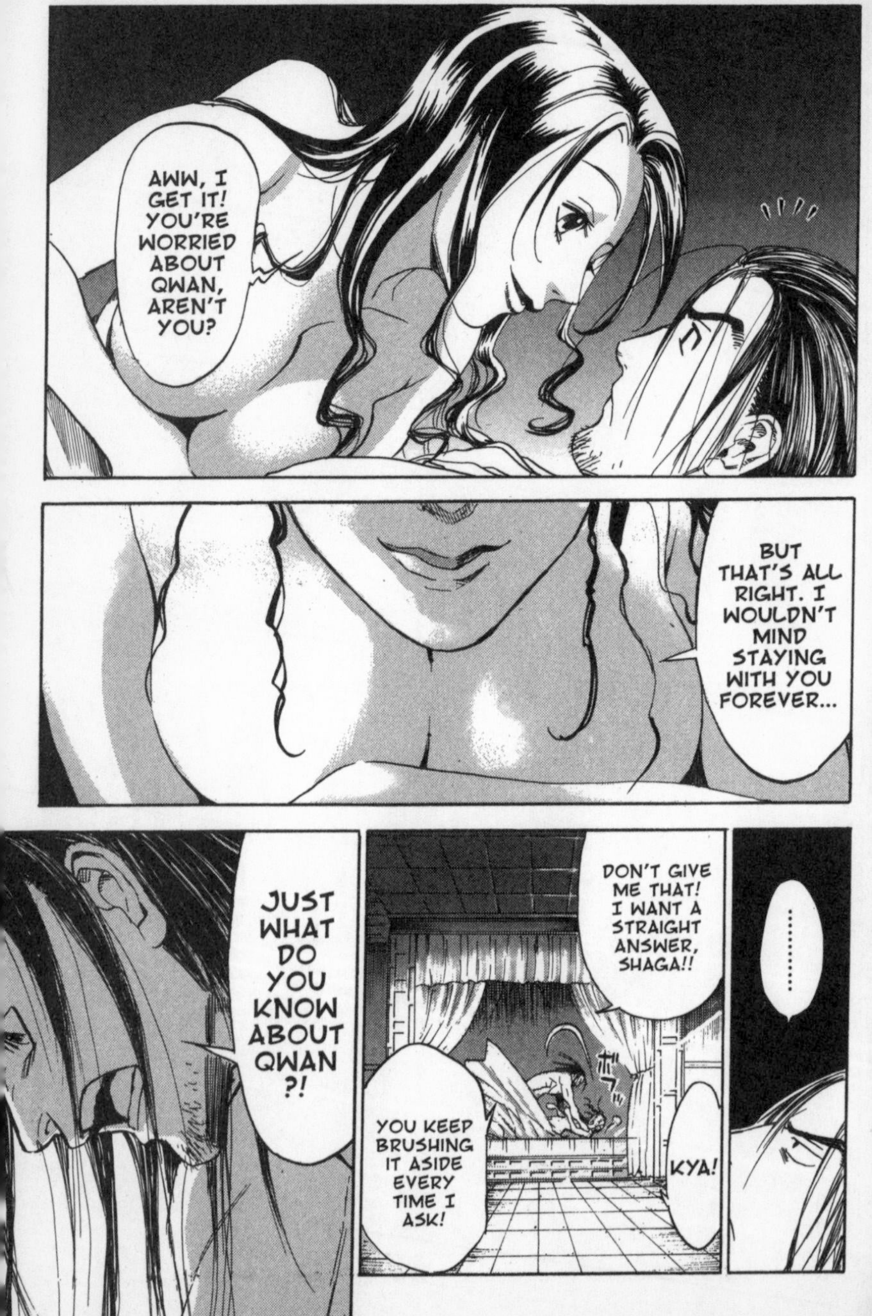
AWW, I GET IT! YOU'RE WORRIED ABOUT QWAN, AREN'T YOU?
BUT THAT'S ALL RIGHT. I WOULDN'T MIND STAYING WITH YOU FOREVER...
....
DON'T GIVE ME THAT! I WANT A STRAIGHT ANSWER, SHAGA!!
KYA!
YOU KEEP BRUSHING IT ASIDE EVERY TIME I ASK!
JUST WHAT DO YOU KNOW ABOUT QWAN?!

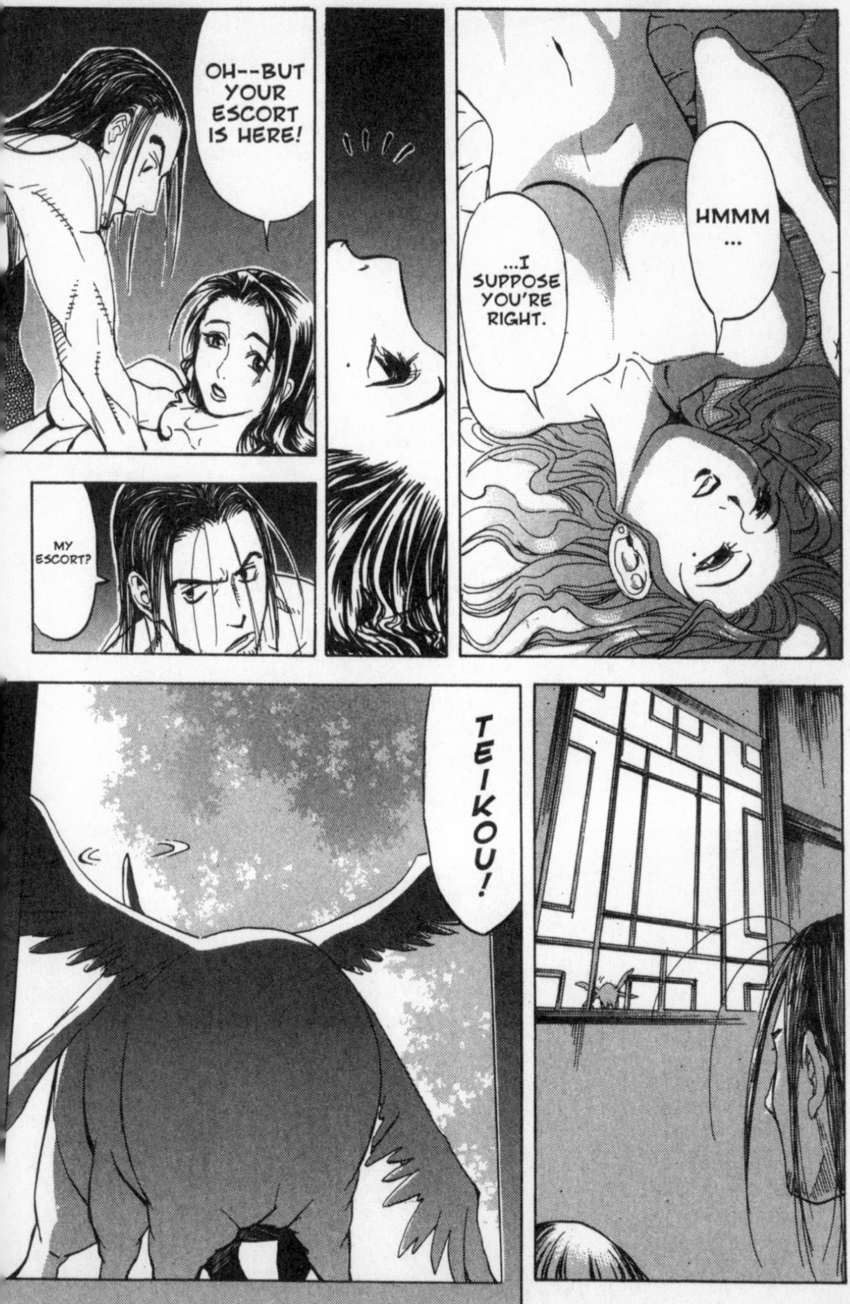
HMMM...
...I SUPPOSE YOU'RE RIGHT.
OH--BUT YOUR ESCORT IS HERE!
MY ESCORT?
TEIKOU!

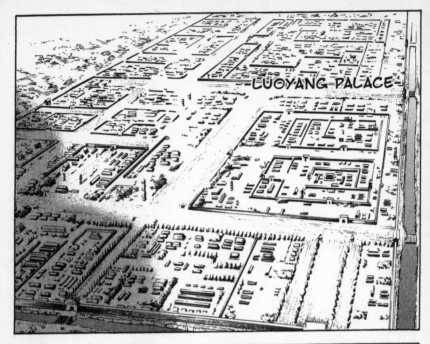

LUOYANG PALACE

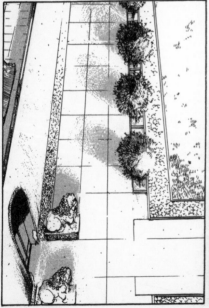

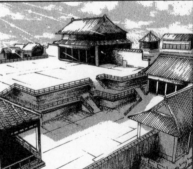

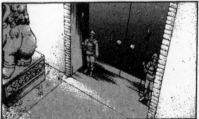

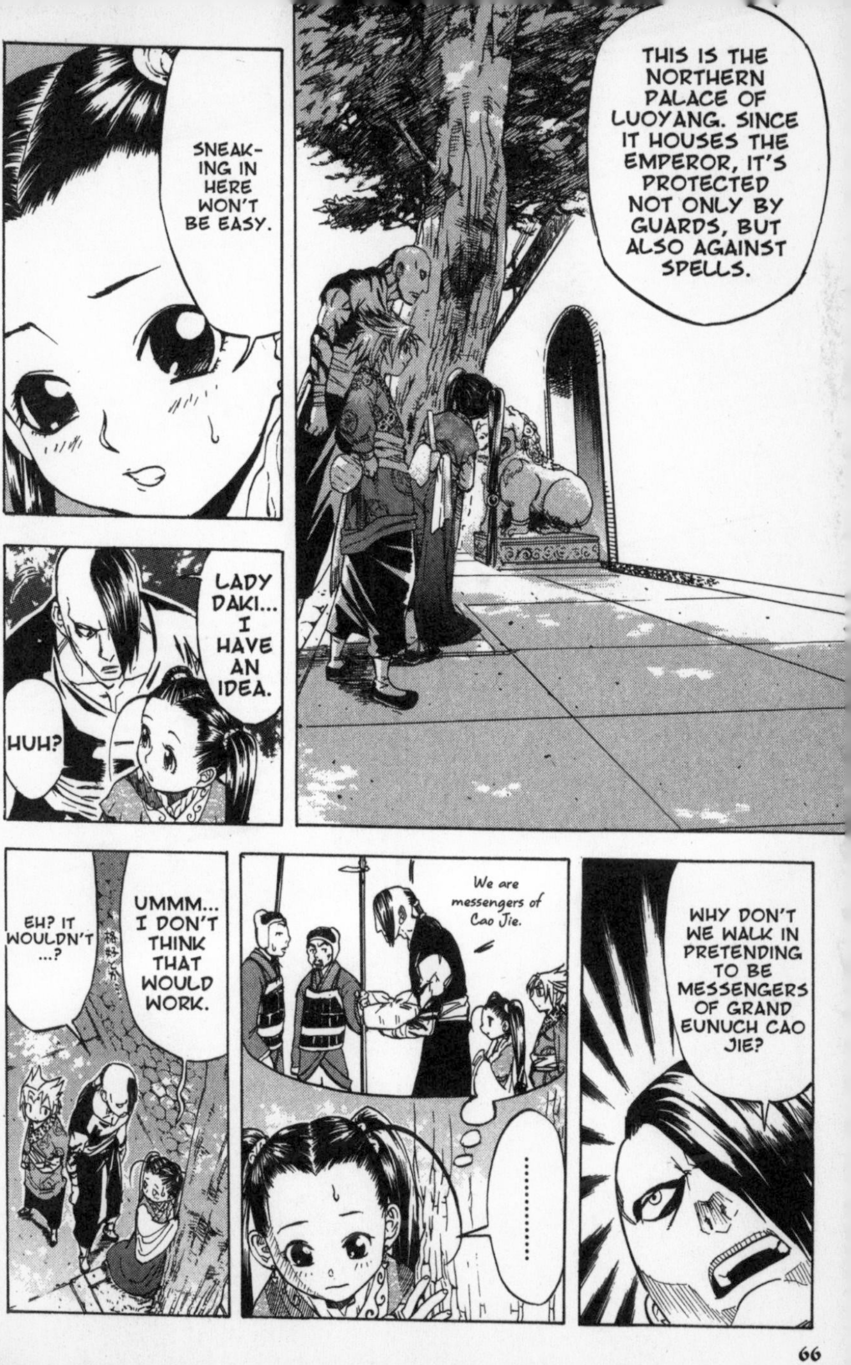
THIS IS THE NORTHERN PALACE OF LUOYANG. SINCE IT HOUSES THE EMPEROR, IT'S PROTECTED NOT ONLY BY GUARDS, BUT ALSO AGAINST SPELLS.
SNEAK-ING IN HERE WON'T BE EASY.
LADY DAKI... I HAVE AN IDEA.
HUH?
WHY DON'T WE WALK IN PRETENDING TO BE MESSENGERS OF GRAND EUNUCH CAO JIE?
We are messengers of Cao Jie.
....
UMMM... I DON'T THINK THAT WOULD WORK.
EH? IT WOULDN'T ...?

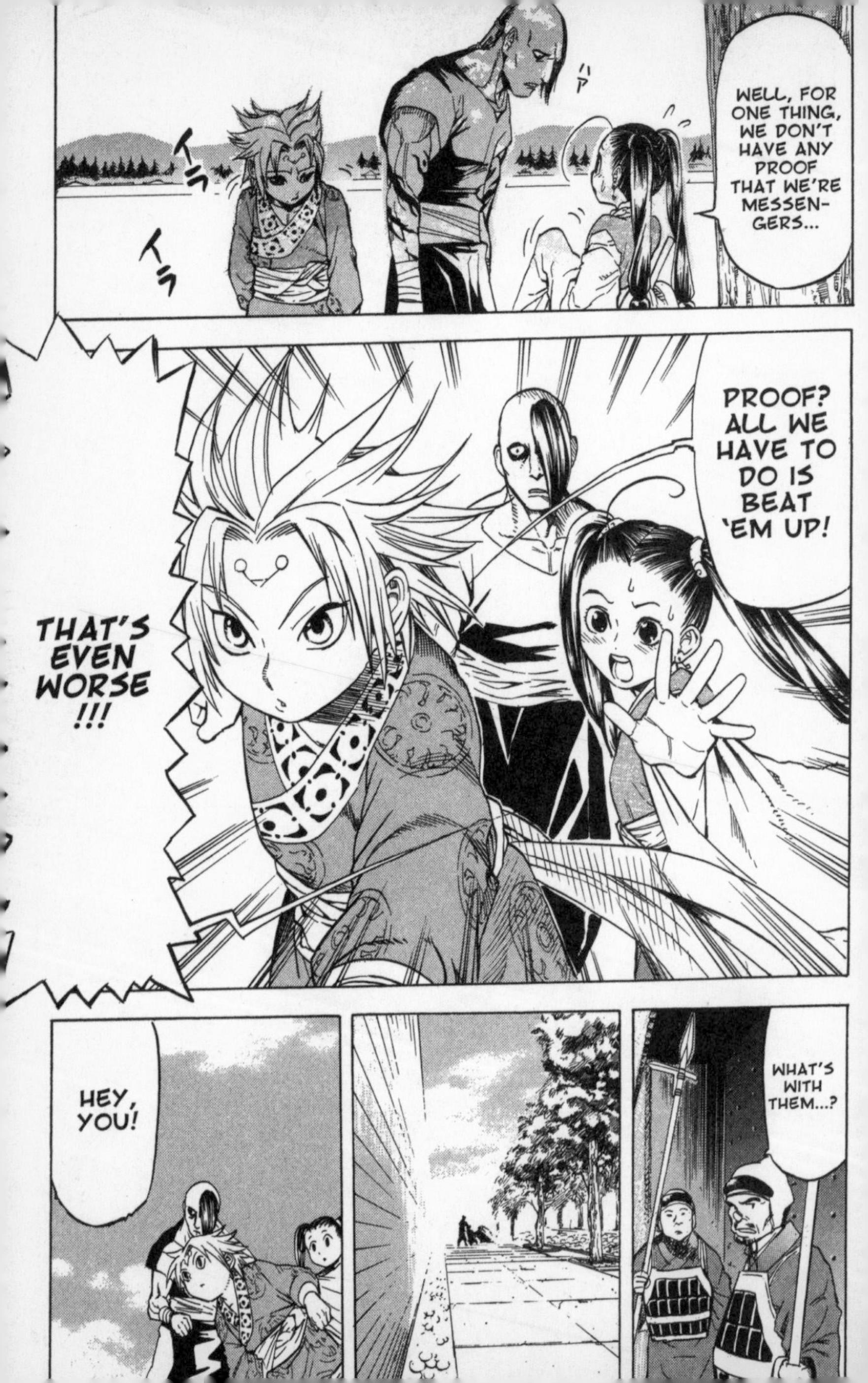
WELL, FOR ONE THING, WE DON'T HAVE ANY PROOF THAT WE'RE MESSEN-GERS...
イラ
イラ
PROOF? ALL WE HAVE TO DO IS BEAT 'EM UP!
THAT'S EVEN WORSE !!!
WHAT'S WITH THEM...?
HEY, YOU!

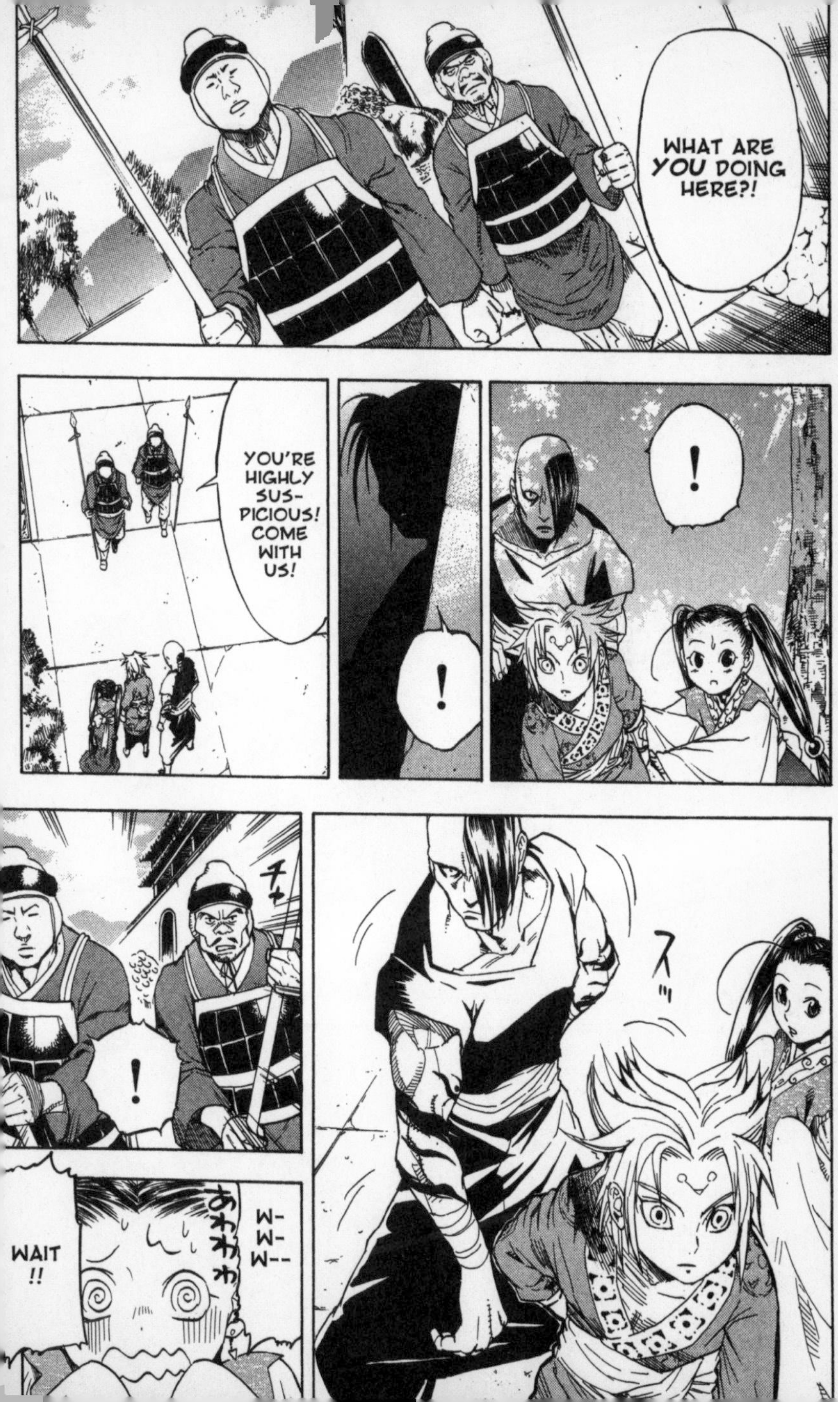
WHAT ARE *YOU* DOING HERE?!
!
!
YOU'RE HIGHLY SUS-PICIOUS! COME WITH US!
スッ
チャ
!
W-W-W--
あわわわ
WAIT !!

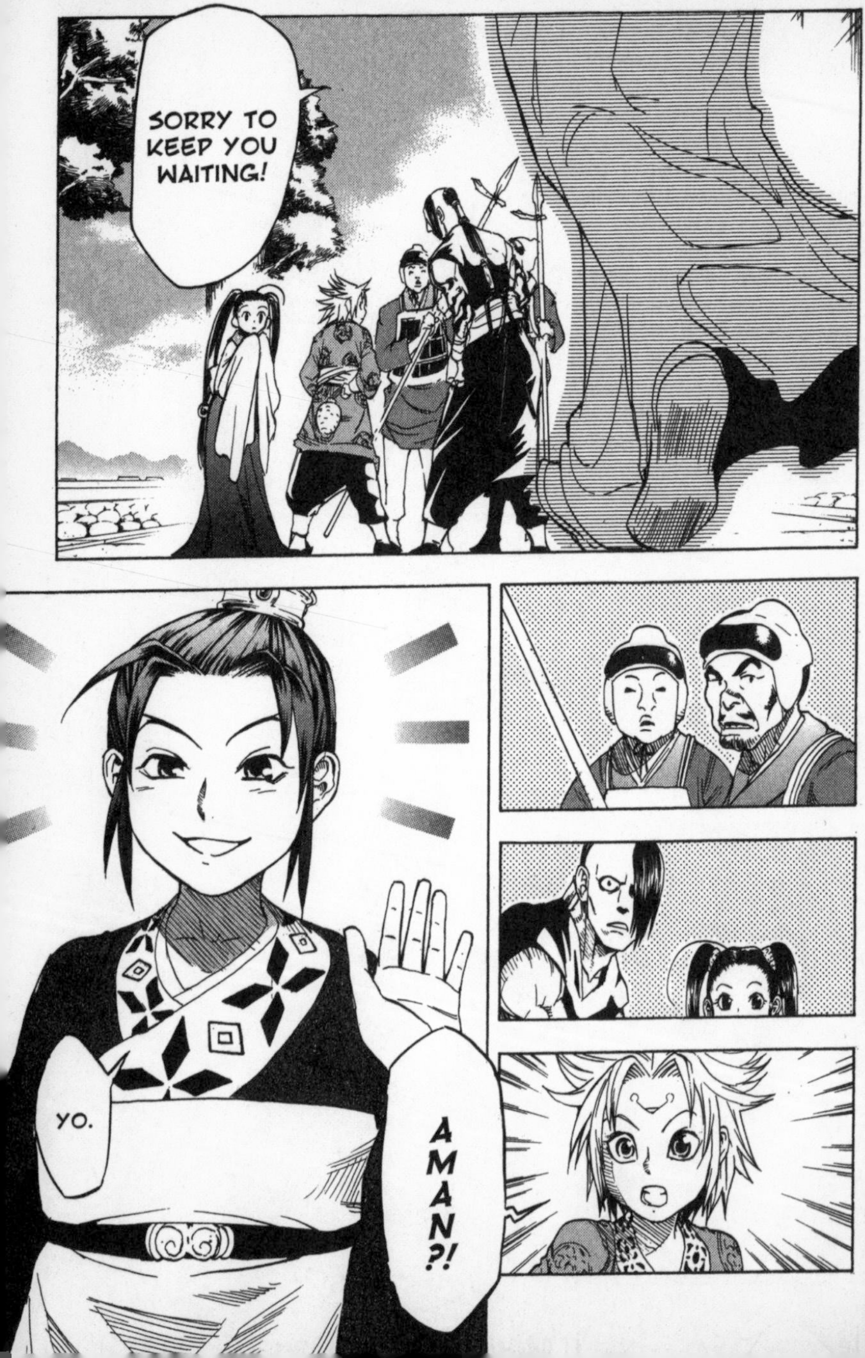
SORRY TO KEEP YOU WAITING!
AMAN?!
YO.

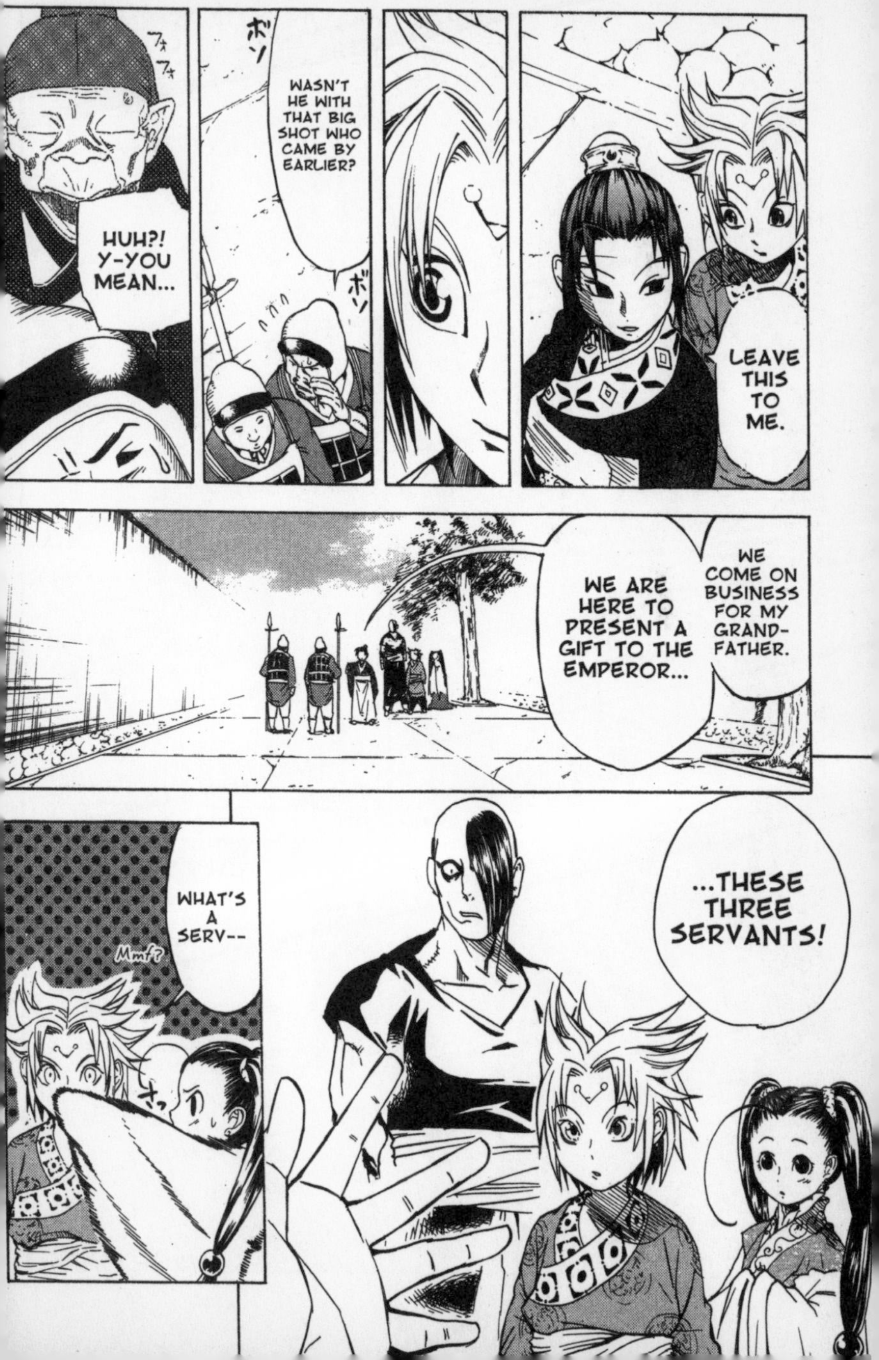
LEAVE THIS TO ME.
ボソ
WASN'T HE WITH THAT BIG SHOT WHO CAME BY EARLIER?
ボソ
HUH?! Y-YOU MEAN...
WE COME ON BUSINESS FOR MY GRANDFATHER.
WE ARE HERE TO PRESENT A GIFT TO THE EMPEROR...
...THESE THREE SERVANTS!
WHAT'S A SERV--
Mmf?

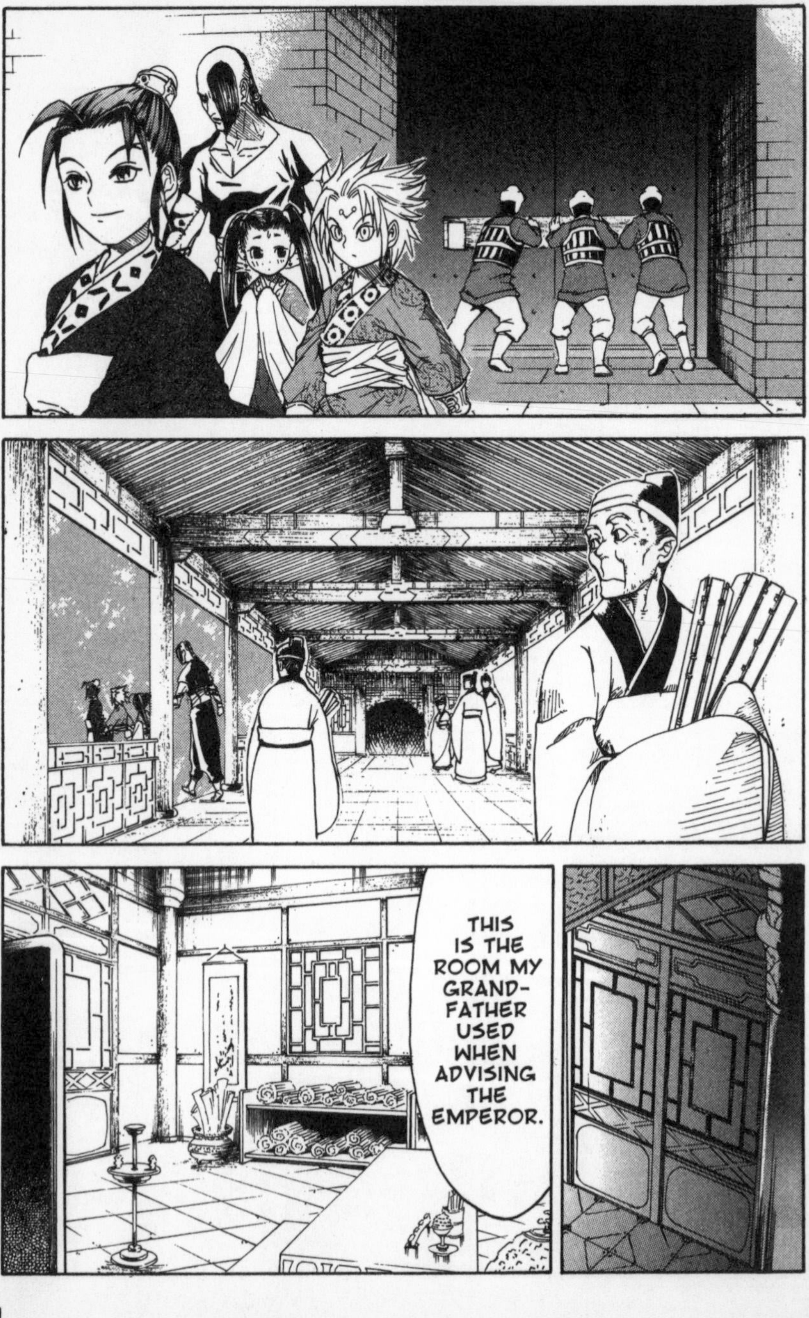
THIS IS THE ROOM MY GRAND-FATHER USED WHEN ADVISING THE EMPEROR.

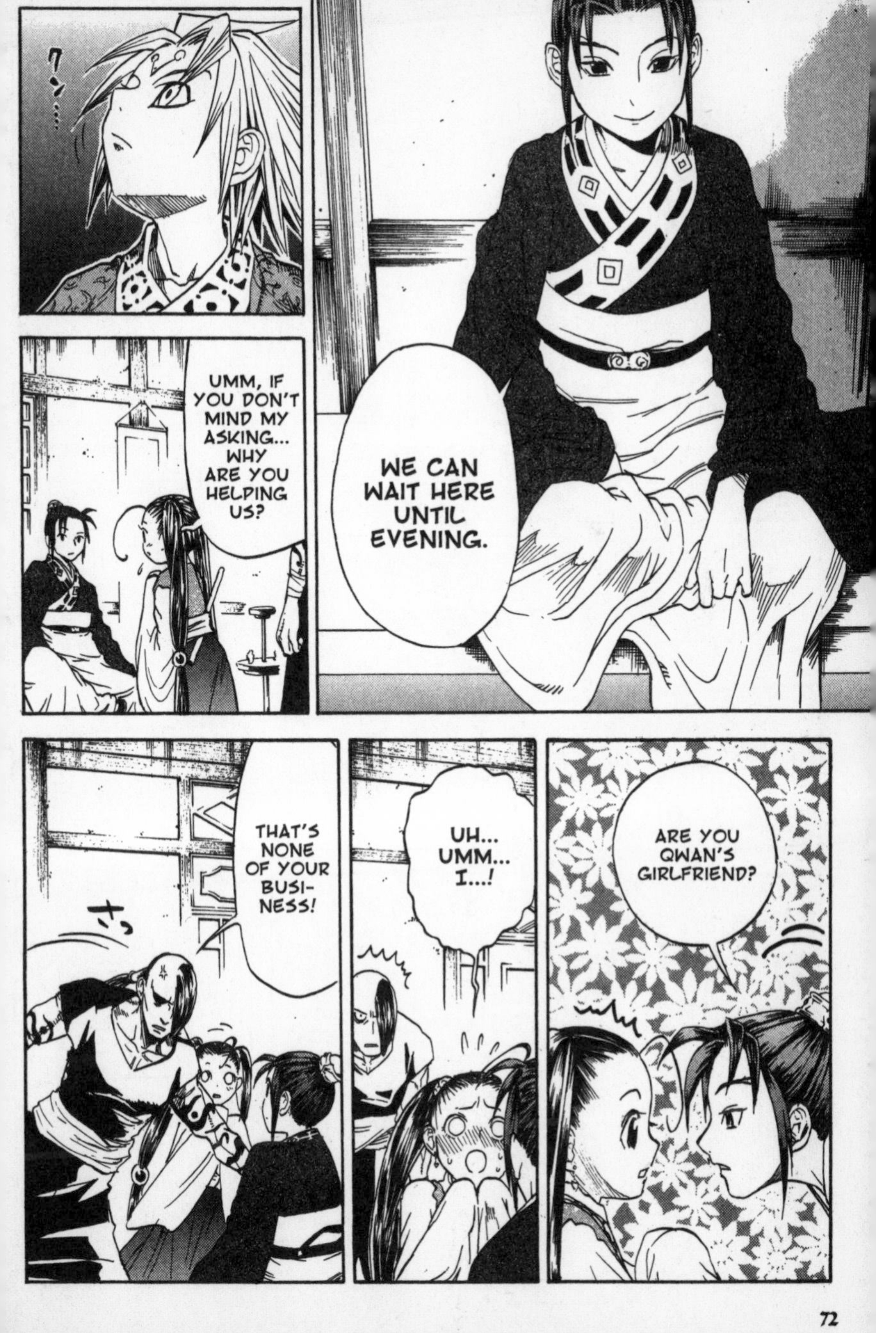
WE CAN WAIT HERE UNTIL EVENING.
UMM, IF YOU DON'T MIND MY ASKING... WHY ARE YOU HELPING US?
ARE YOU QWAN'S GIRLFRIEND?
UH... UMM... I...!
THAT'S NONE OF YOUR BUSI-NESS!

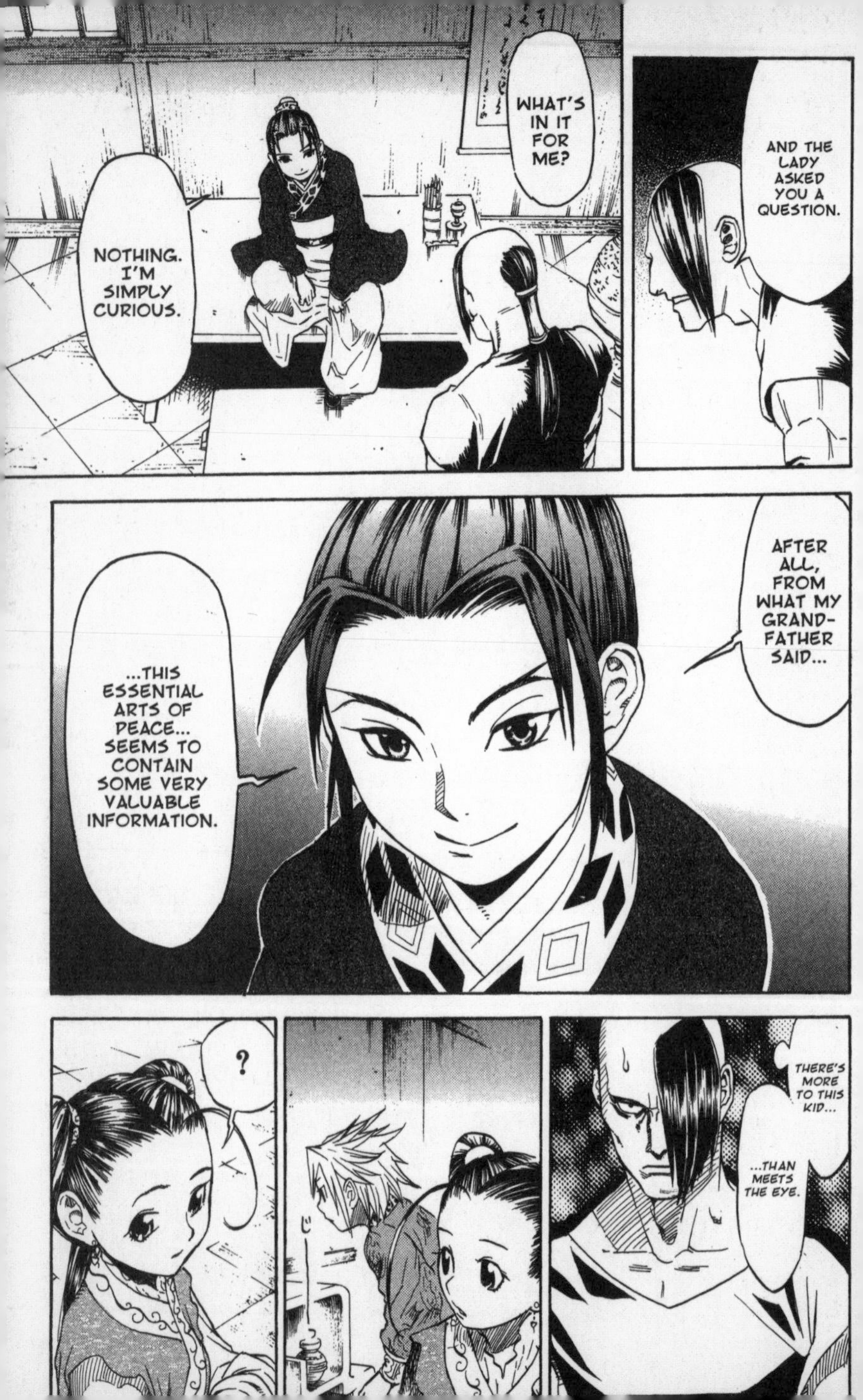
AND THE LADY ASKED YOU A QUESTION.
WHAT'S IN IT FOR ME?
NOTHING. I'M SIMPLY CURIOUS.
AFTER ALL, FROM WHAT MY GRAND-FATHER SAID...
...THIS ESSENTIAL ARTS OF PEACE... SEEMS TO CONTAIN SOME VERY VALUABLE INFORMATION.
THERE'S MORE TO THIS KID...
...THAN MEETS THE EYE.
?

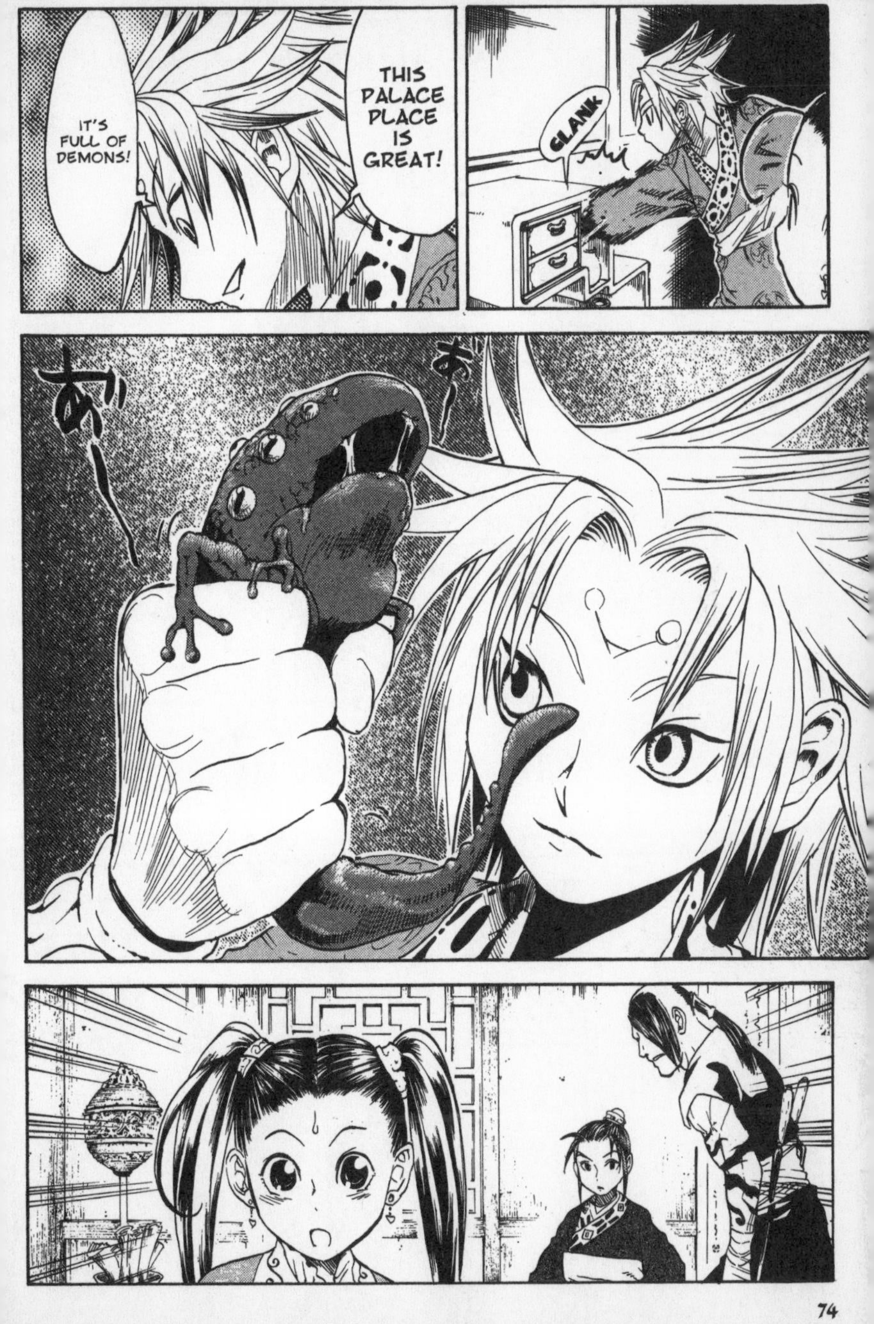
CLANK
THIS PALACE PLACE IS GREAT!
IT'S FULL OF DEMONS!

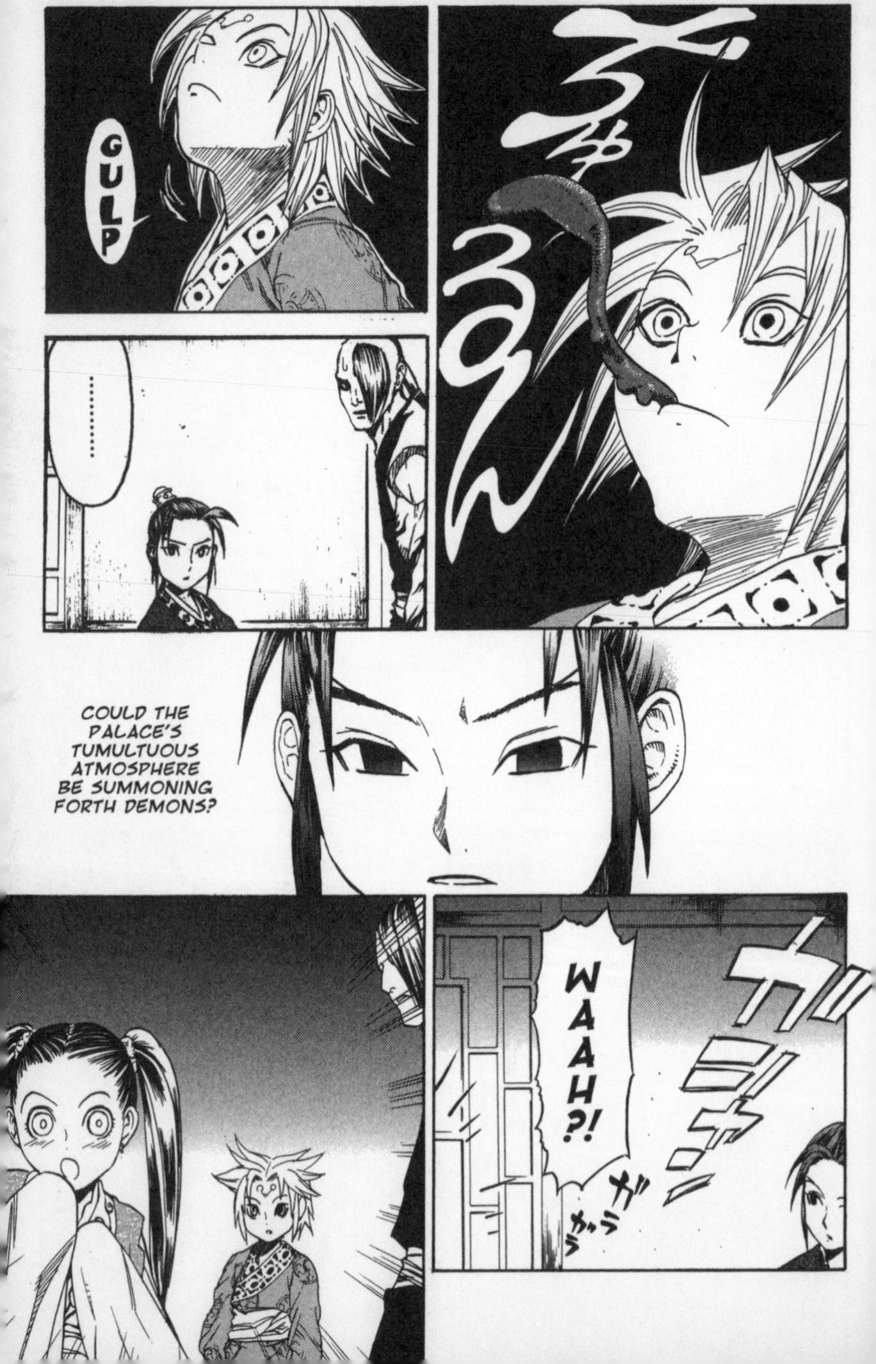
GULP
......
COULD THE PALACE'S TUMULTUOUS ATMOSPHERE BE SUMMONING FORTH DEMONS?
WAAAH?!
ガラガラ

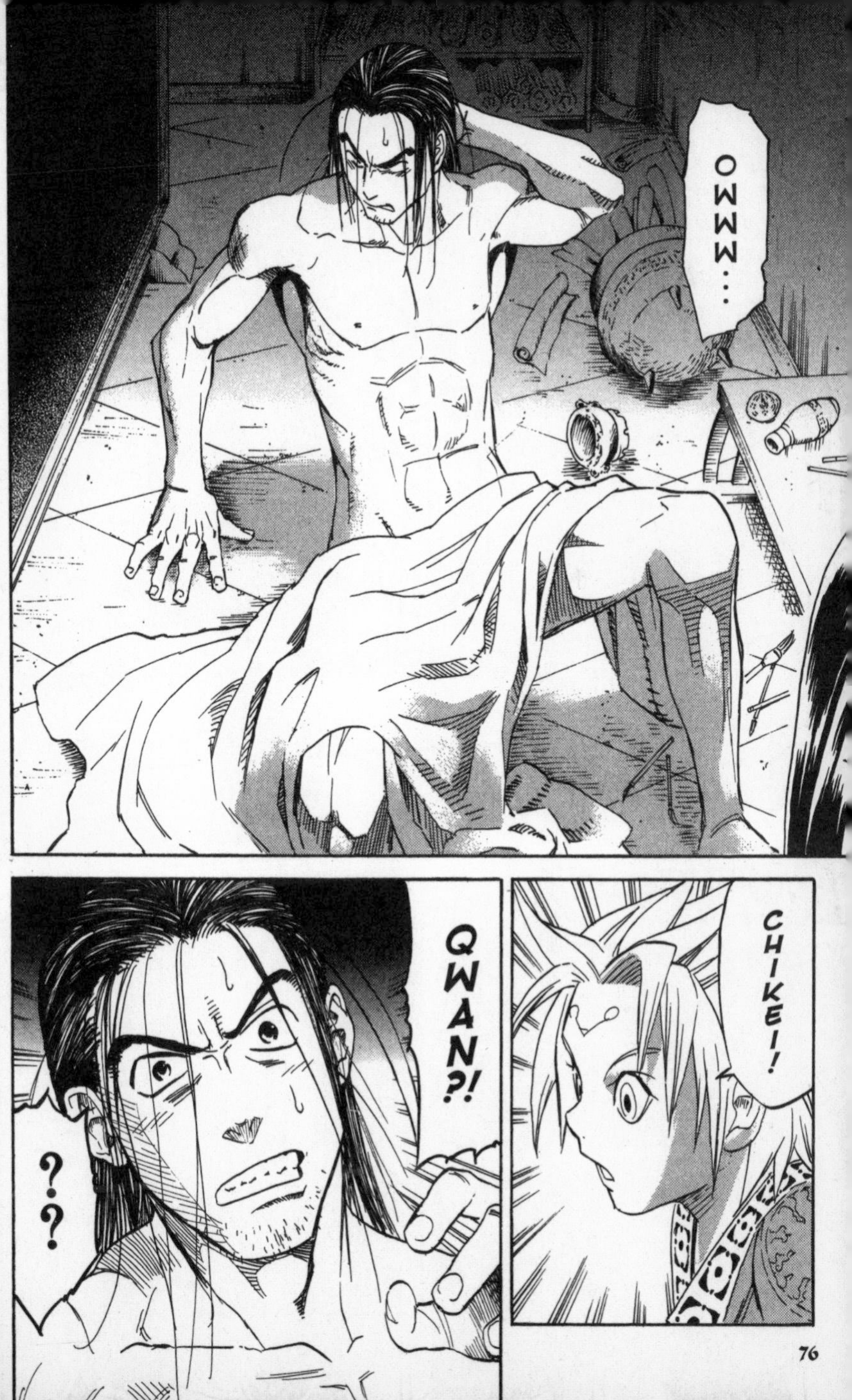
OWWW...
CHIKE!!
QWAN?!
??

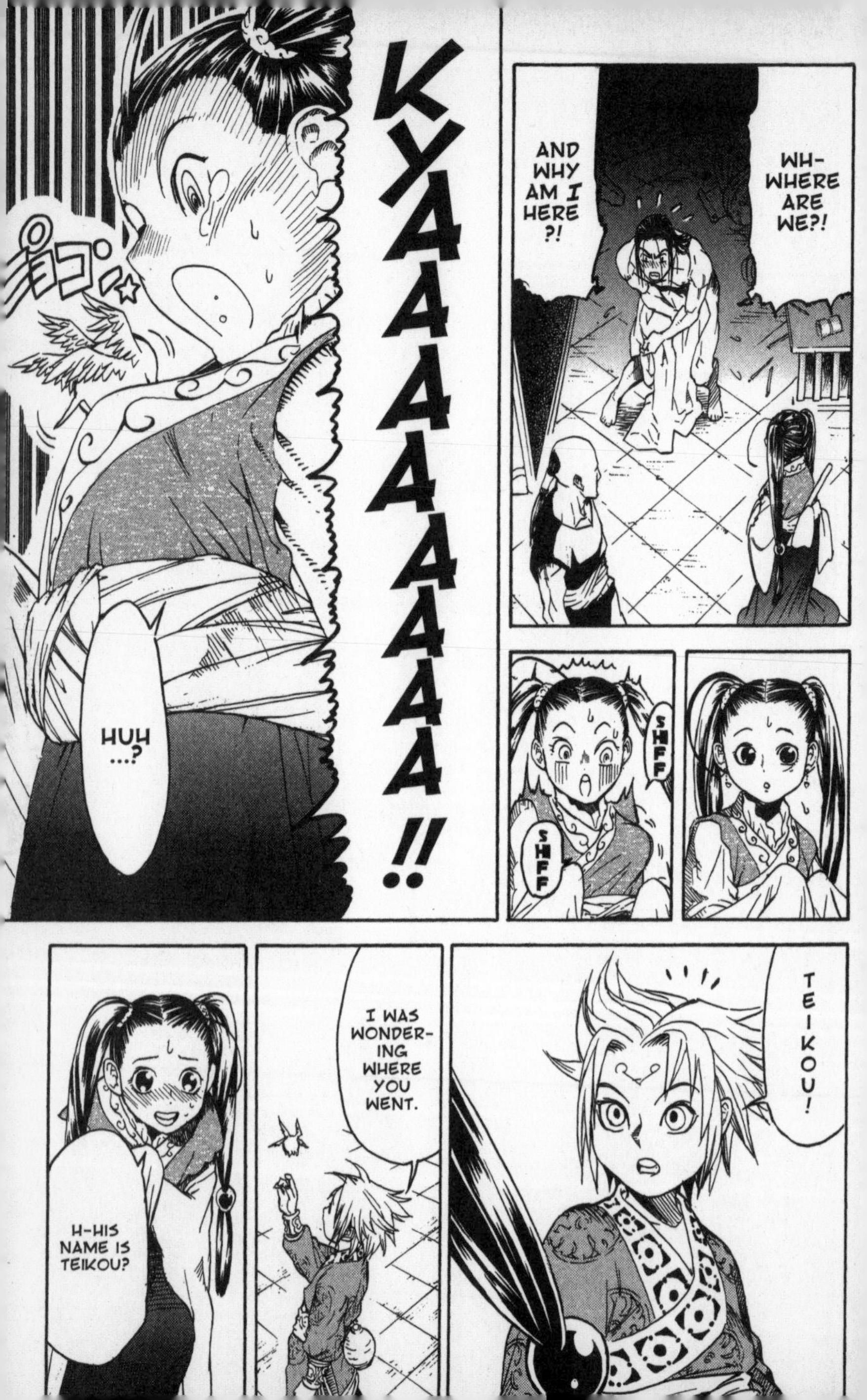
WH-WHERE ARE WE?!
AND WHY AM I HERE?!
SHFF
SHFF
KYAAAAAAA!!
HUH ...?
TEIKOU!
I WAS WONDER-ING WHERE YOU WENT.
H-HIS NAME IS TEIKOU?

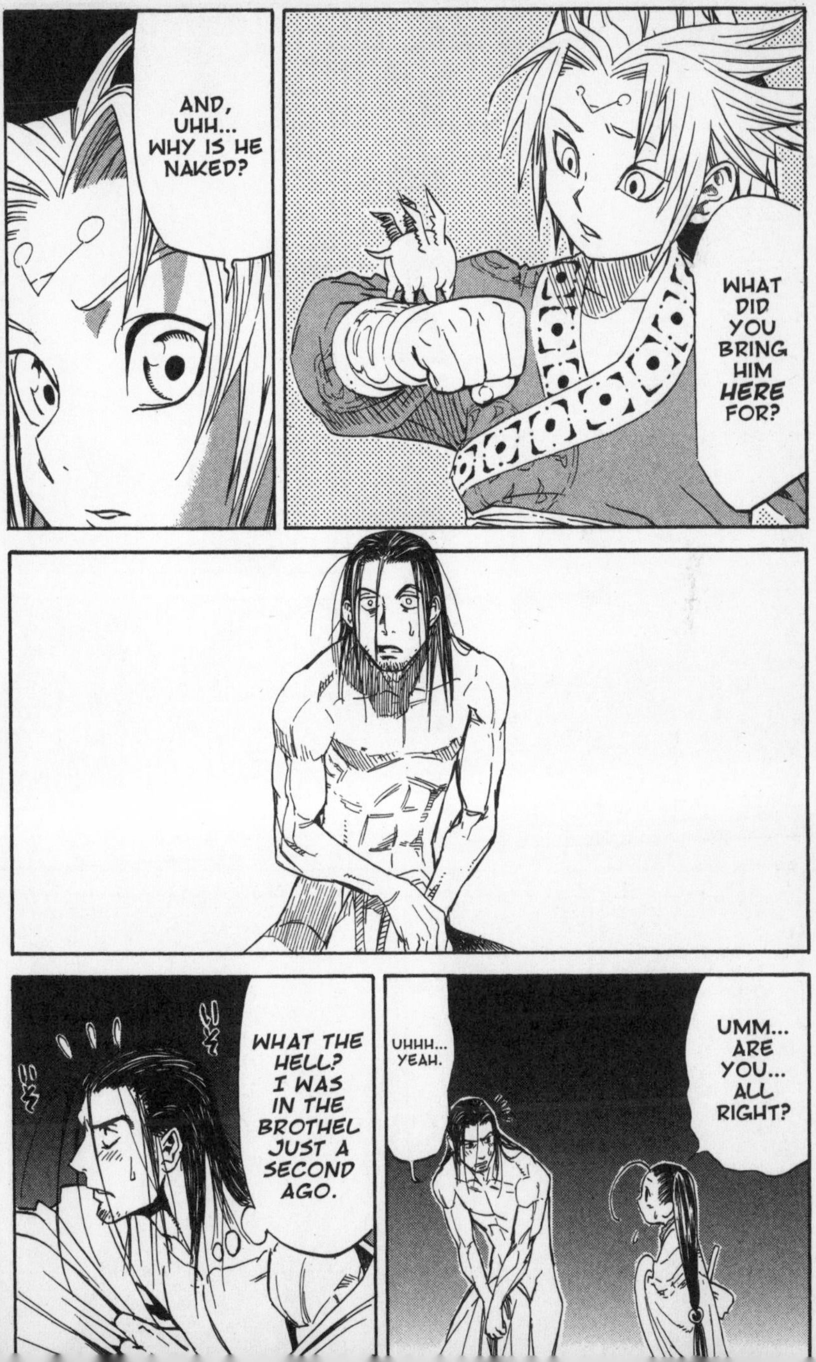
WHAT DID YOU BRING HIM HERE FOR?
AND, UHH... WHY IS HE NAKED?
UMM... ARE YOU... ALL RIGHT?
UHHH... YEAH.
WHAT THE HELL? I WAS IN THE BROTHEL JUST A SECOND AGO.

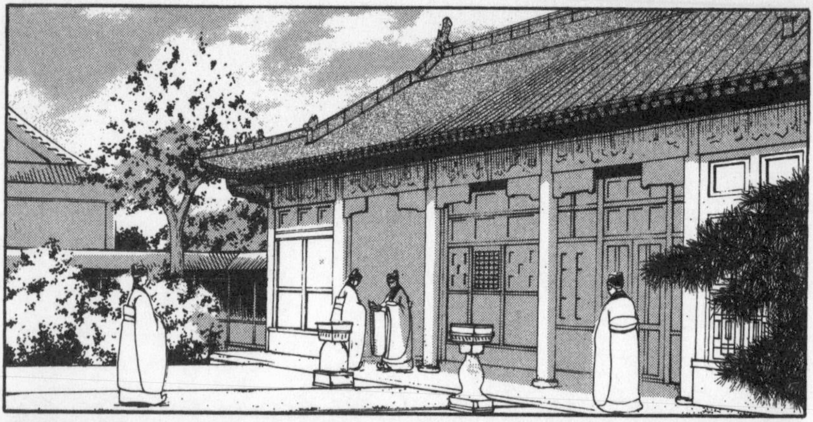
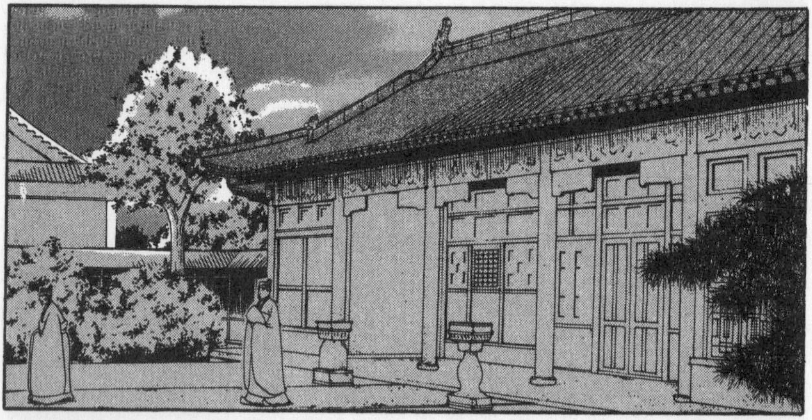
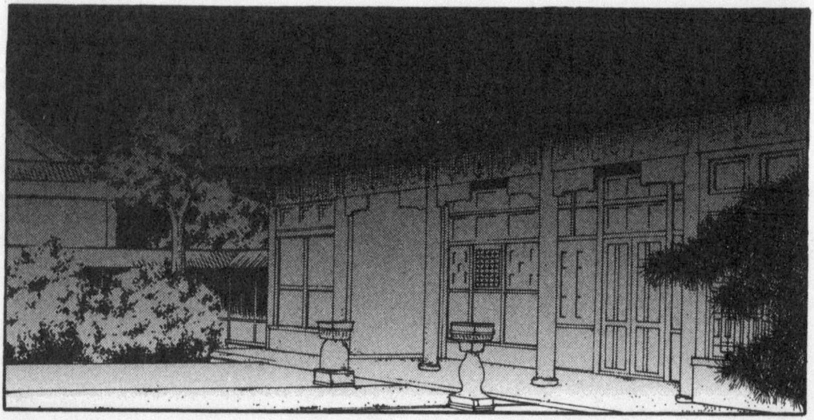

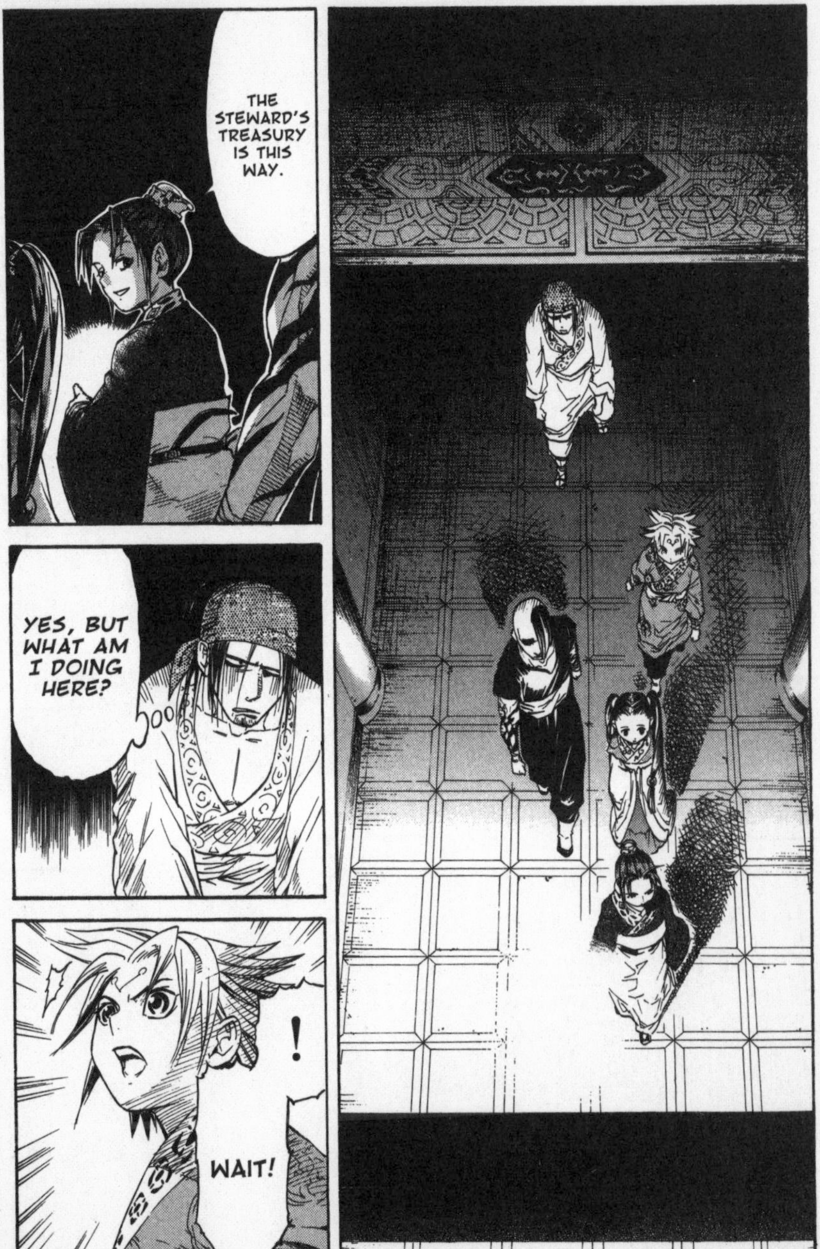
THE STEWARD'S TREASURY IS THIS WAY.
YES, BUT WHAT AM I DOING HERE?
!
WAIT!

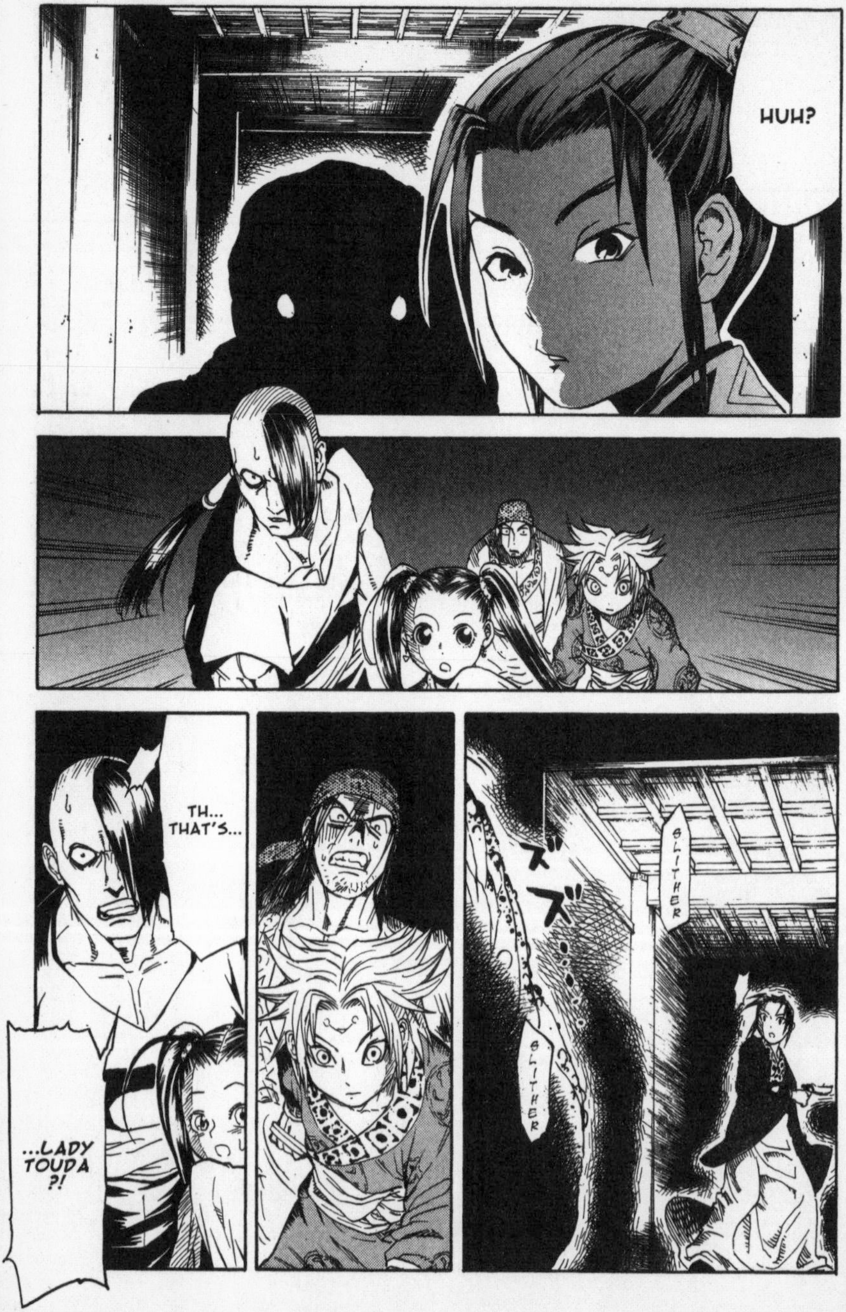
HUH?
SLITHER
SLITHER
TH... THAT'S...
...LADY TOUDA ?!

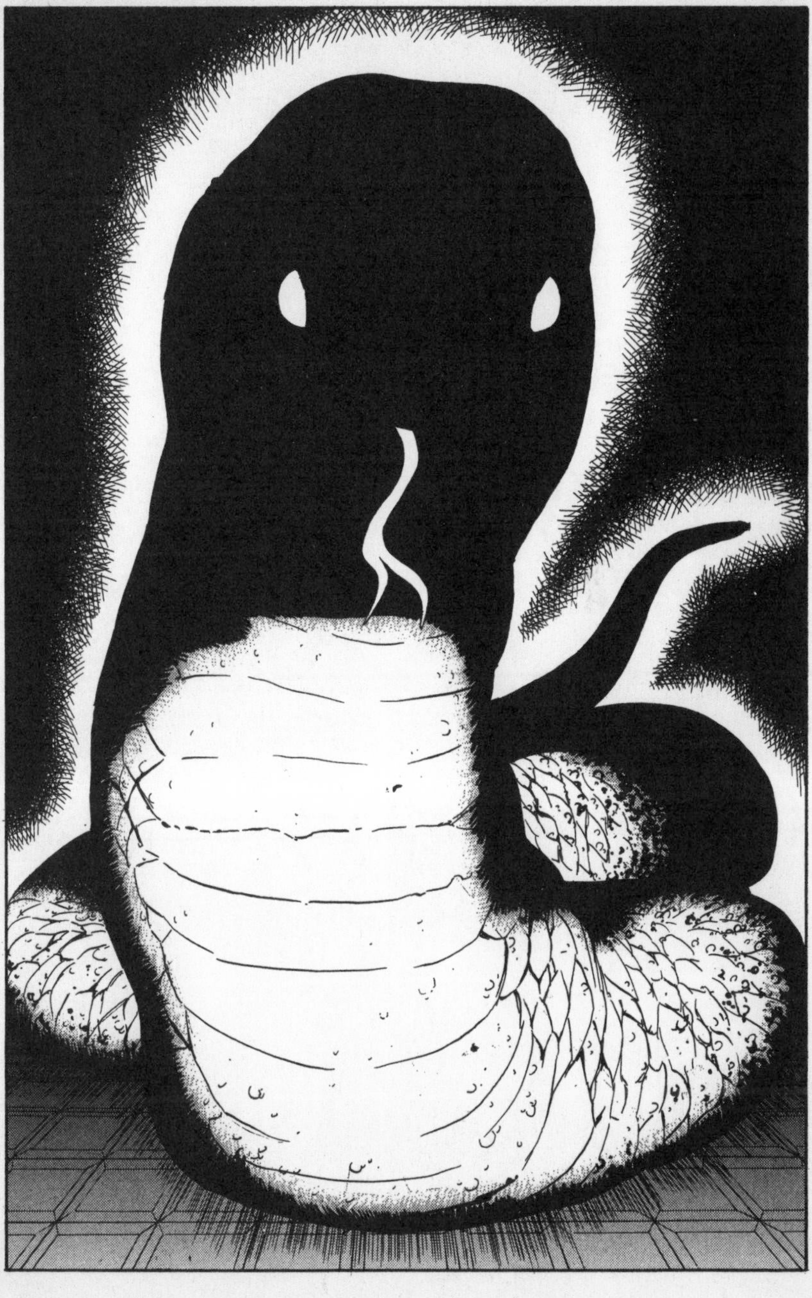

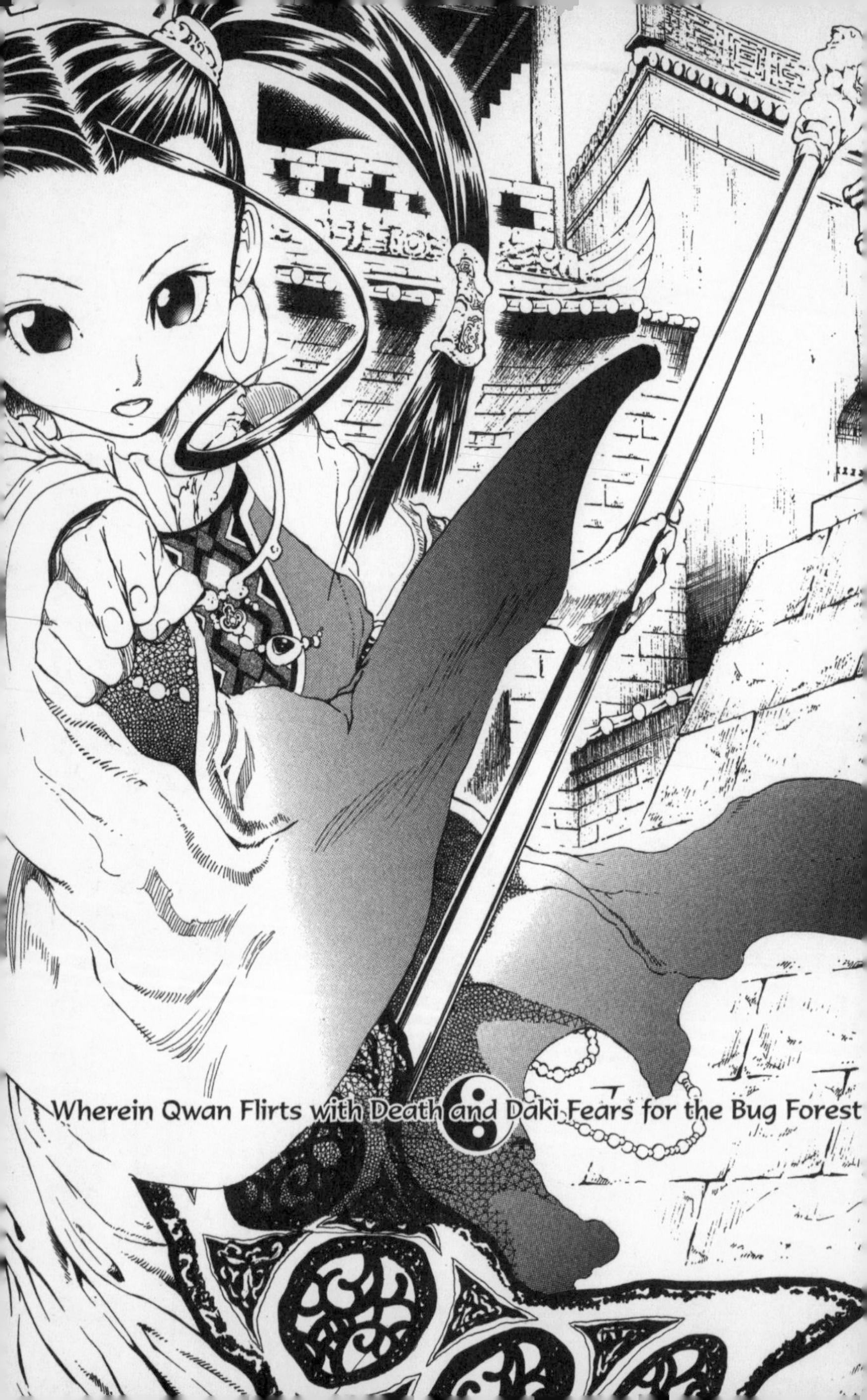
Wherein Qwan Flirts with Death and Daki Fears for the Bug Forest

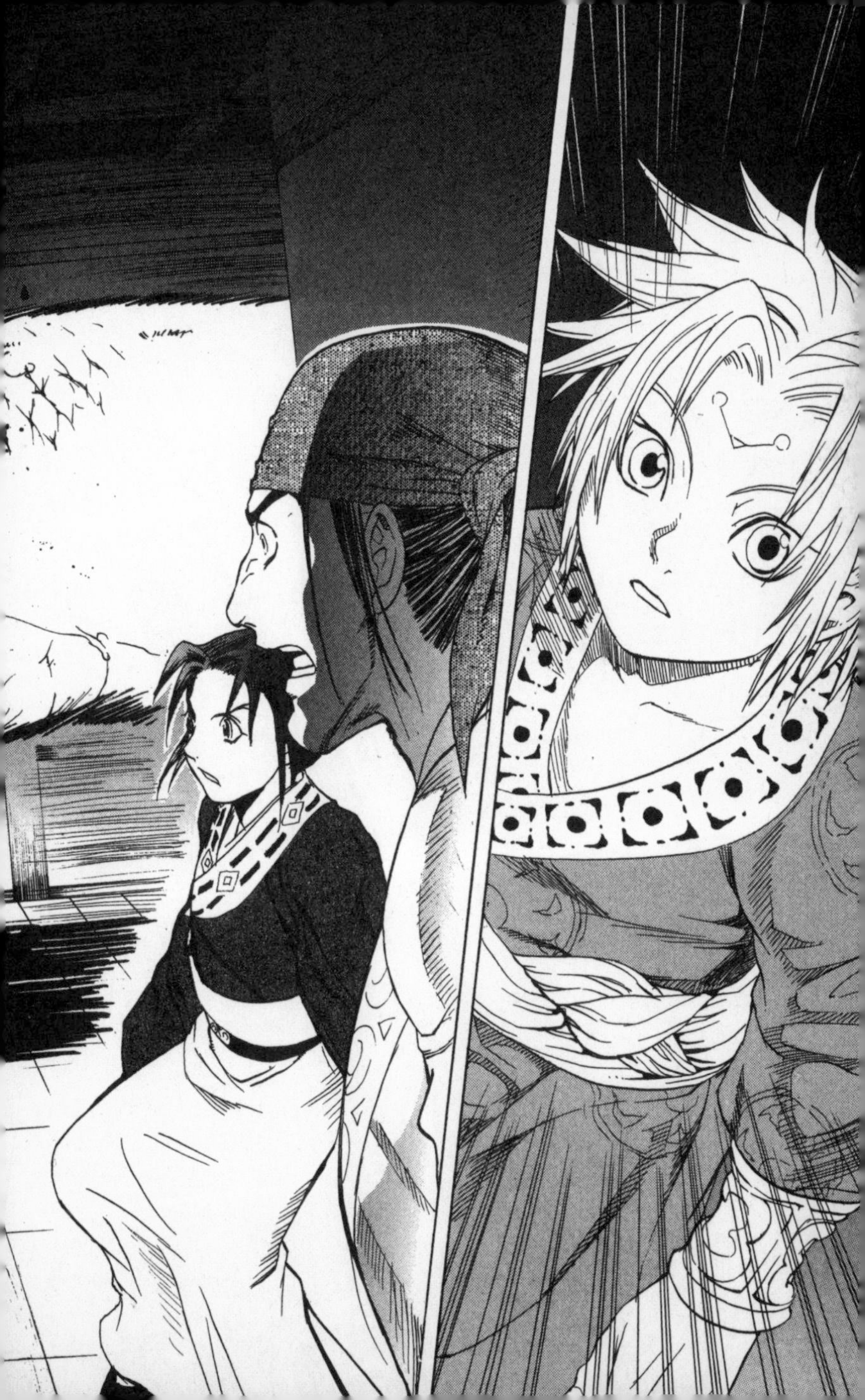

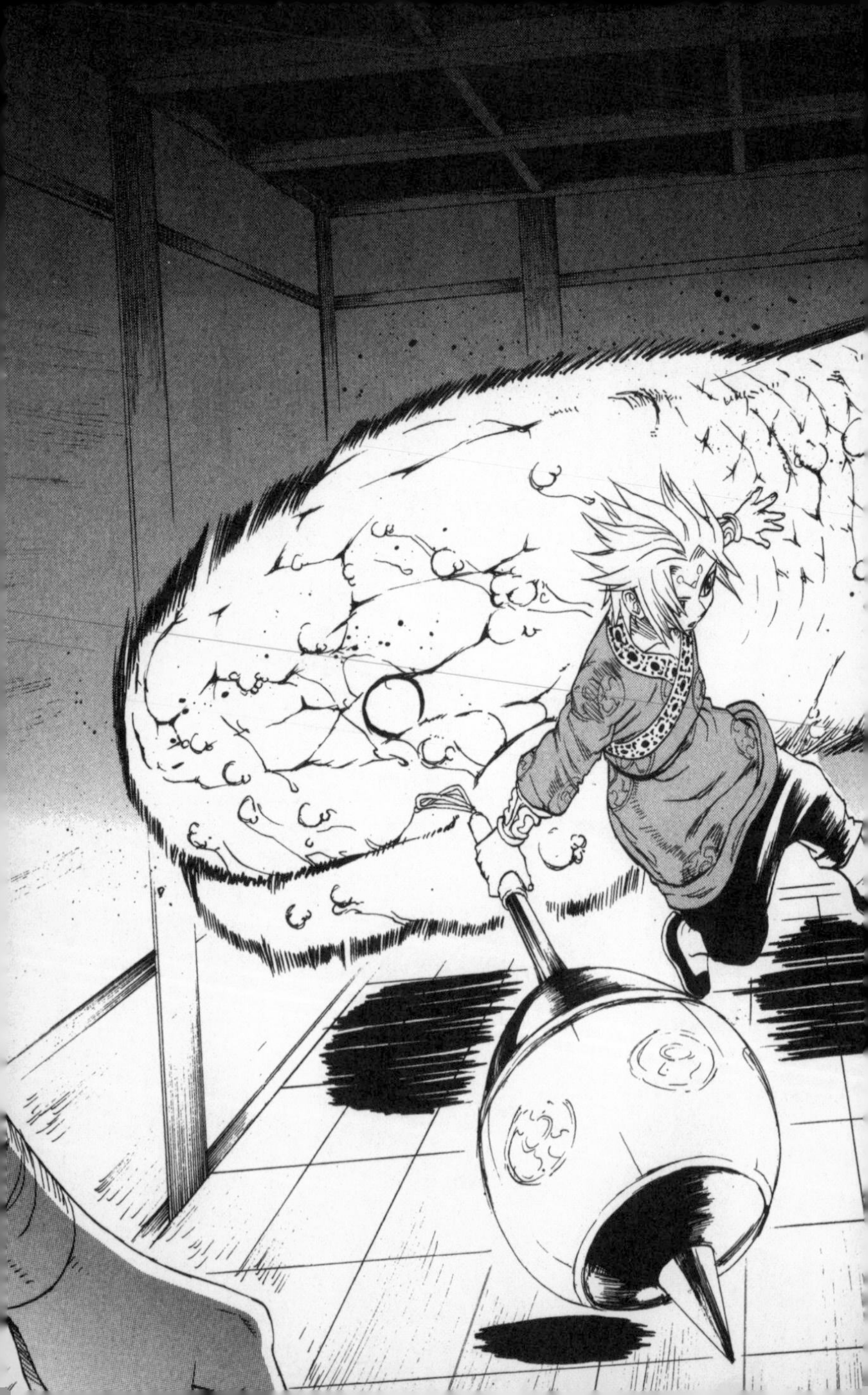

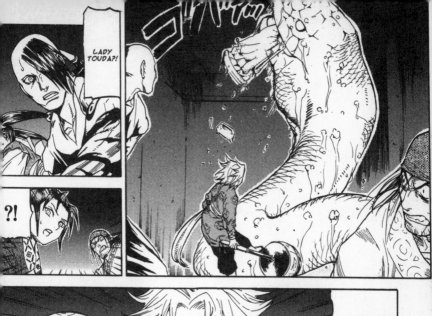

LADY TOUDA?!

?!

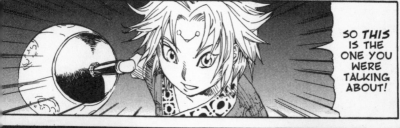

SO *THIS* IS THE ONE YOU WERE TALKING ABOUT!

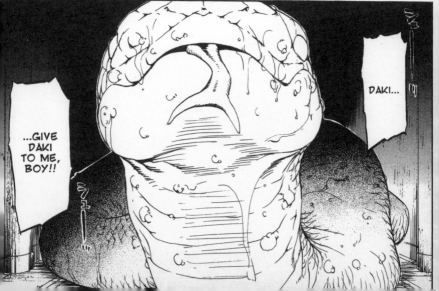

DAKI...

...GIVE DAKI TO ME, BOY!!

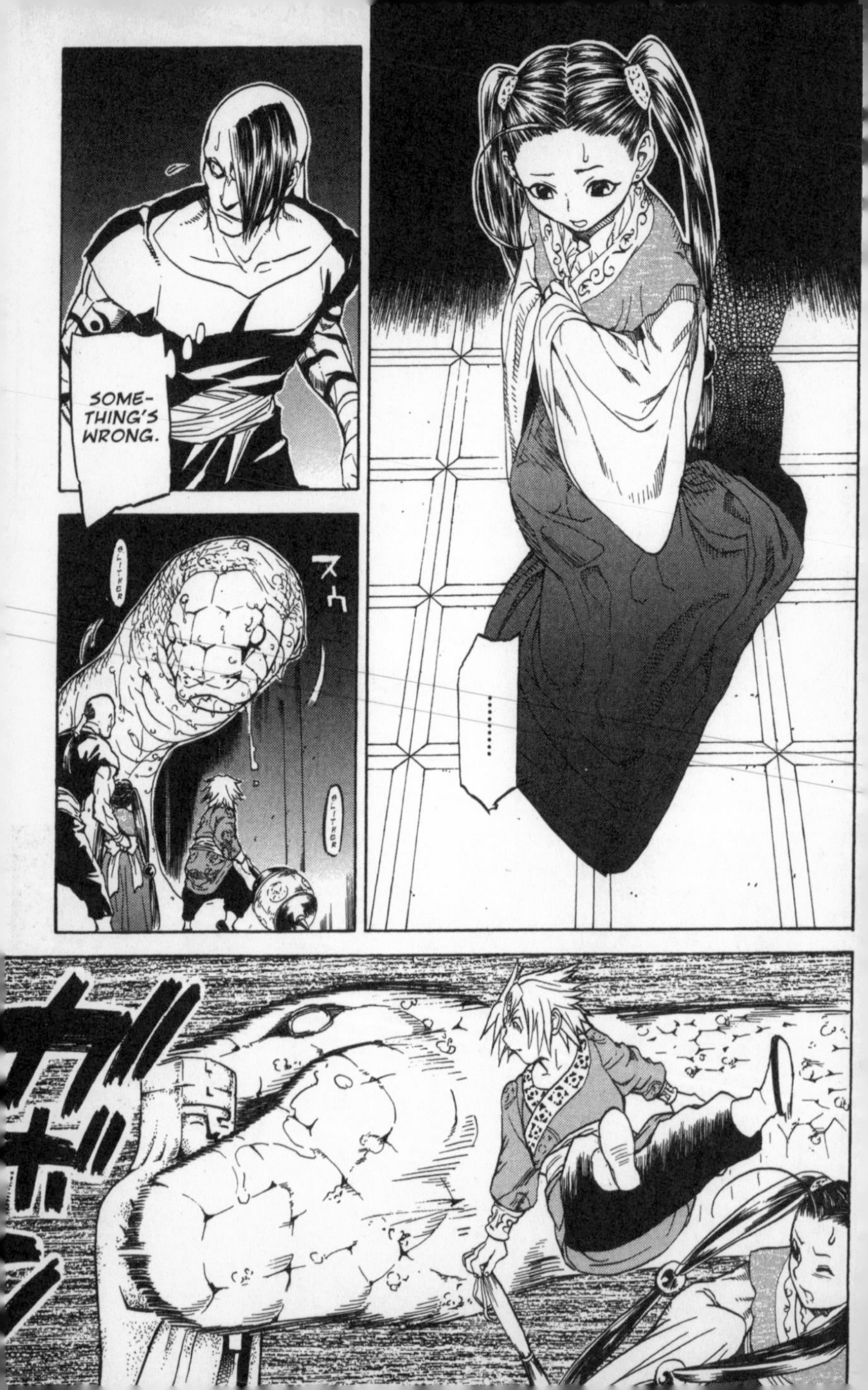
......
SOME-THING'S WRONG.
SLITHER
SLITHER

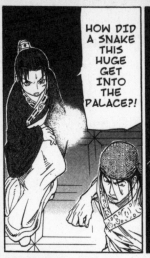

HOW DID A SNAKE THIS HUGE GET INTO THE PALACE?!

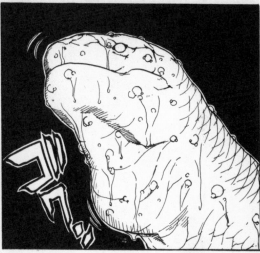

WHAT?!

IT HAS ALREADY EATEN SEVERAL PEOPLE.

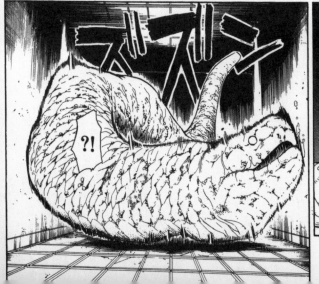

?!

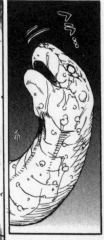

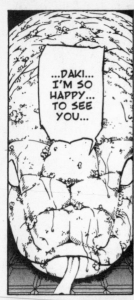

ズズ
ズ
DA...
...DAKI... I'M SO HAPPY... TO SEE YOU...
SLITHER
COME CLOSER... LET ME SEE YOUR FACE...
...I CAN'T SEE VERY WELL.
SLITHER
....
DAKI...? WHAT'S WRONG?

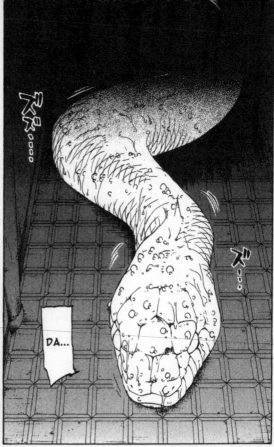

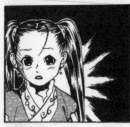

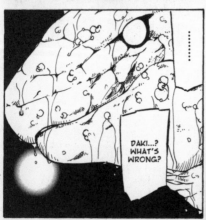

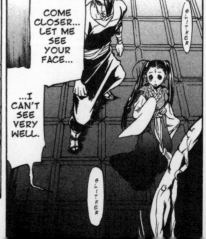

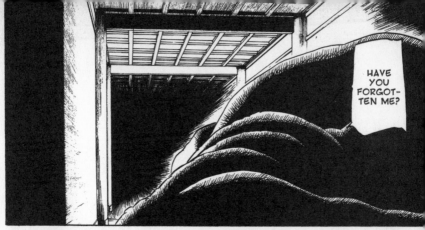

HAVE YOU FORGOTTEN ME?

M...

MOTHER...?

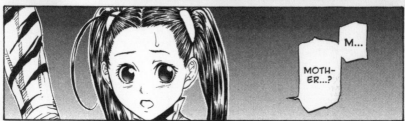

I DON'T BLAME HER... WITH LADY TOUDA LOOKING LIKE THIS.

....

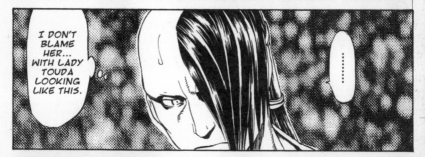

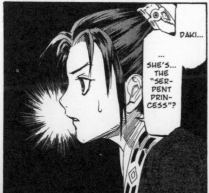

DAKI...

...SHE'S... THE "SERPENT PRINCESS"?

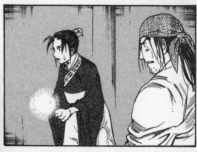

90

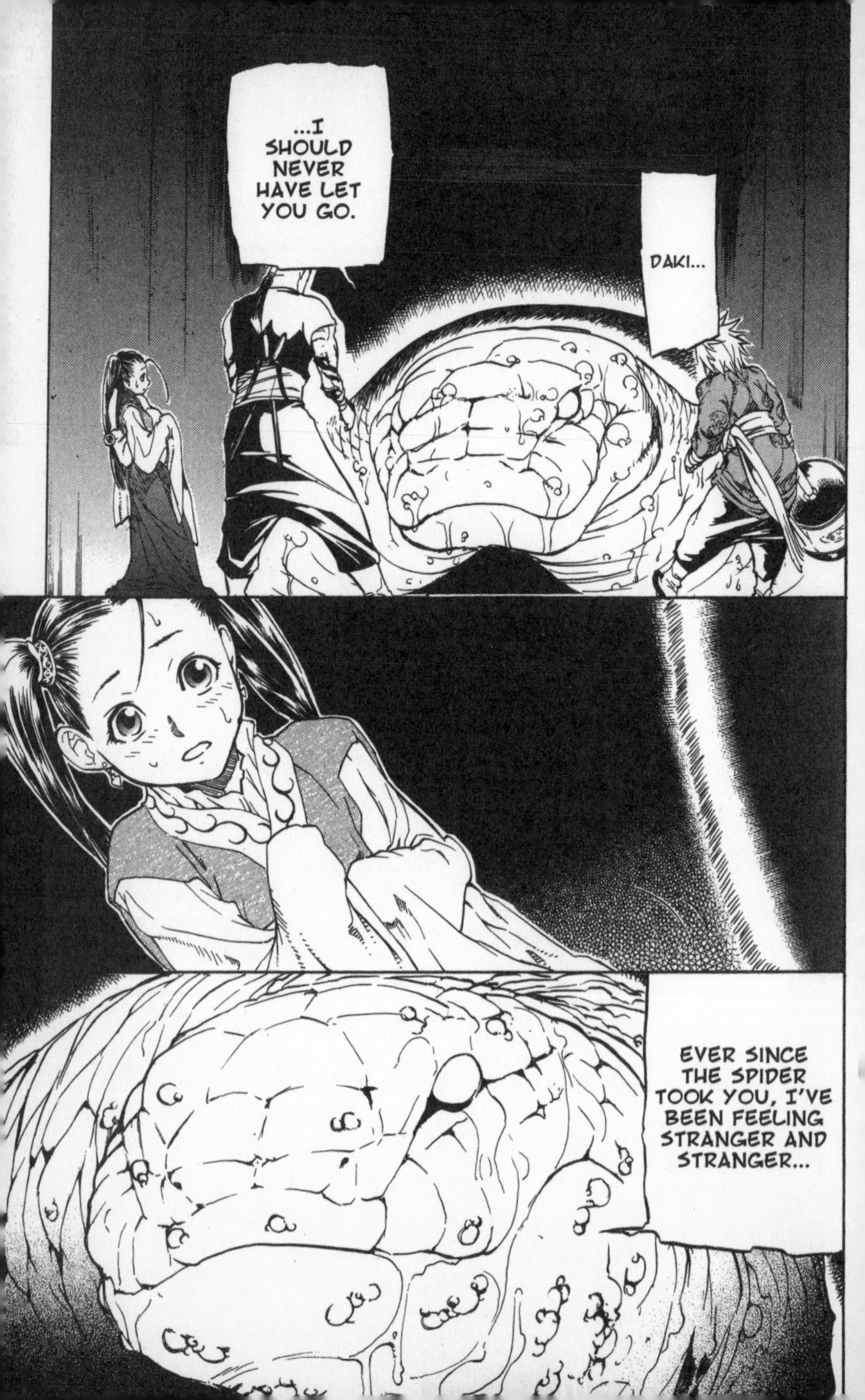
DAKI...
...I SHOULD NEVER HAVE LET YOU GO.
EVER SINCE THE SPIDER TOOK YOU, I'VE BEEN FEELING STRANGER AND STRANGER...

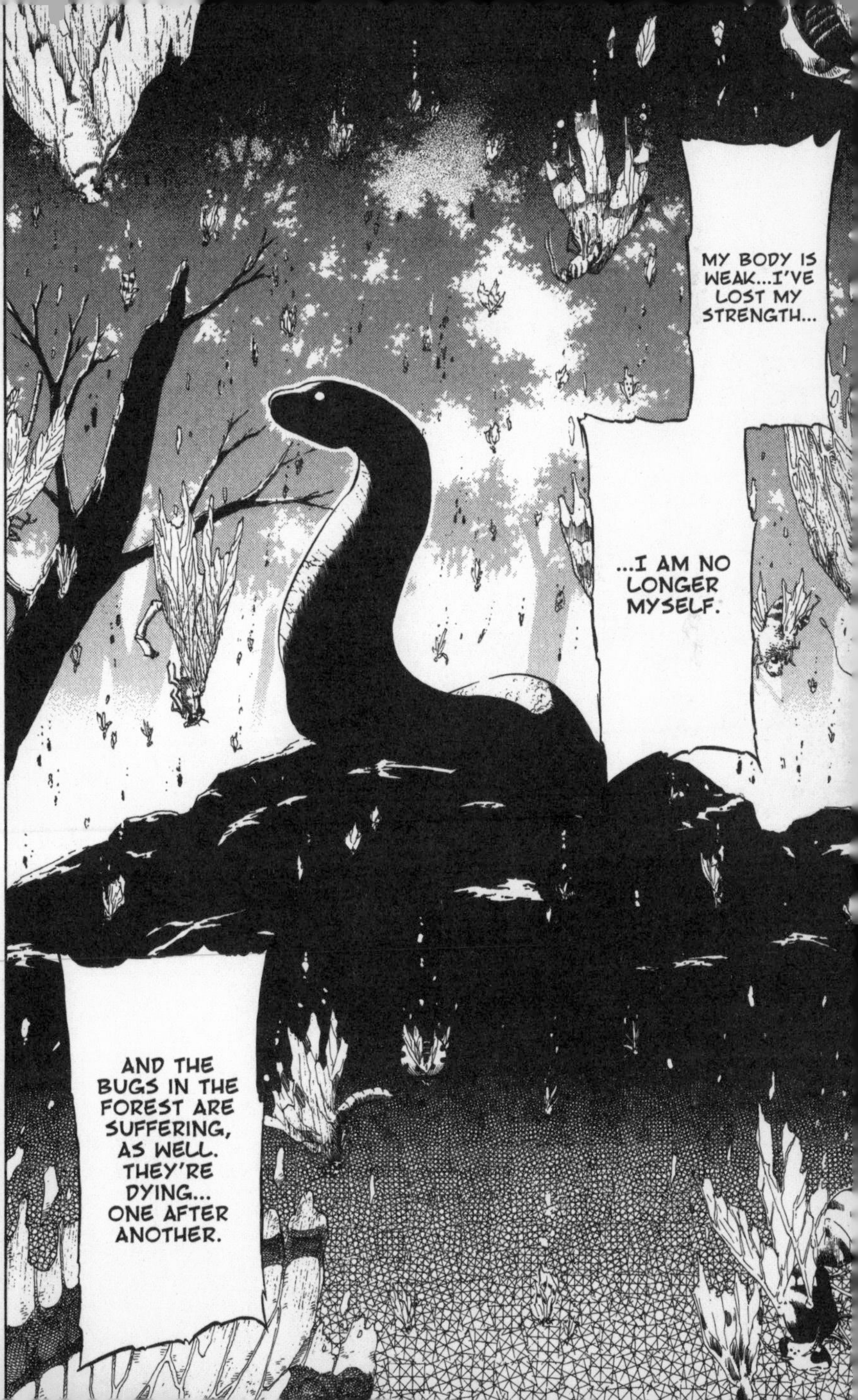
MY BODY IS WEAK...I'VE LOST MY STRENGTH...
...I AM NO LONGER MYSELF.
AND THE BUGS IN THE FOREST ARE SUFFERING, AS WELL. THEY'RE DYING... ONE AFTER ANOTHER.

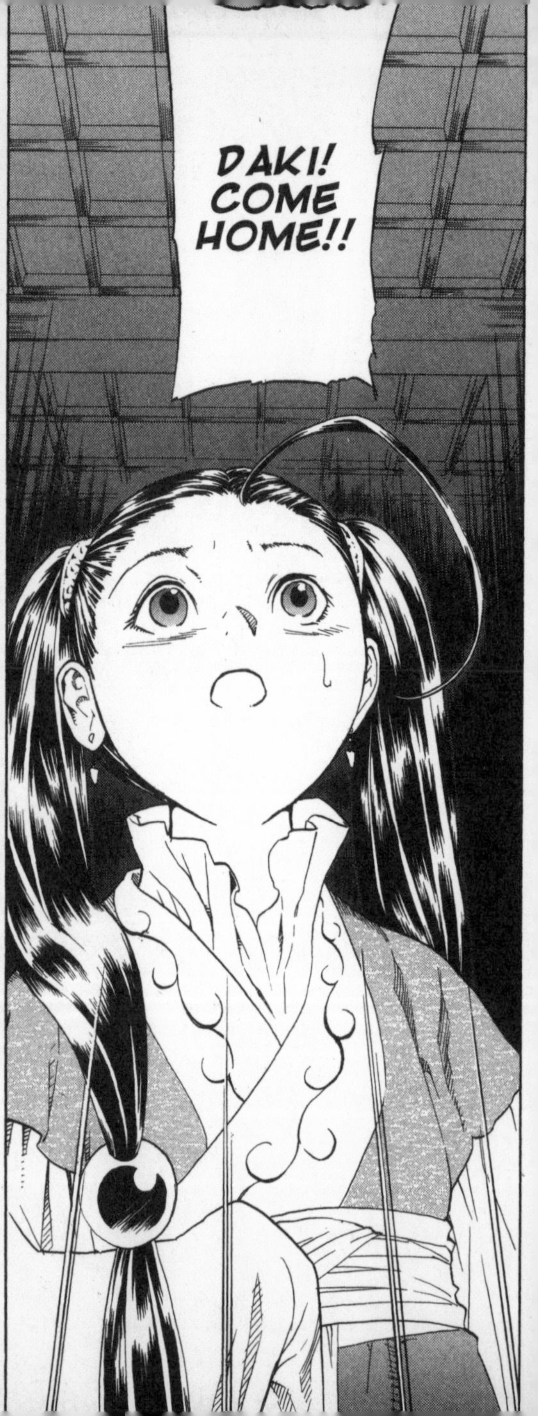
DAKI! COME HOME!!

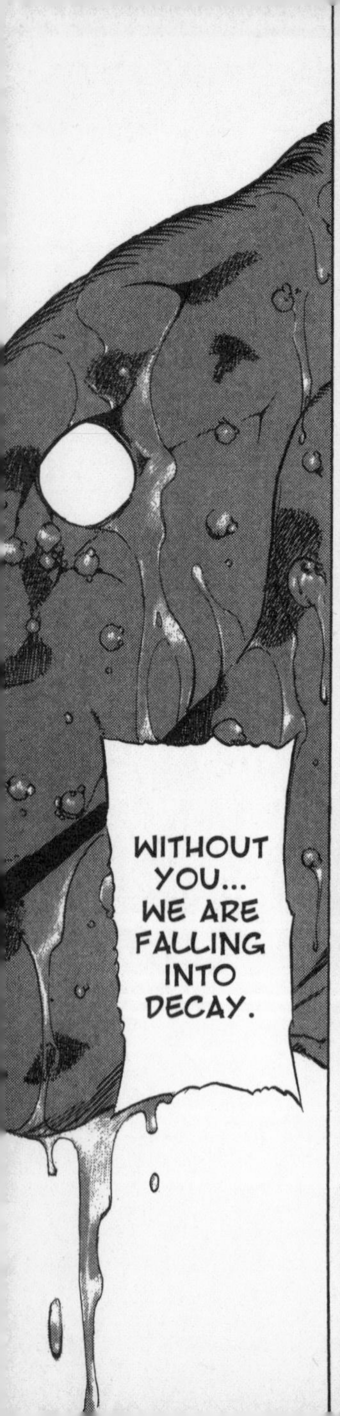
WITHOUT YOU... WE ARE FALLING INTO DECAY.

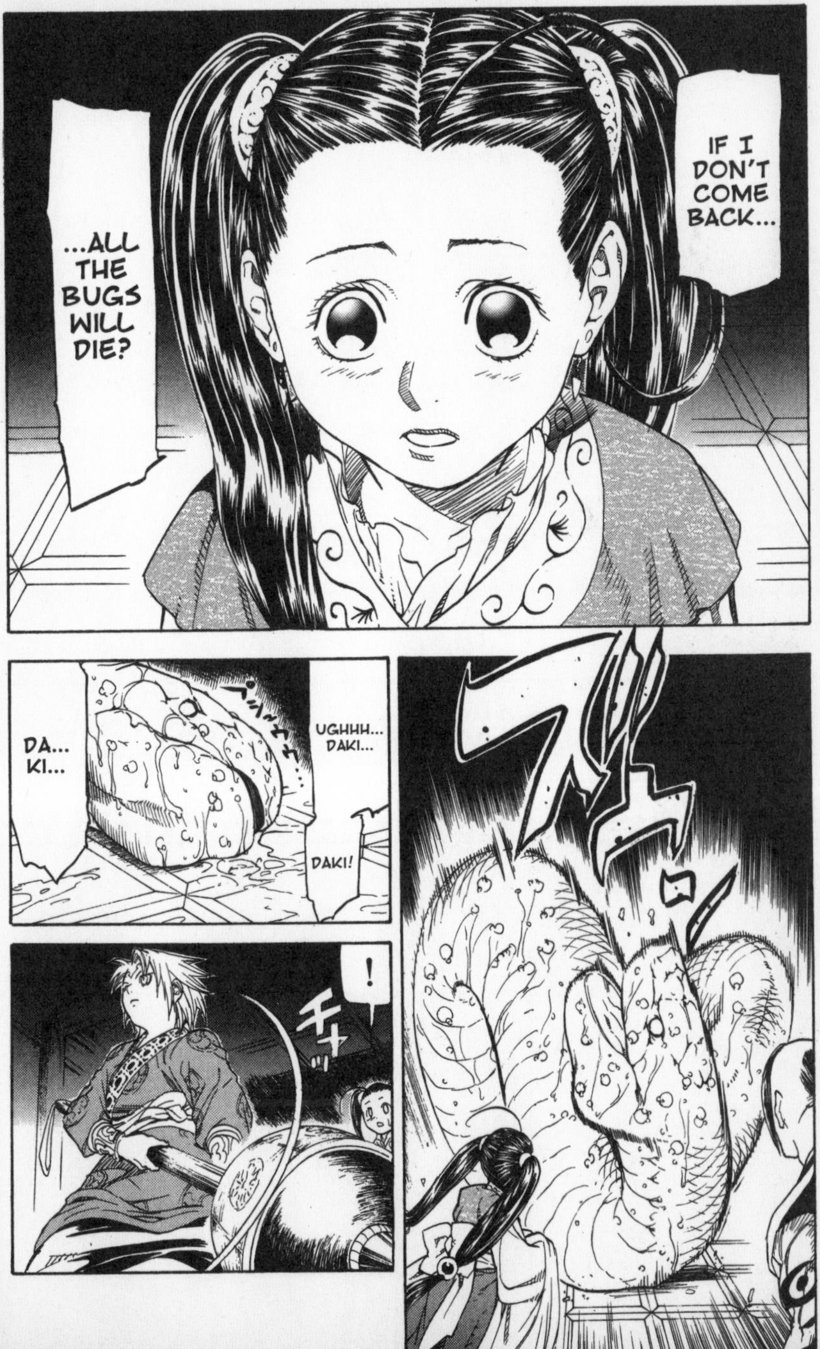
IF I DON'T COME BACK...
...ALL THE BUGS WILL DIE?
UGHHH... DAKI...
DAKI!
DA... KI...
!

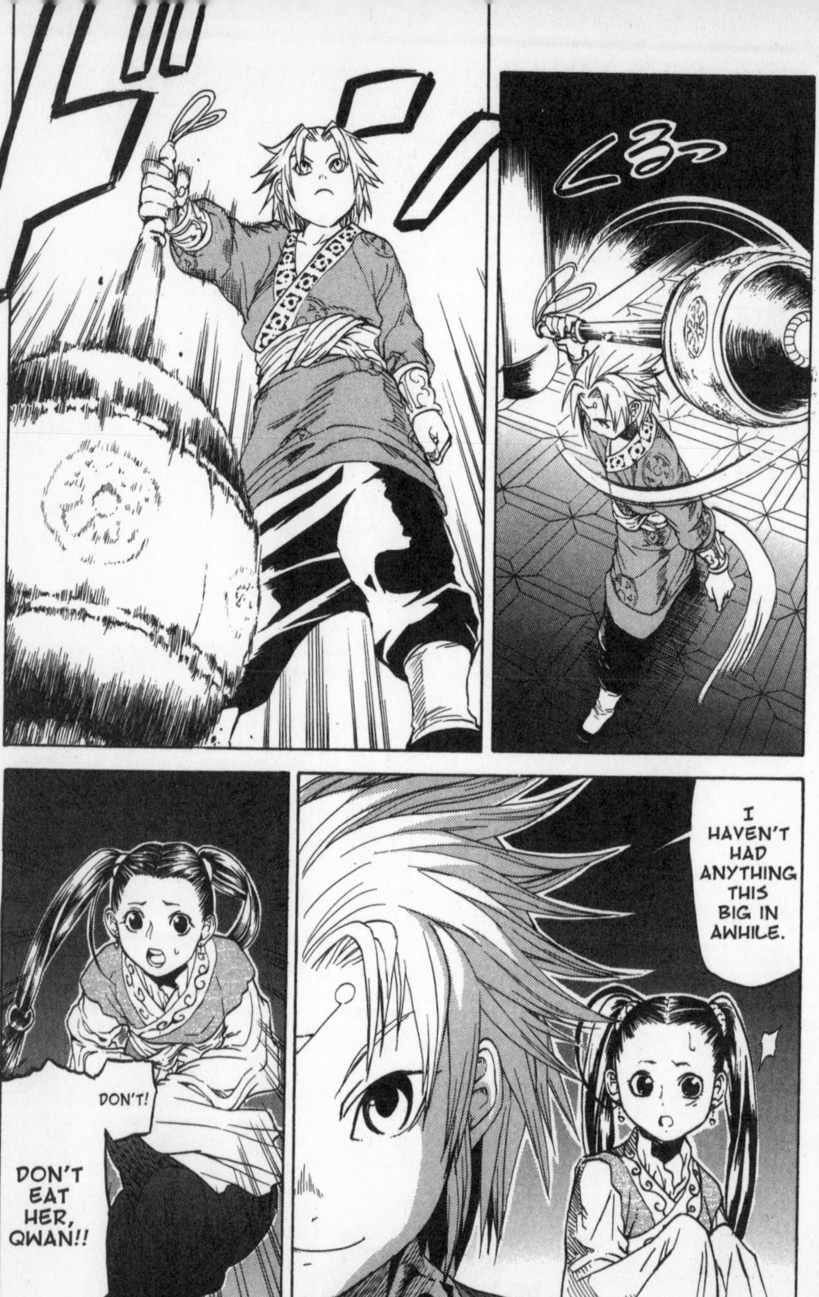
くるっ
I HAVEN'T HAD ANYTHING THIS BIG IN AWHILE.
DON'T!
DON'T EAT HER, QWAN!!

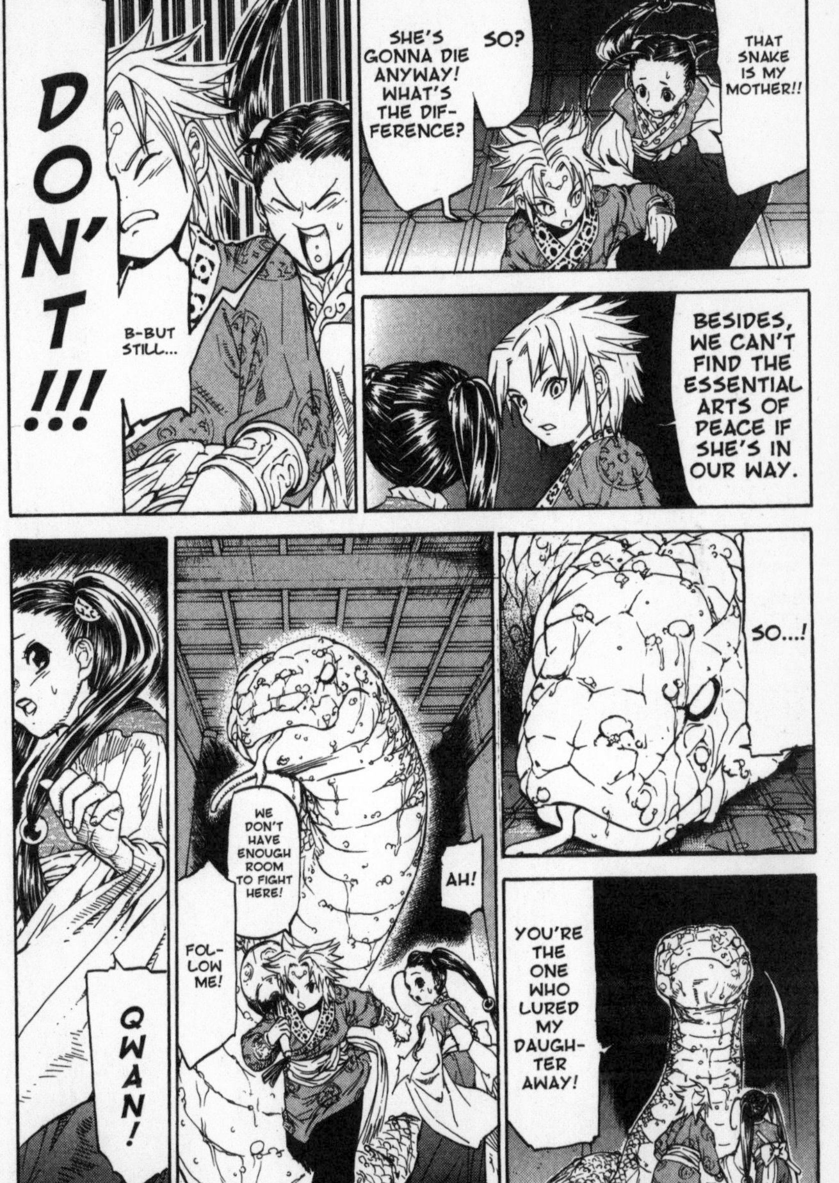
THAT SNAKE IS MY MOTHER!!
SO?
SHE'S GONNA DIE ANYWAY! WHAT'S THE DIF-FERENCE?
BESIDES, WE CAN'T FIND THE ESSENTIAL ARTS OF PEACE IF SHE'S IN OUR WAY.
DON'T!!!
B-BUT STILL...
SO...!
YOU'RE THE ONE WHO LURED MY DAUGH-TER AWAY!
AH!
WE DON'T HAVE ENOUGH ROOM TO FIGHT HERE!
FOL-LOW ME!
QWAN!

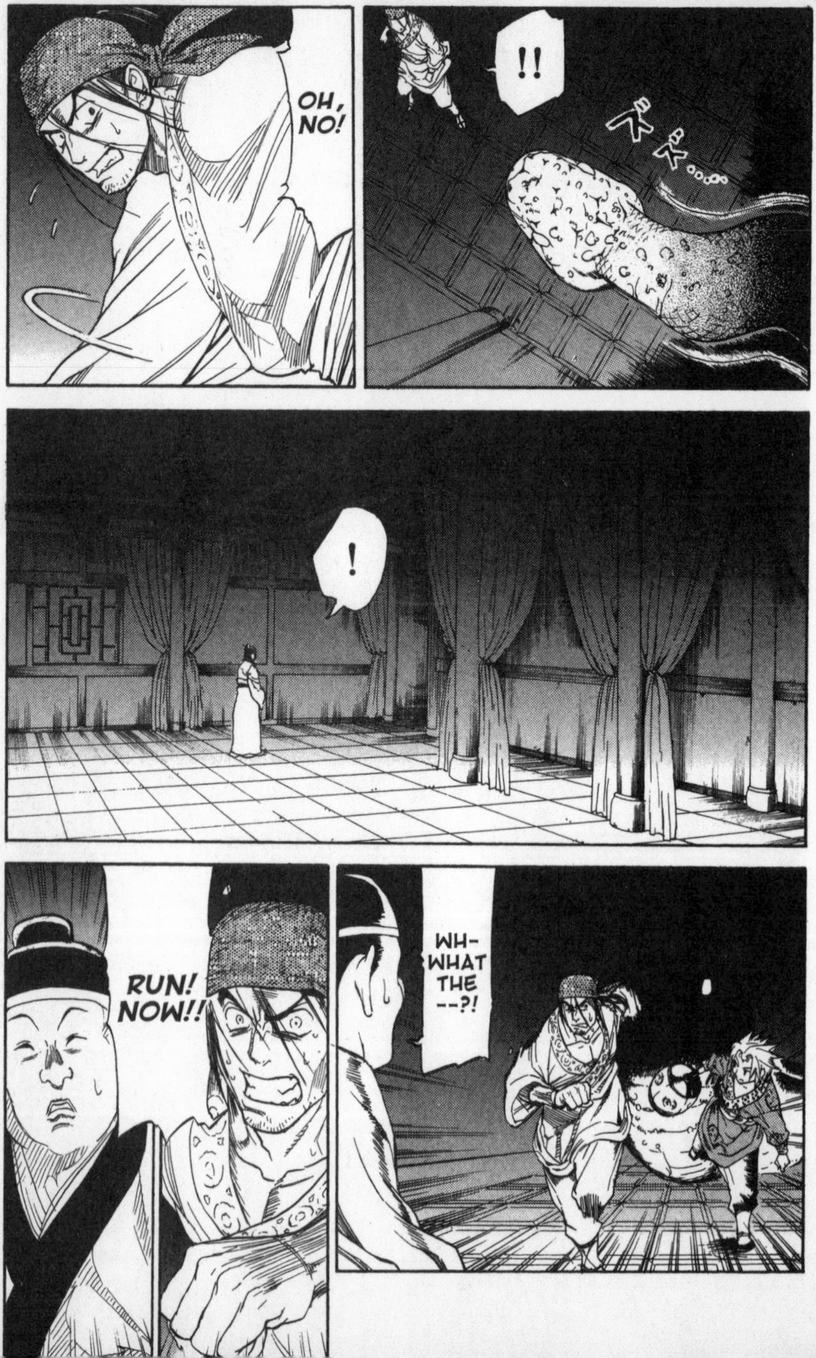
!!
ズズ
OH, NO!
!
WH-WHAT THE--?!
RUN! NOW!!

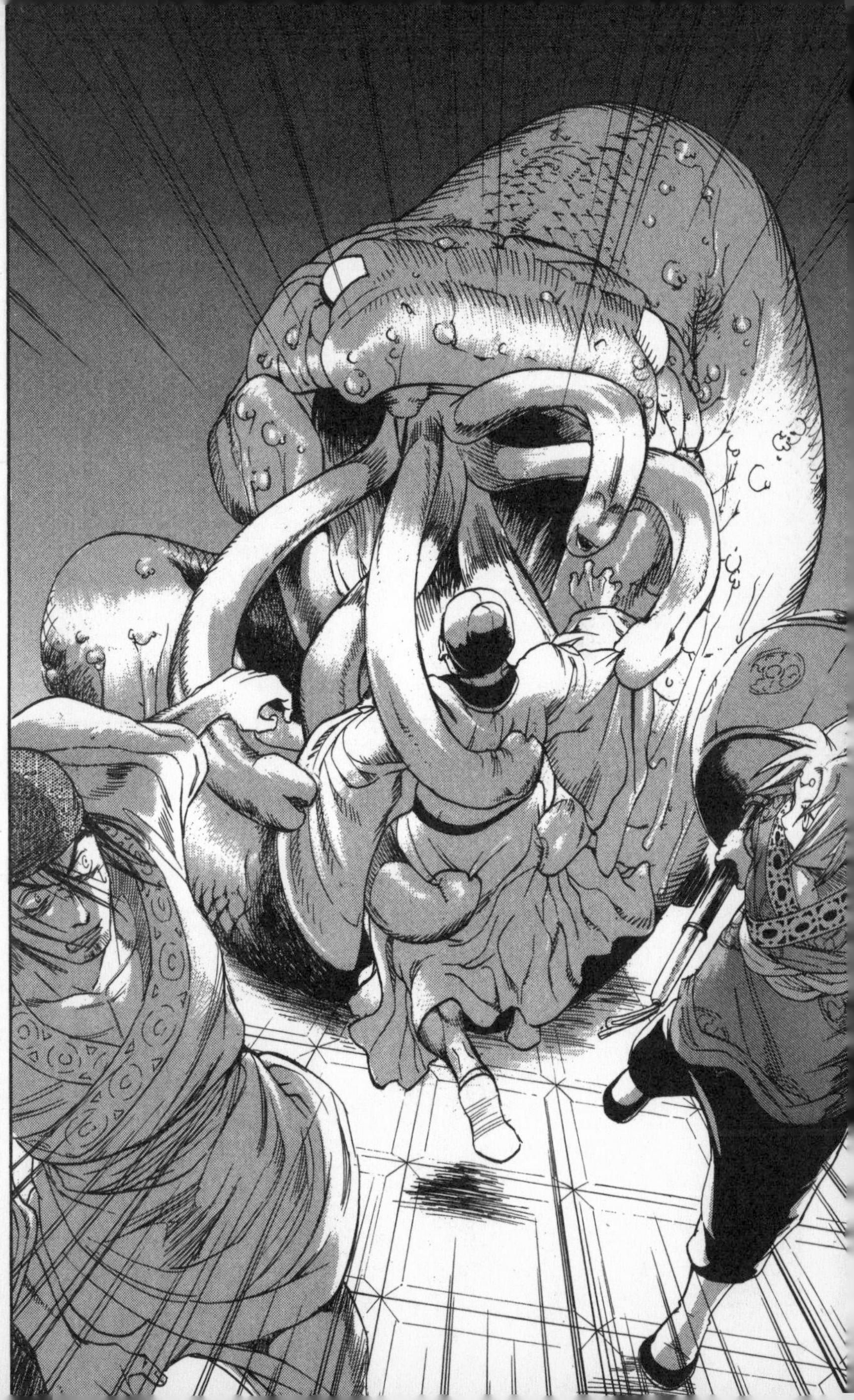

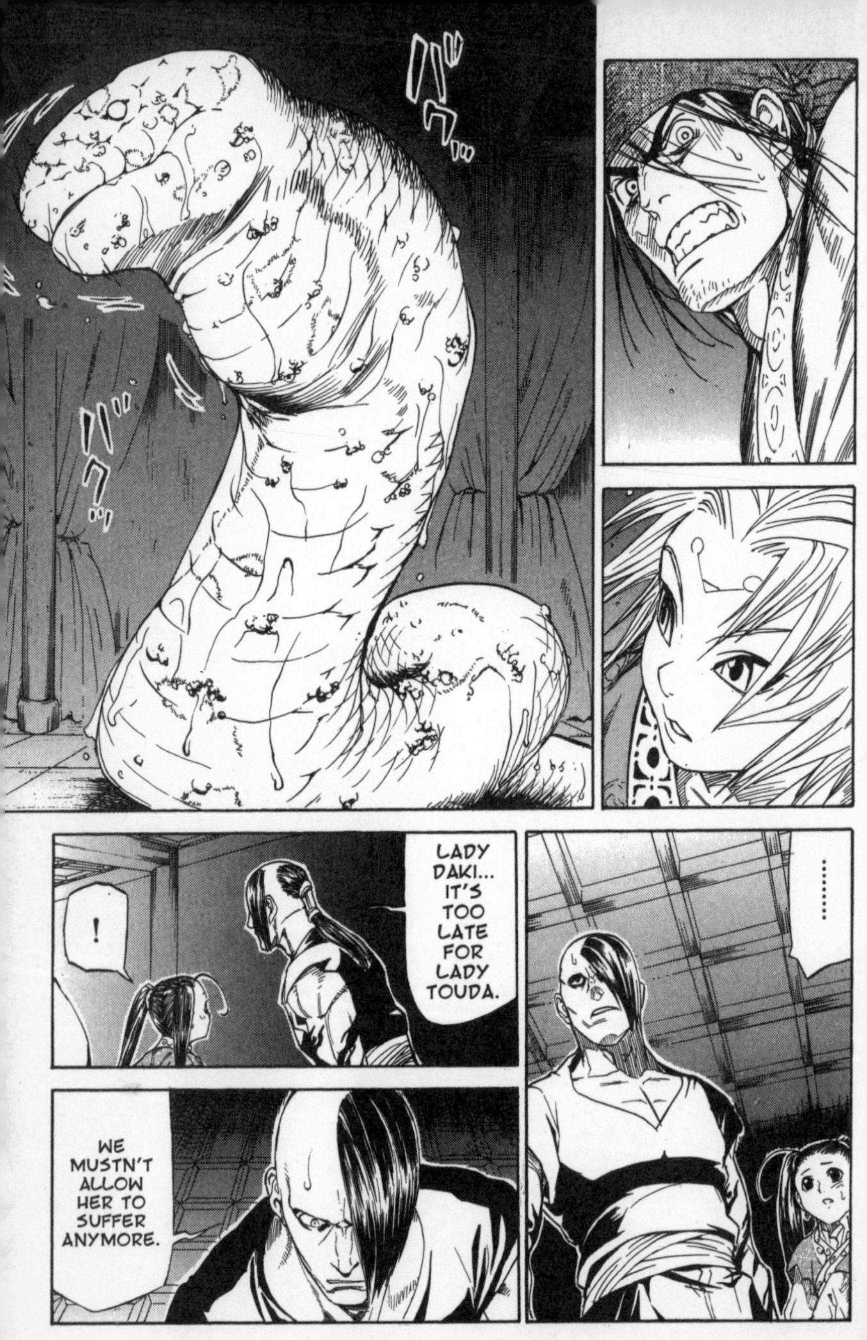
......
LADY DAKI... IT'S TOO LATE FOR LADY TOUDA.
!
WE MUSTN'T ALLOW HER TO SUFFER ANYMORE.

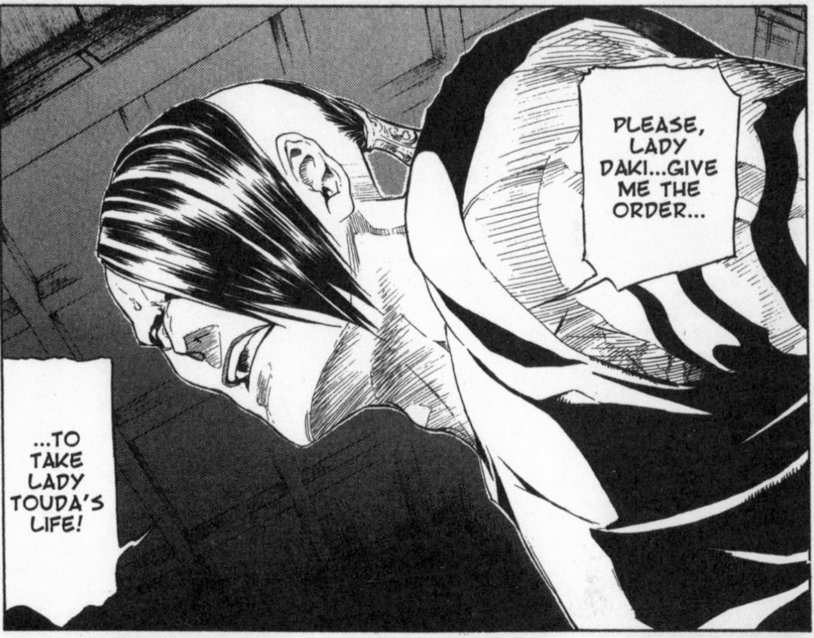
PLEASE, LADY DAKI...GIVE ME THE ORDER...
...TO TAKE LADY TOUDA'S LIFE!

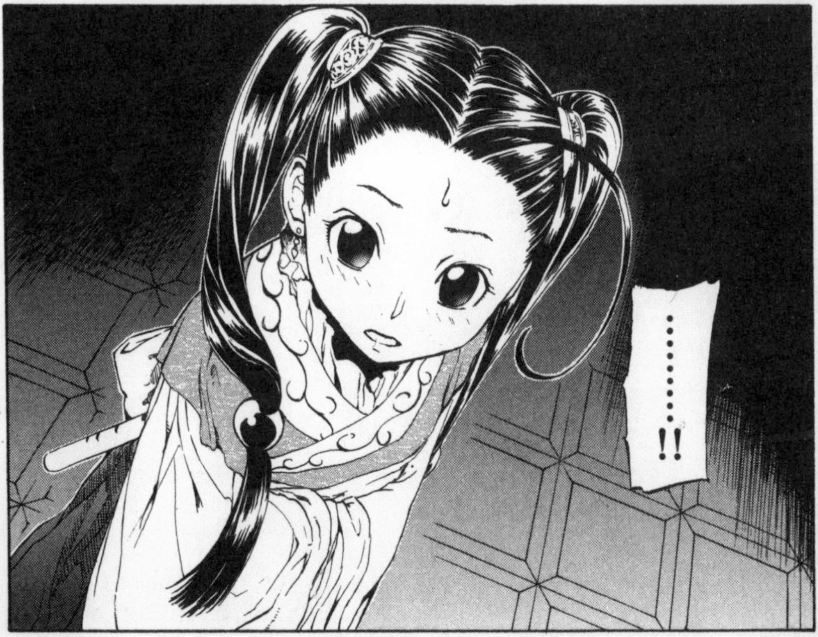
........!!

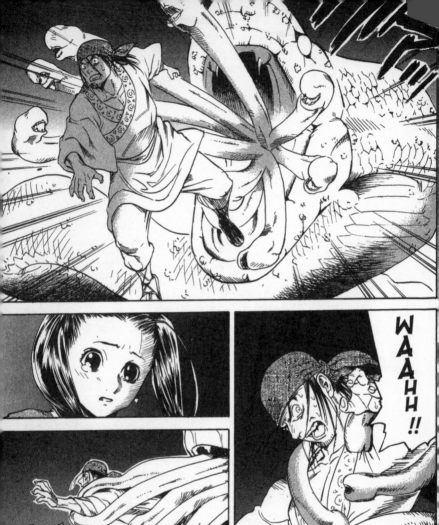

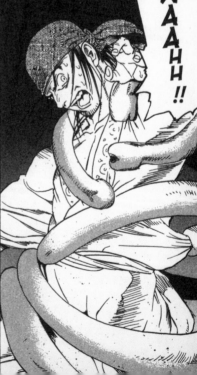

WAAHH!!

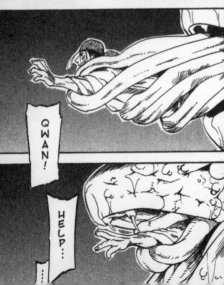

QWAN!

HELP...

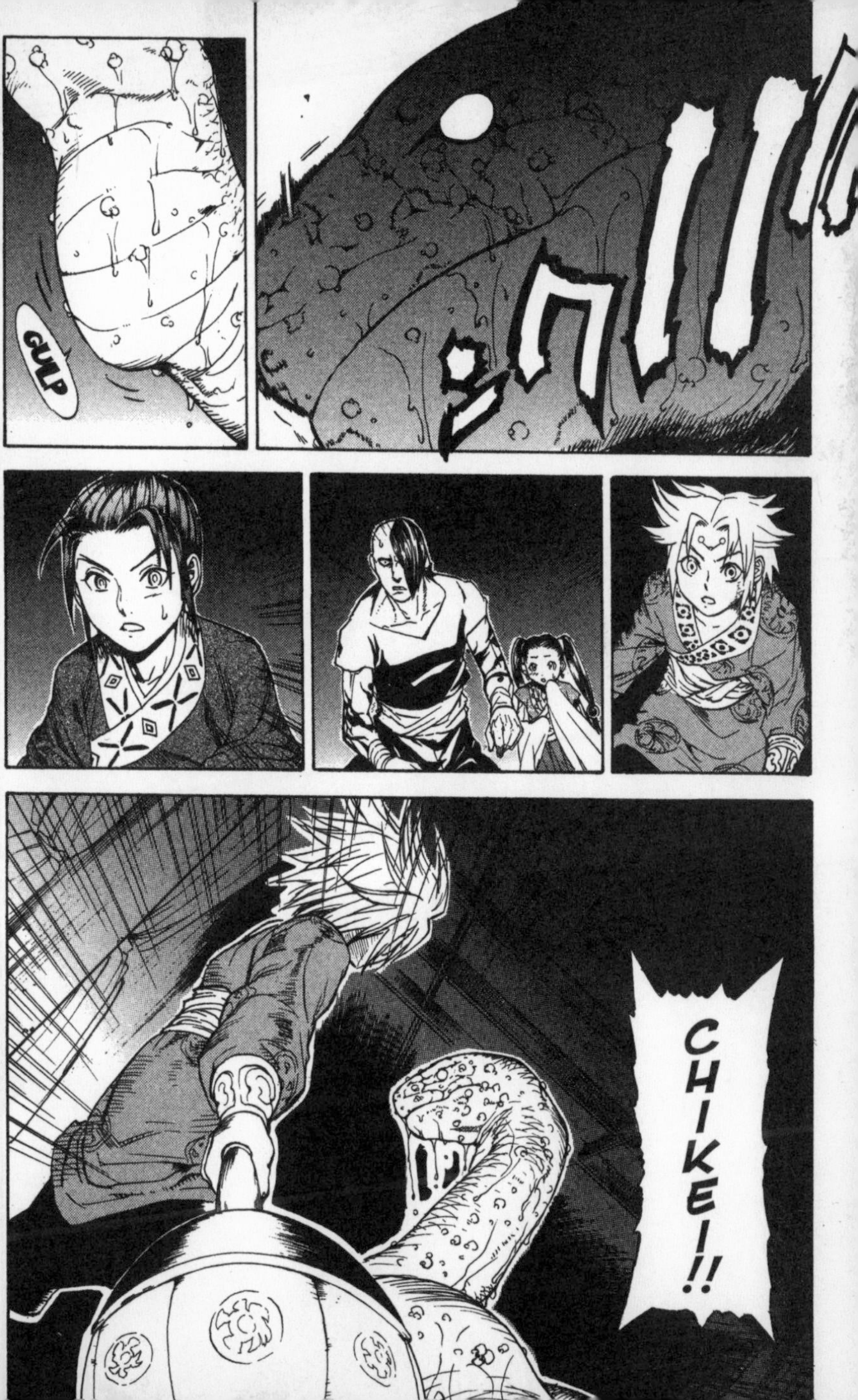
GULP
CHIKEI!!

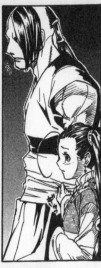

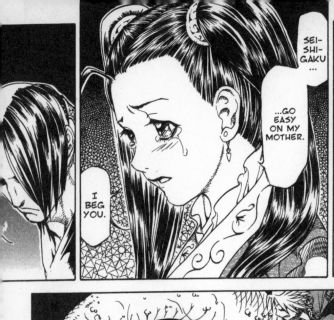

SEI-
SHI-
GAKU
...

...GO
EASY
ON MY
MOTHER.

I BEG
YOU.

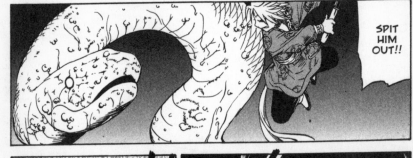

SPIT
HIM
OUT!!

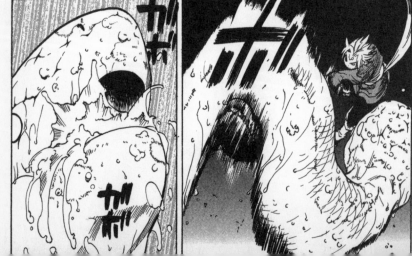

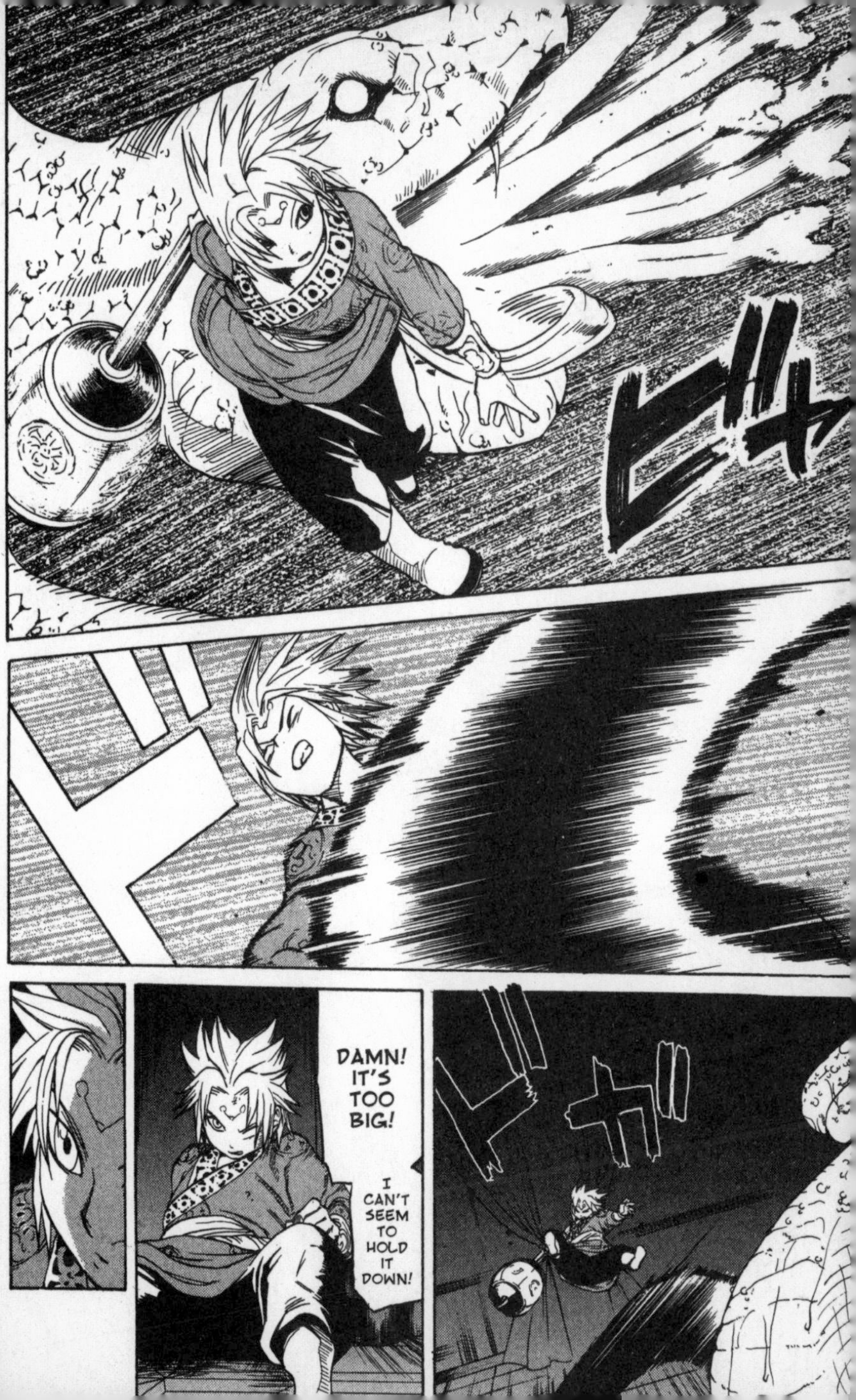
DAMN! IT'S TOO BIG!
I CAN'T SEEM TO HOLD IT DOWN!

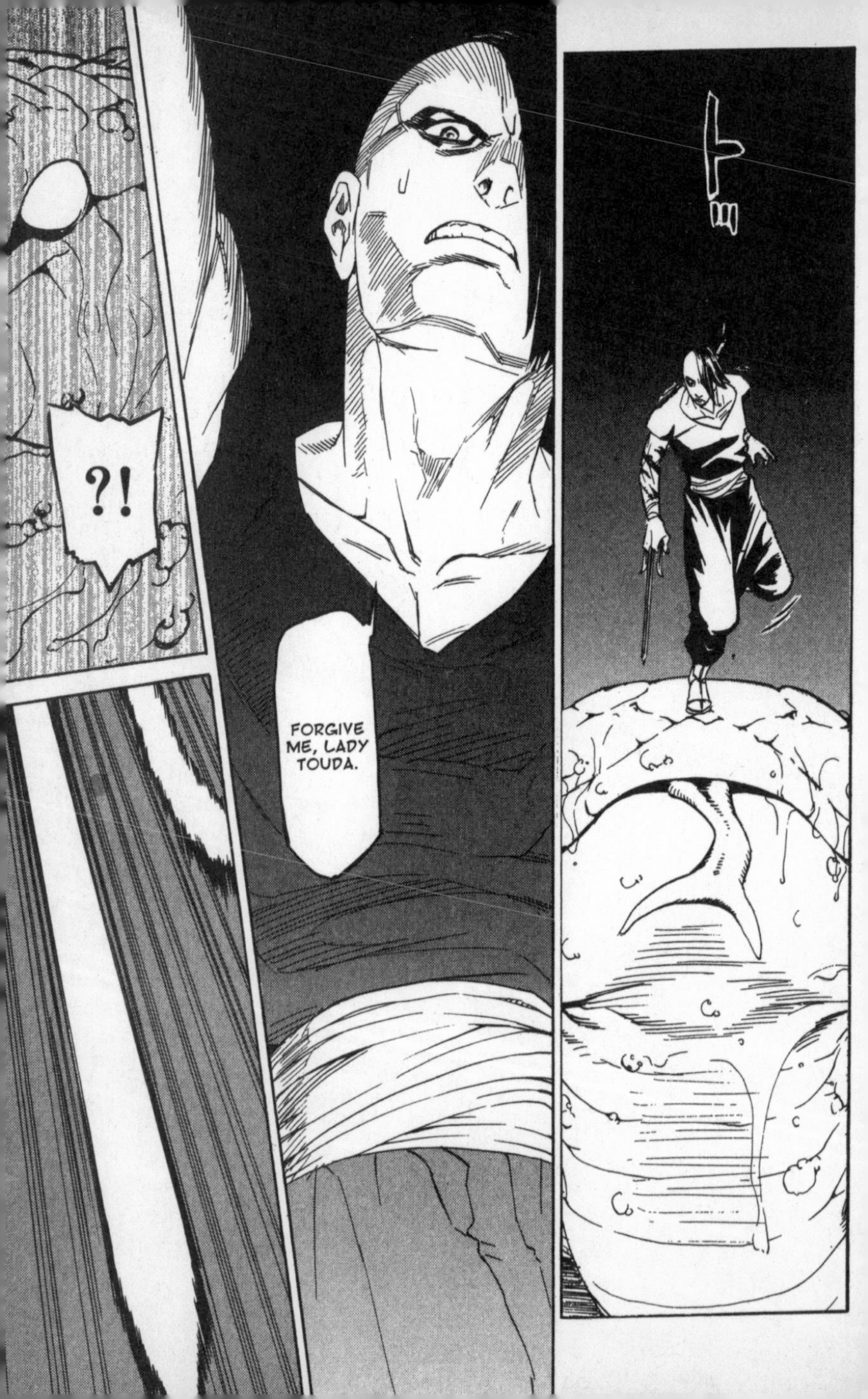
FORGIVE ME, LADY TOUDA.
?!

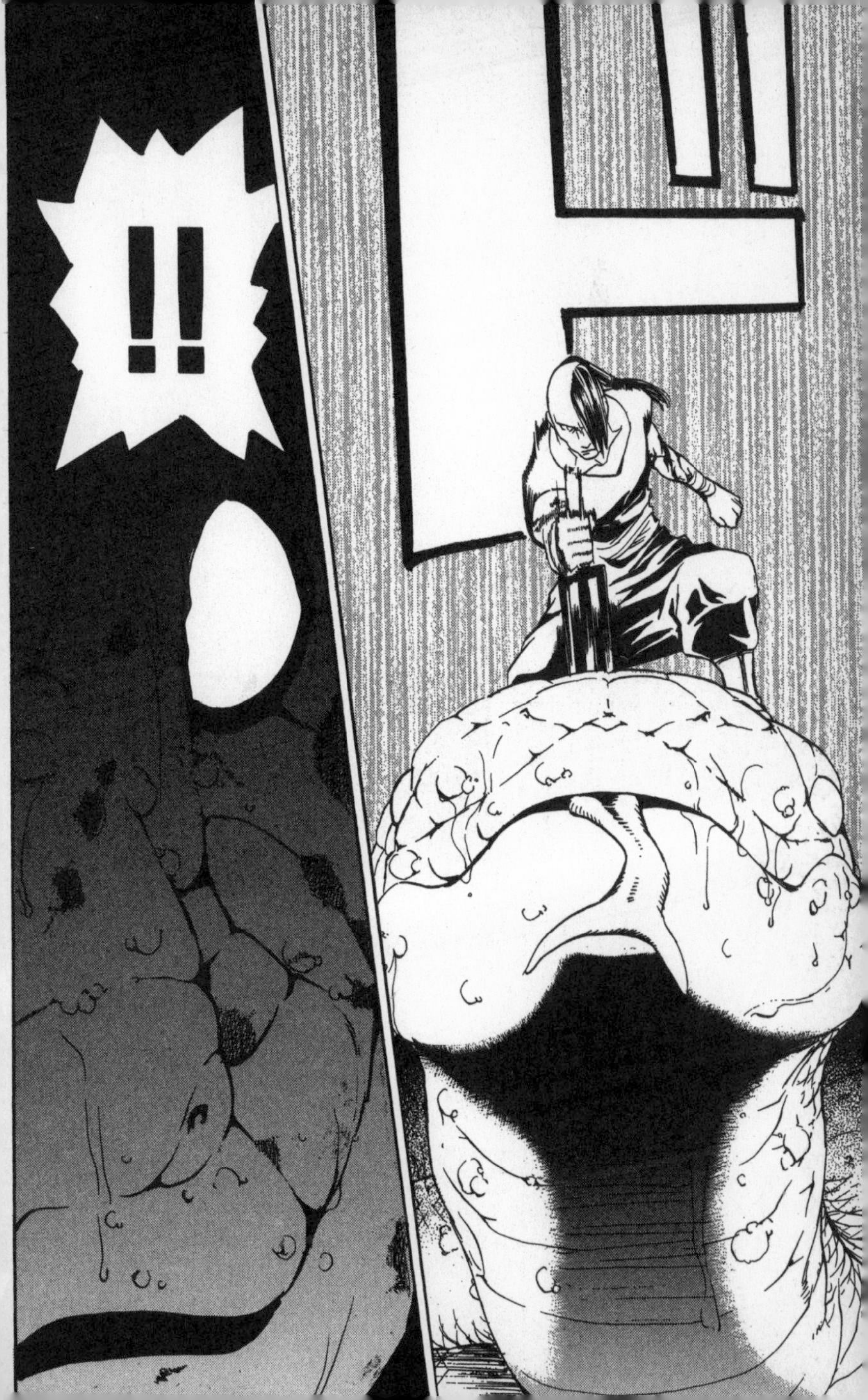
!!

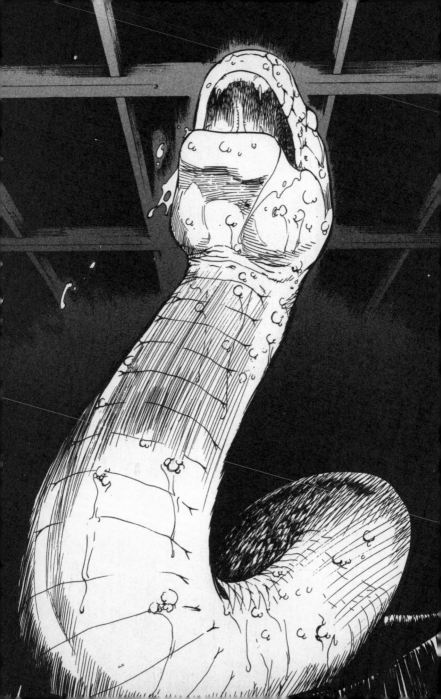

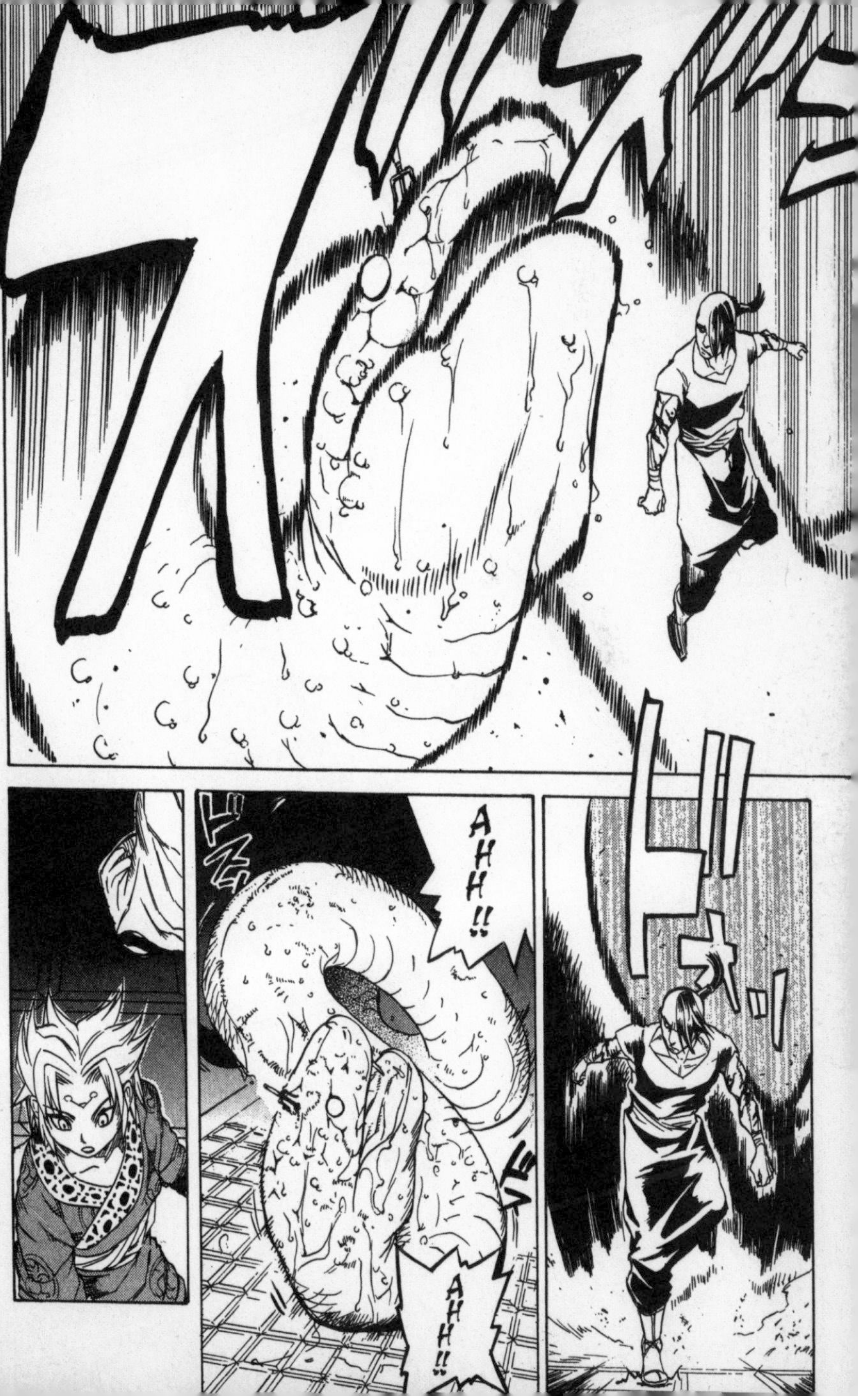
AHH!!
AHH!!

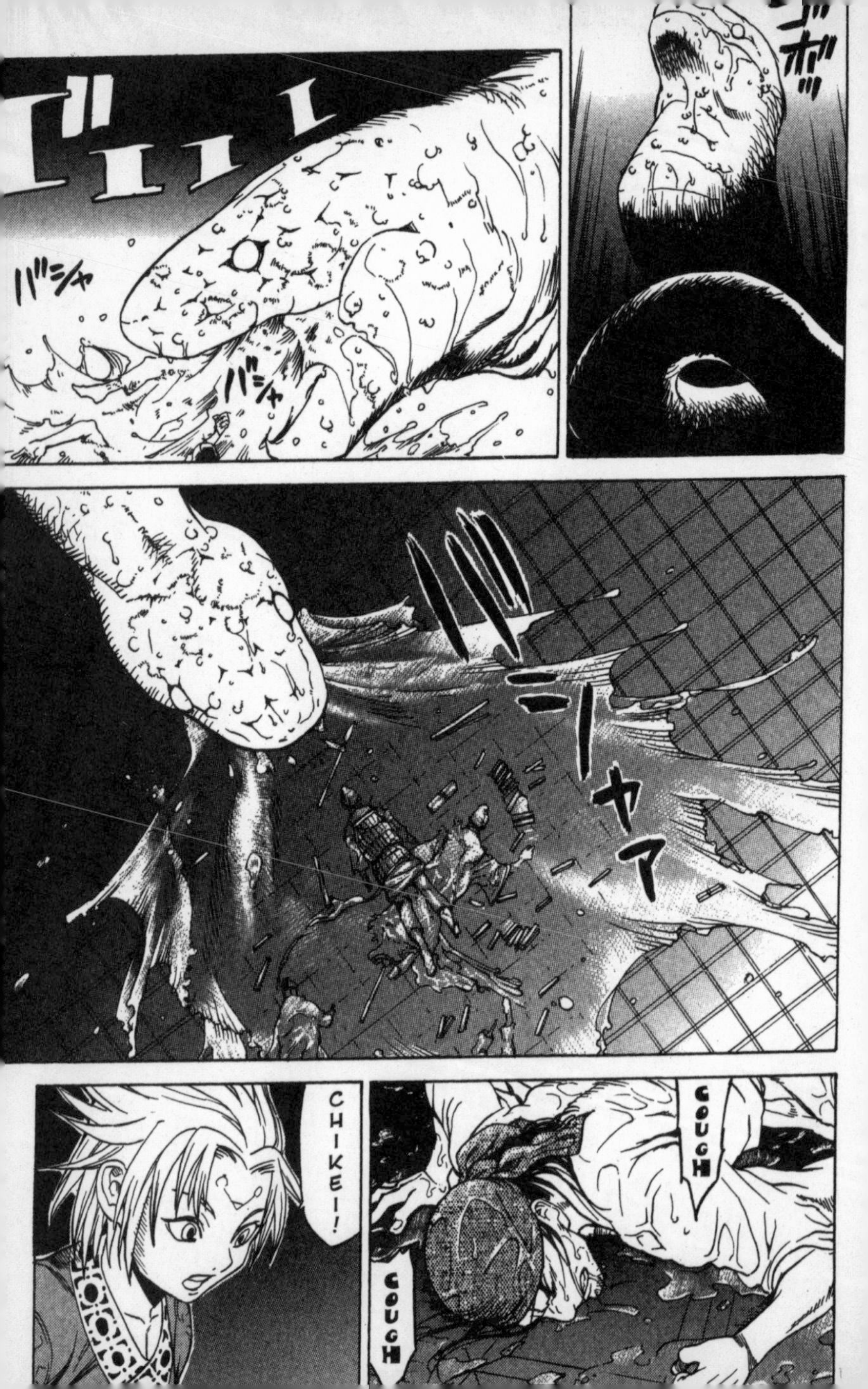
ゴボッ
バシャ
バシャ
COUGH
COUGH
CHIKE!!

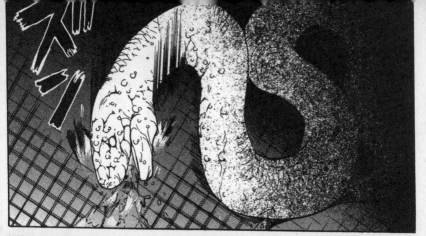

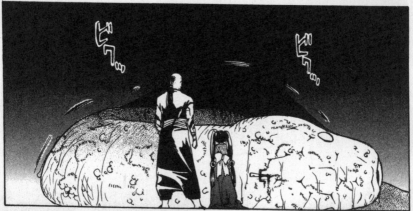

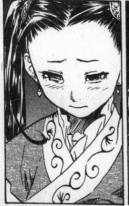

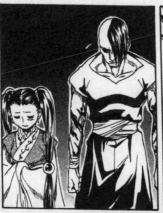

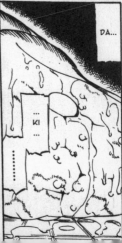

DA...

...KI
...

....

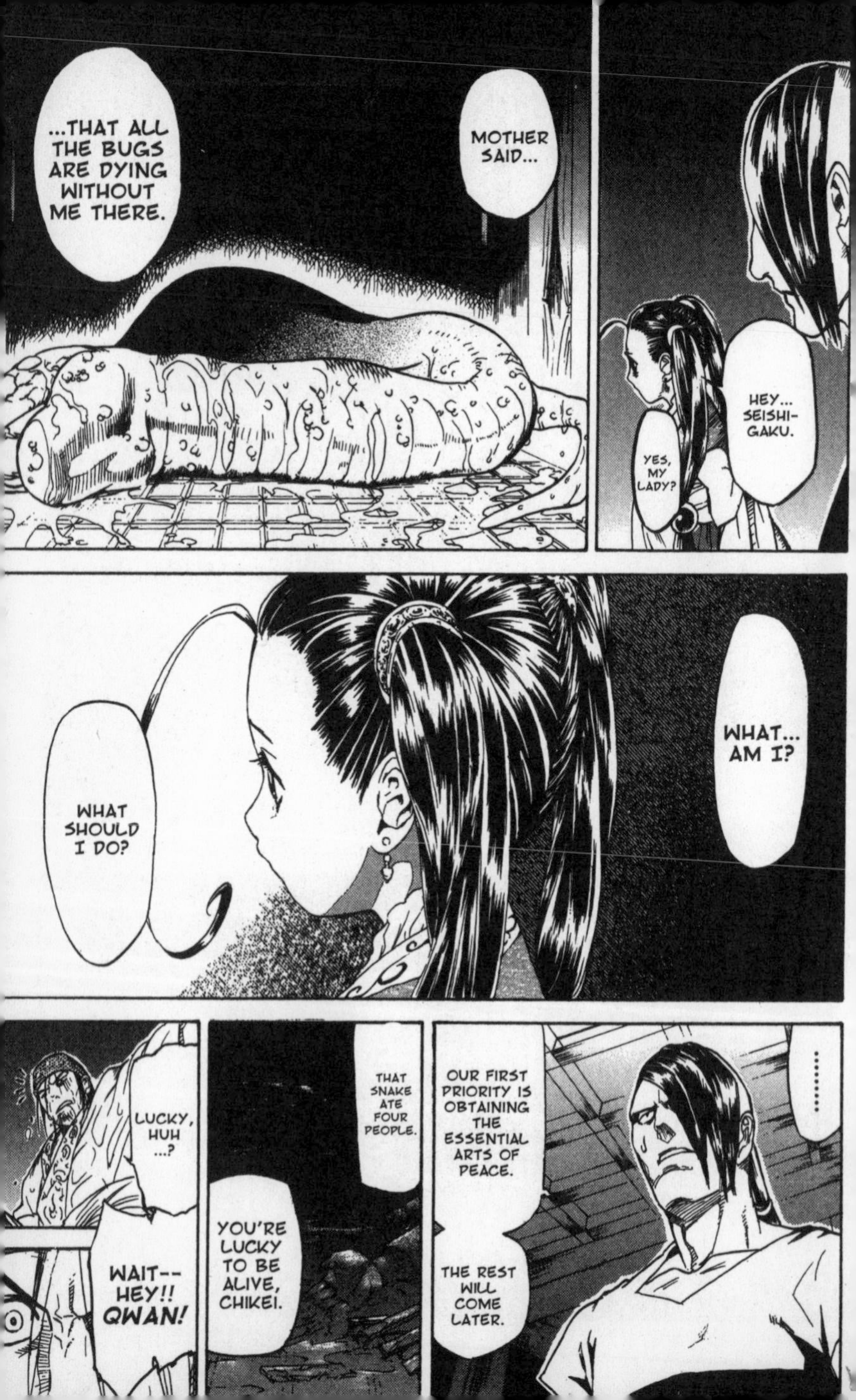
HEY... SEISHI-GAKU.
YES, MY LADY?
MOTHER SAID...
...THAT ALL THE BUGS ARE DYING WITHOUT ME THERE.
WHAT... AM I?
WHAT SHOULD I DO?
......
OUR FIRST PRIORITY IS OBTAINING THE ESSENTIAL ARTS OF PEACE.
THE REST WILL COME LATER.
THAT SNAKE ATE FOUR PEOPLE.
YOU'RE LUCKY TO BE ALIVE, CHIKEI.
LUCKY, HUH ...?
WAIT-- HEY!! QWAN!

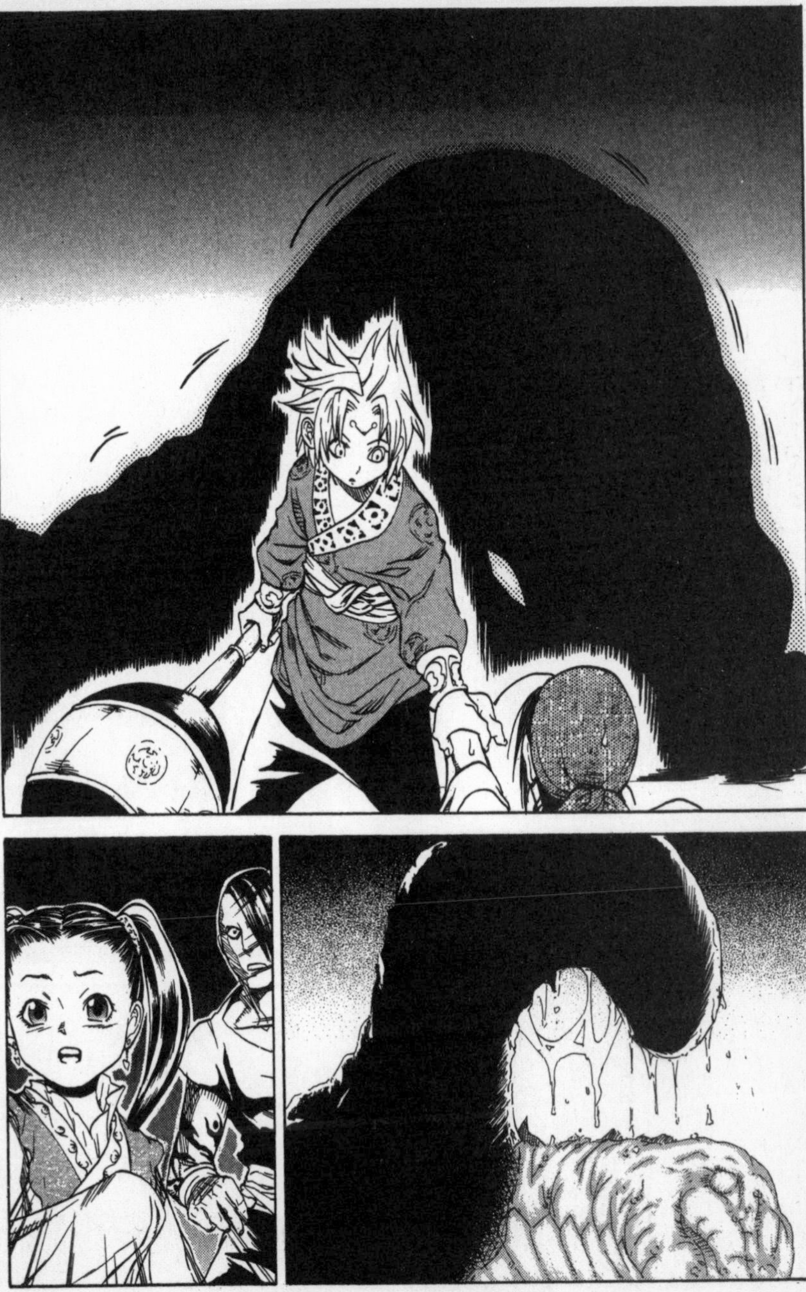

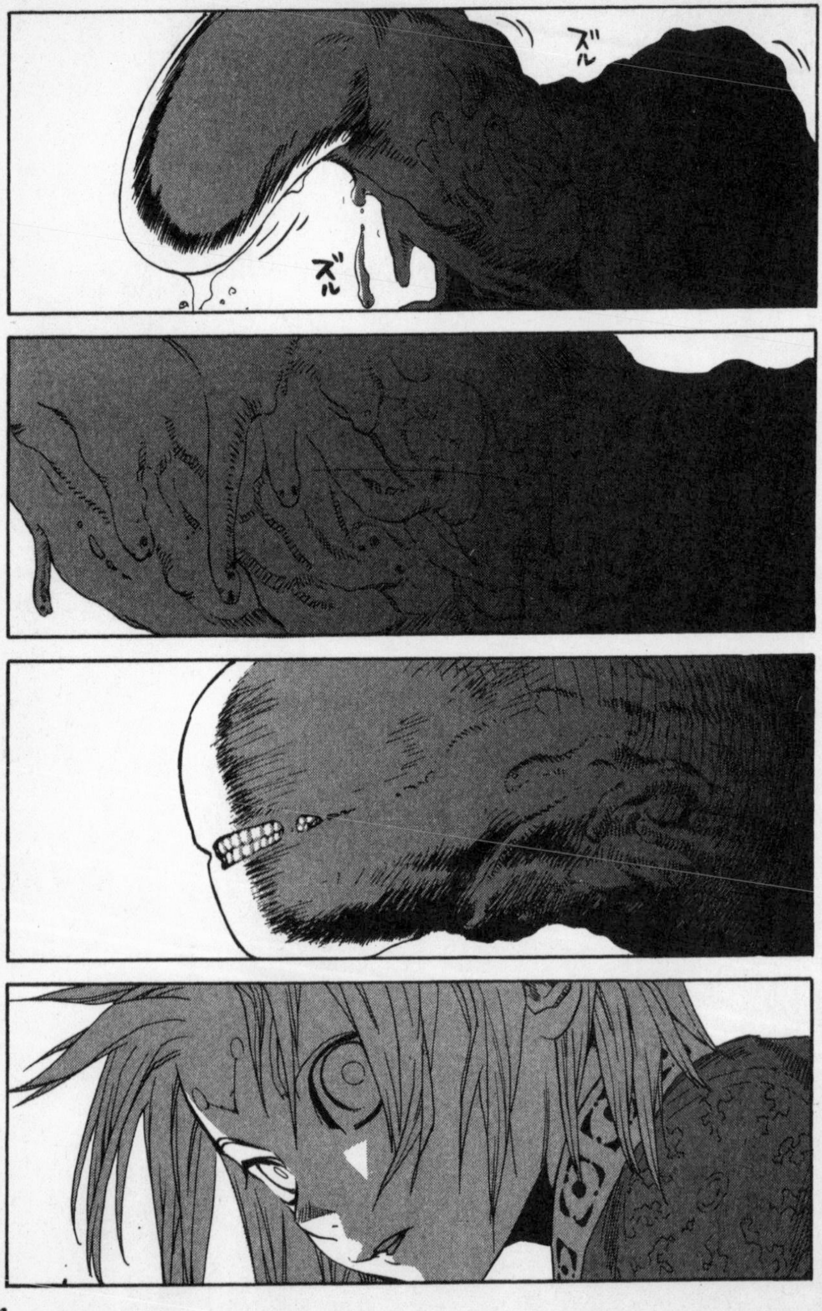
ズル
ズル

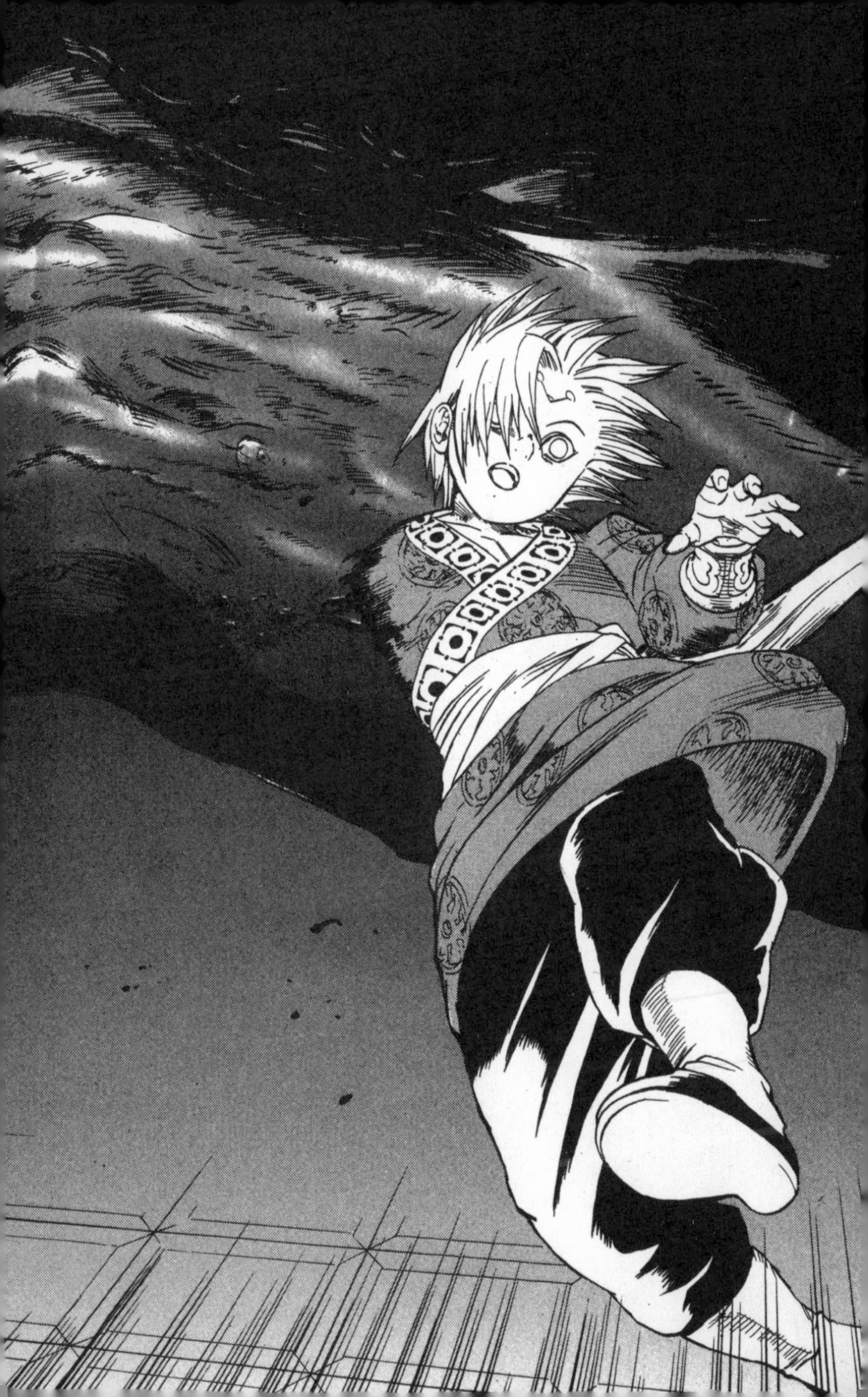

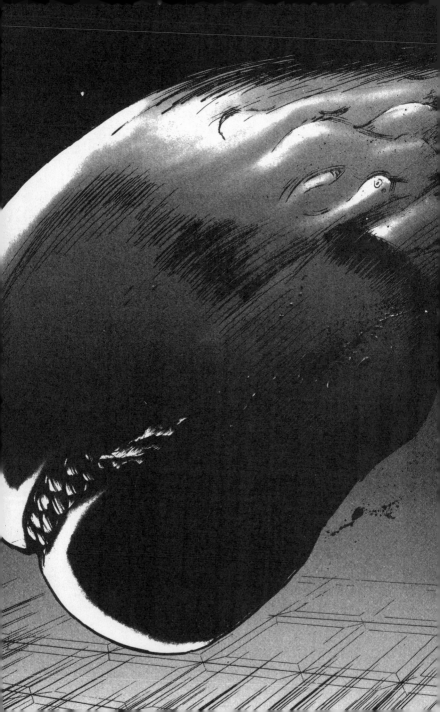

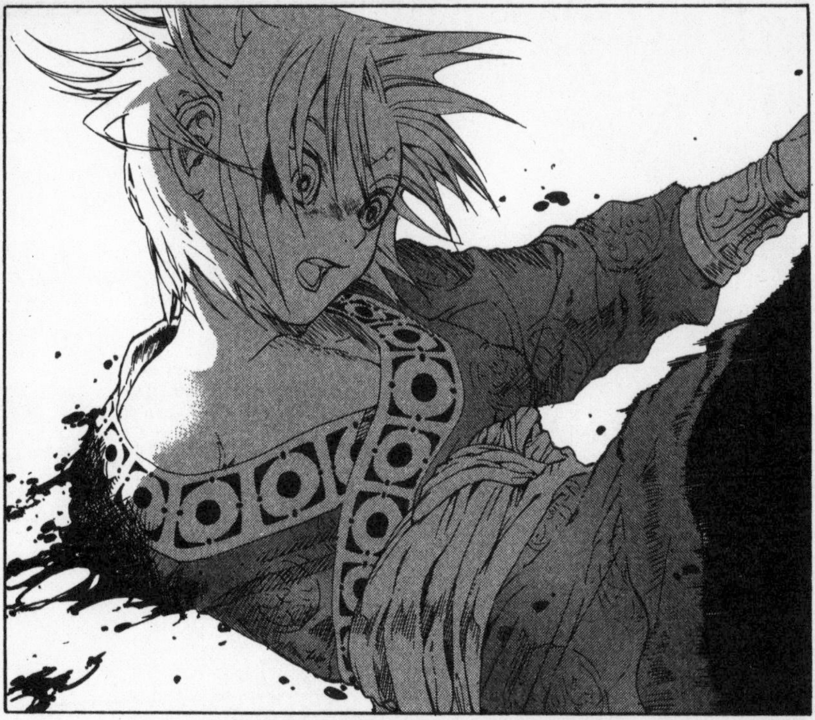
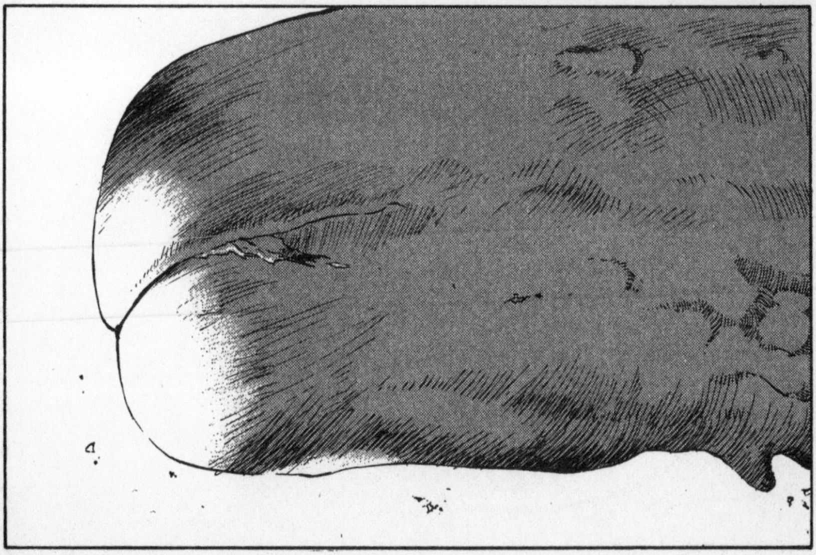

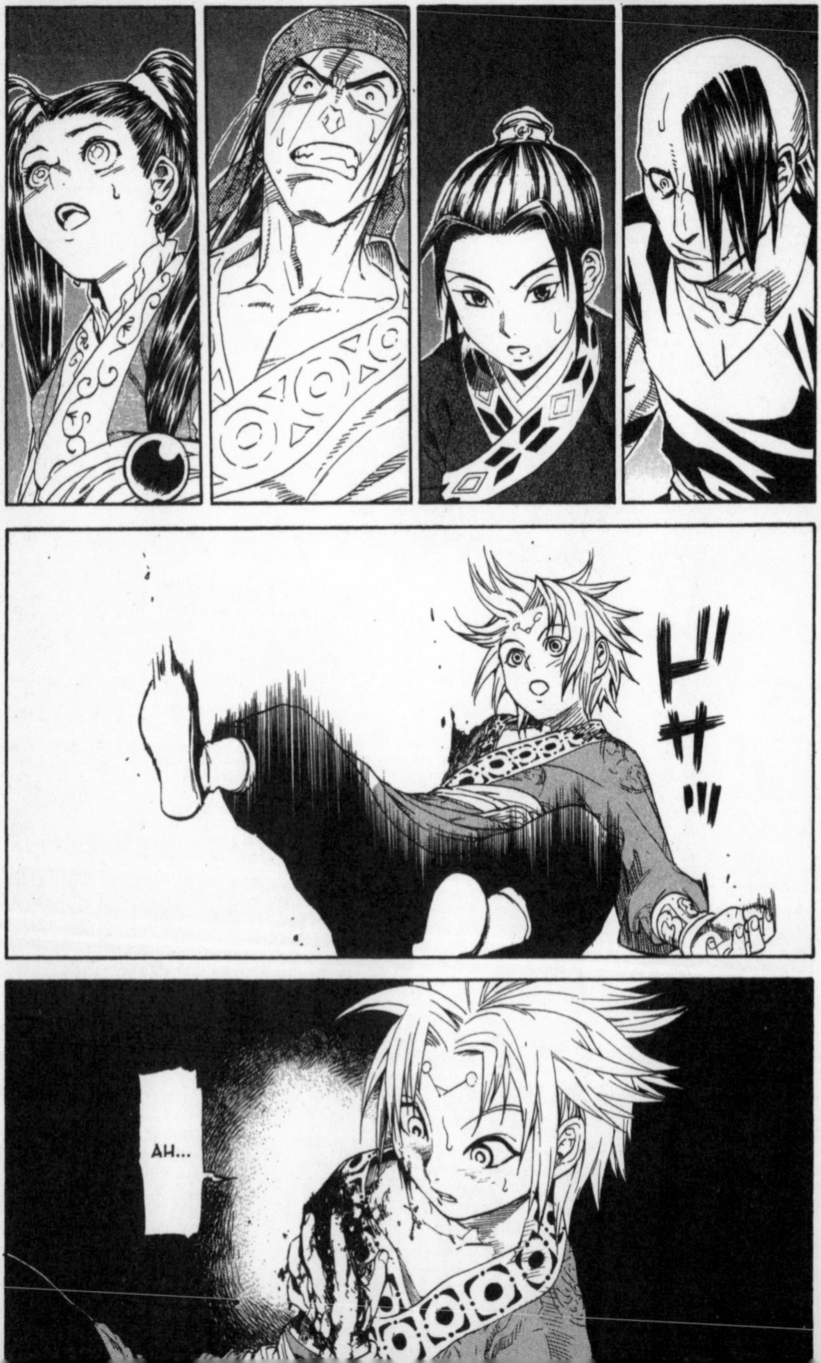
ザザッ
AH...

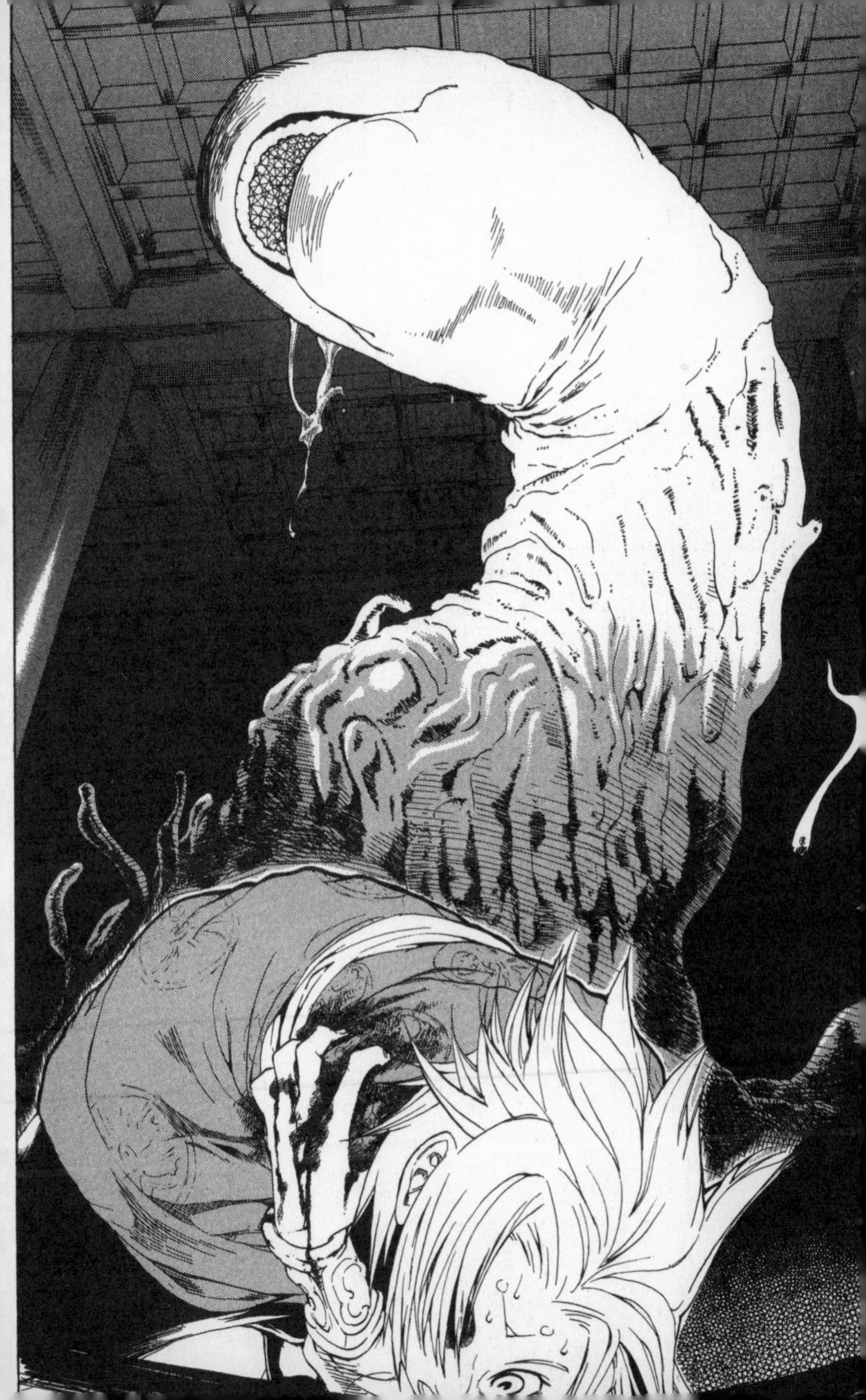

Wherein Daki Sheds Tears Over the Death of Her Mother

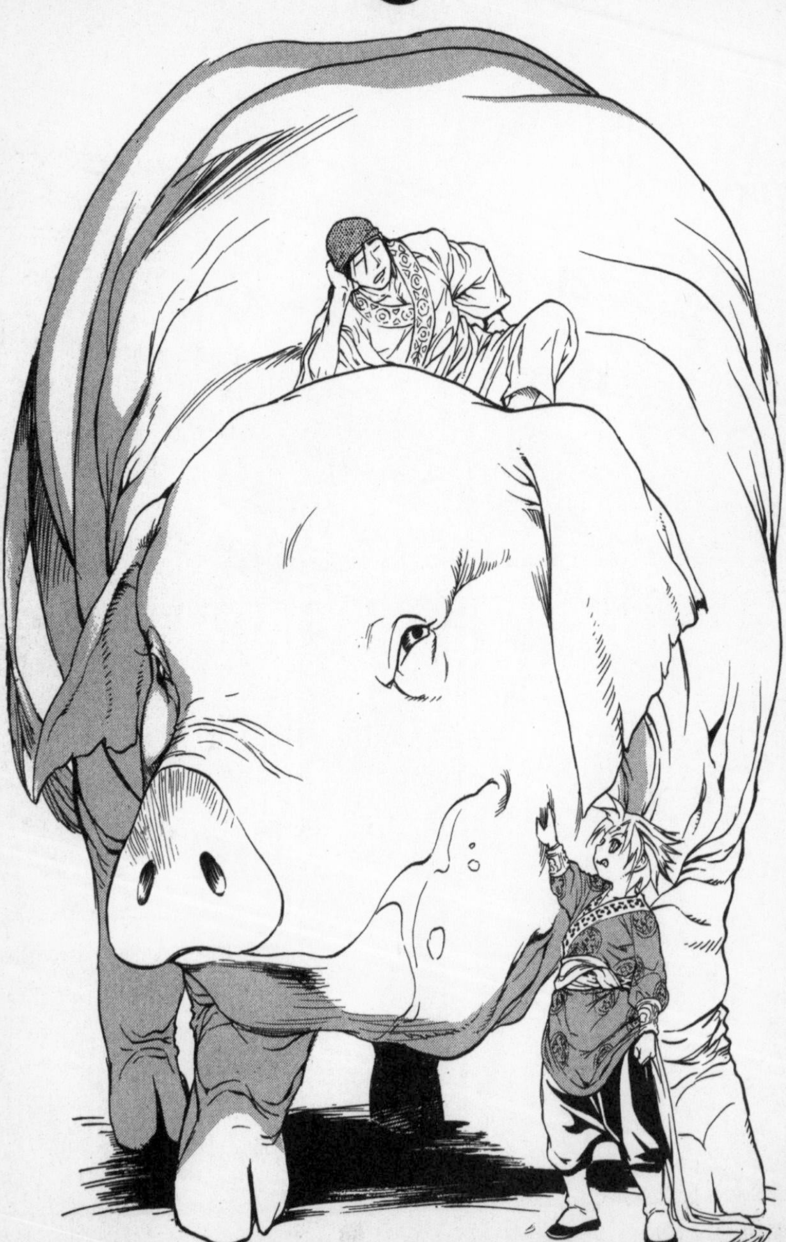

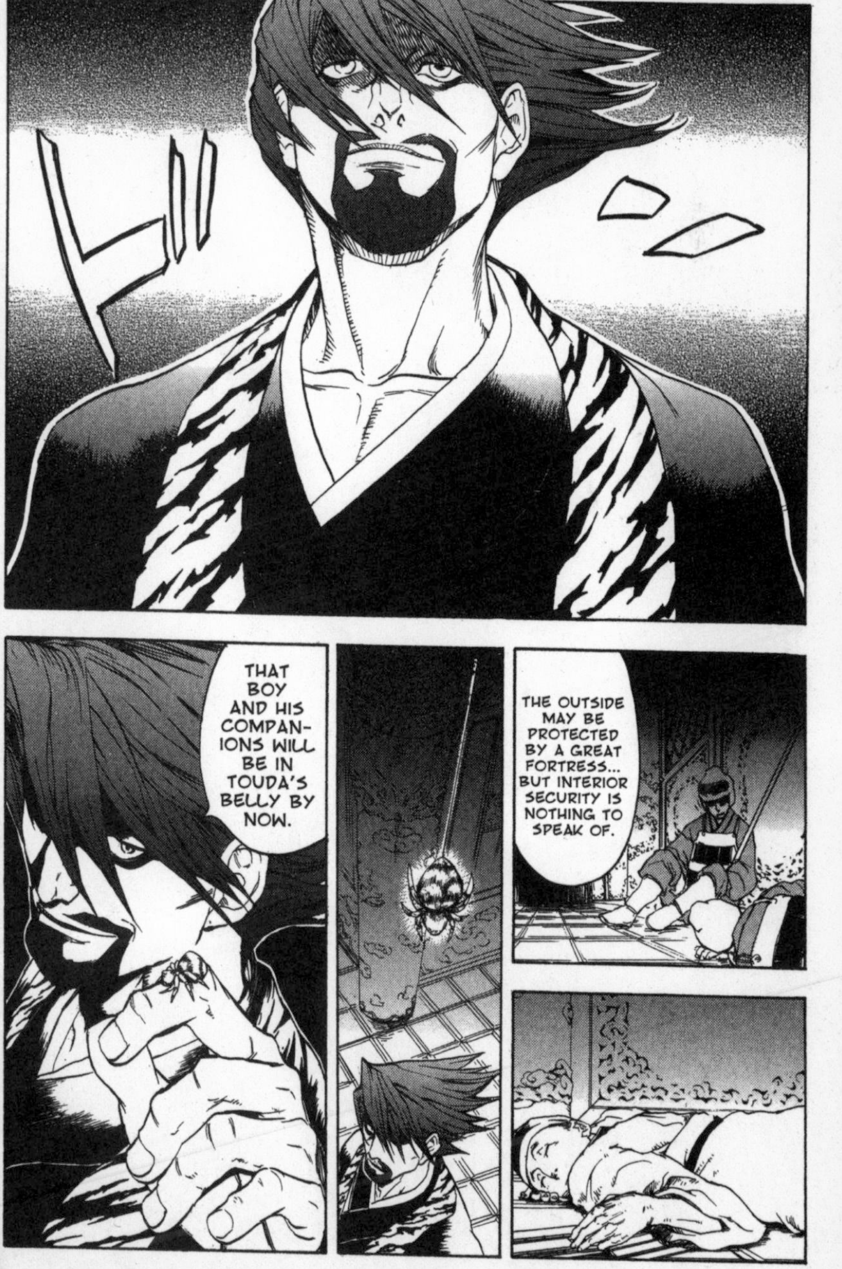
THE OUTSIDE MAY BE PROTECTED BY A GREAT FORTRESS... BUT INTERIOR SECURITY IS NOTHING TO SPEAK OF.
THAT BOY AND HIS COMPANIONS WILL BE IN TOUDA'S BELLY BY NOW.

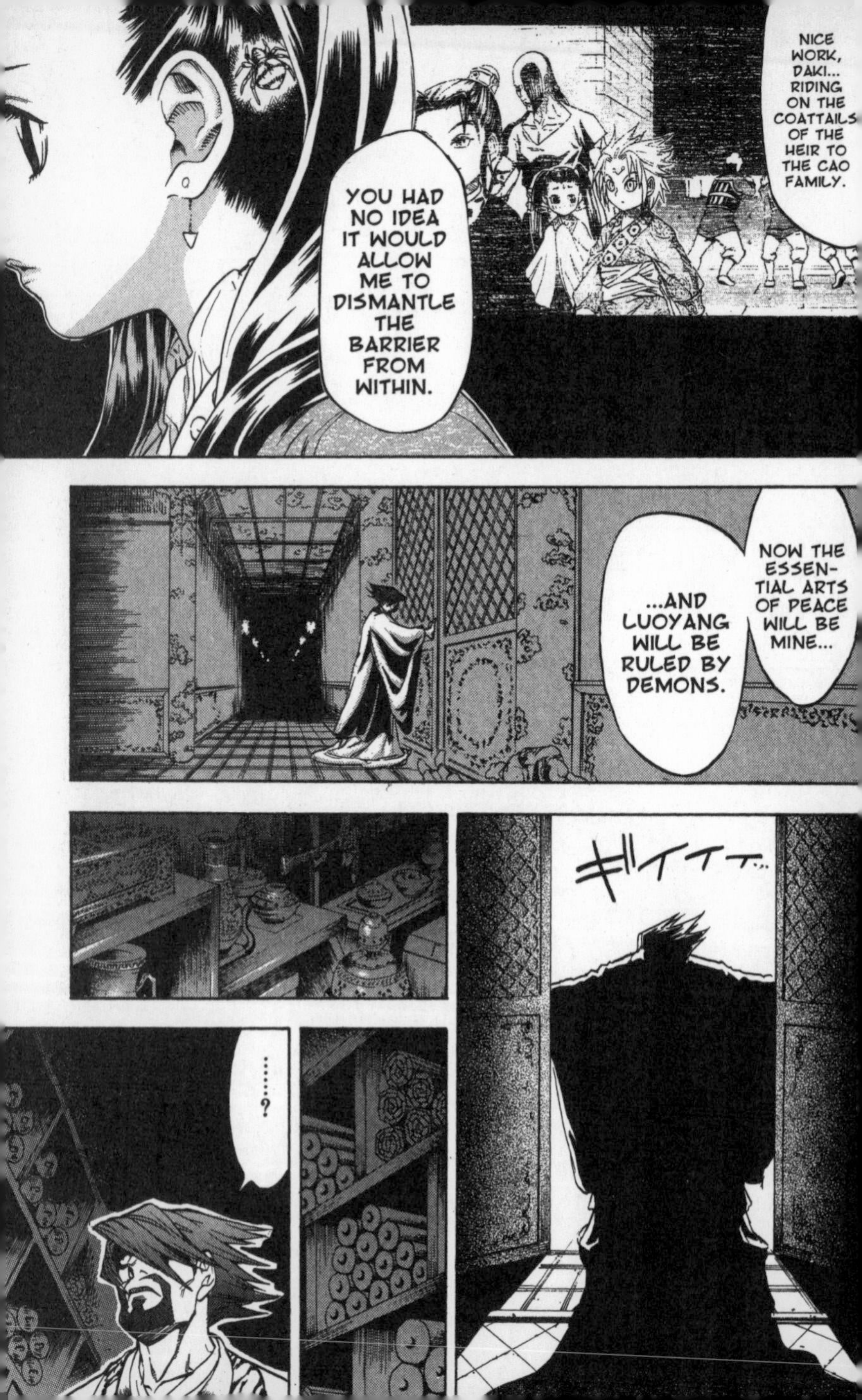
NICE WORK, DAKI... RIDING ON THE COATTAILS OF THE HEIR TO THE CAO FAMILY.
YOU HAD NO IDEA IT WOULD ALLOW ME TO DISMANTLE THE BARRIER FROM WITHIN.
NOW THE ESSEN-TIAL ARTS OF PEACE WILL BE MINE...
...AND LUOYANG WILL BE RULED BY DEMONS.
ギイイイ...
......?

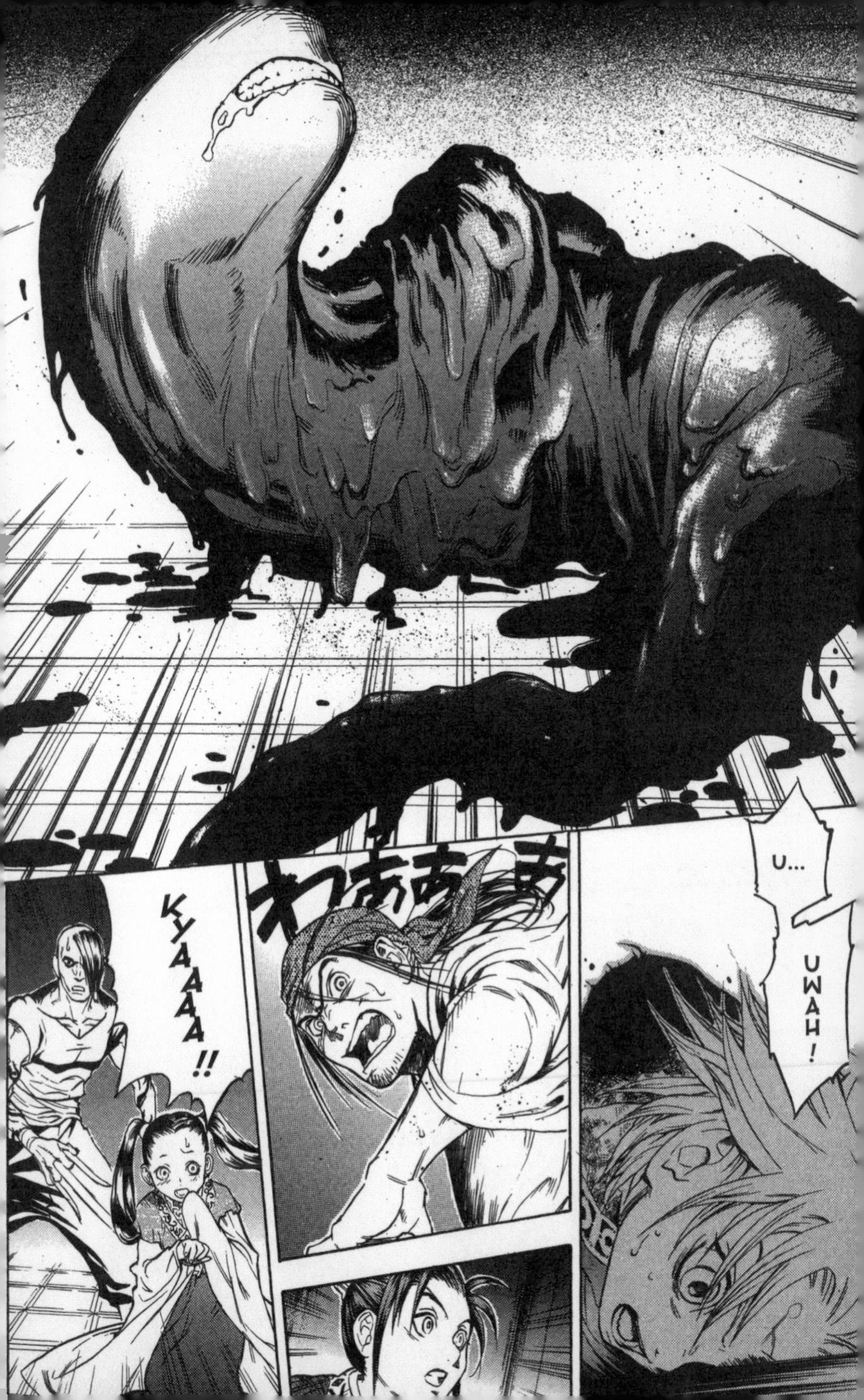
U...
UWAH!
わあああ
KYAAAA!!

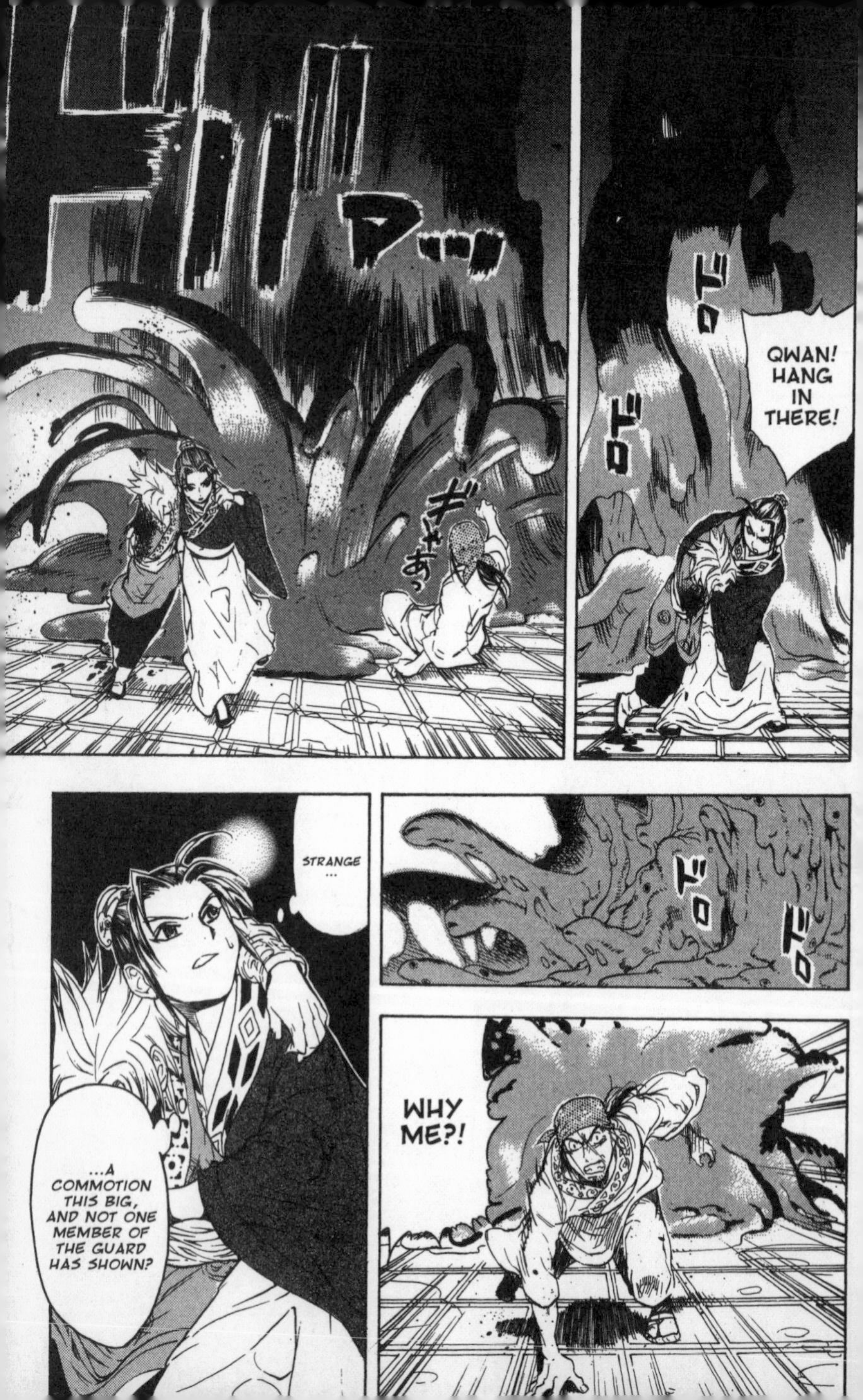

ドロ
ドロ
QWAN! HANG IN THERE!
ドロ
ドロ
WHY ME?!
STRANGE...
...A COMMOTION THIS BIG, AND NOT ONE MEMBER OF THE GUARD HAS SHOWN?

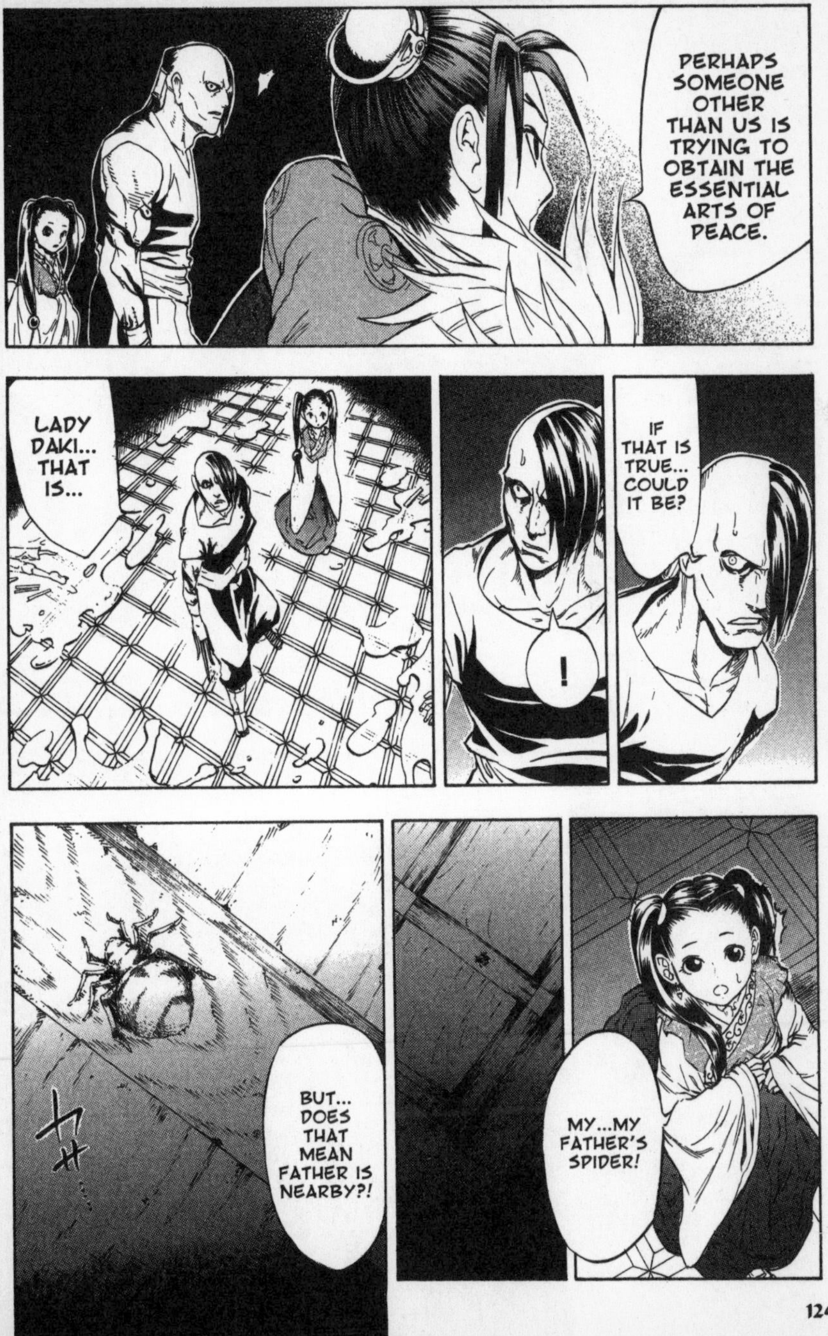
PERHAPS SOMEONE OTHER THAN US IS TRYING TO OBTAIN THE ESSENTIAL ARTS OF PEACE.
IF THAT IS TRUE... COULD IT BE?
!
LADY DAKI... THAT IS...
MY...MY FATHER'S SPIDER!
BUT... DOES THAT MEAN FATHER IS NEARBY?!

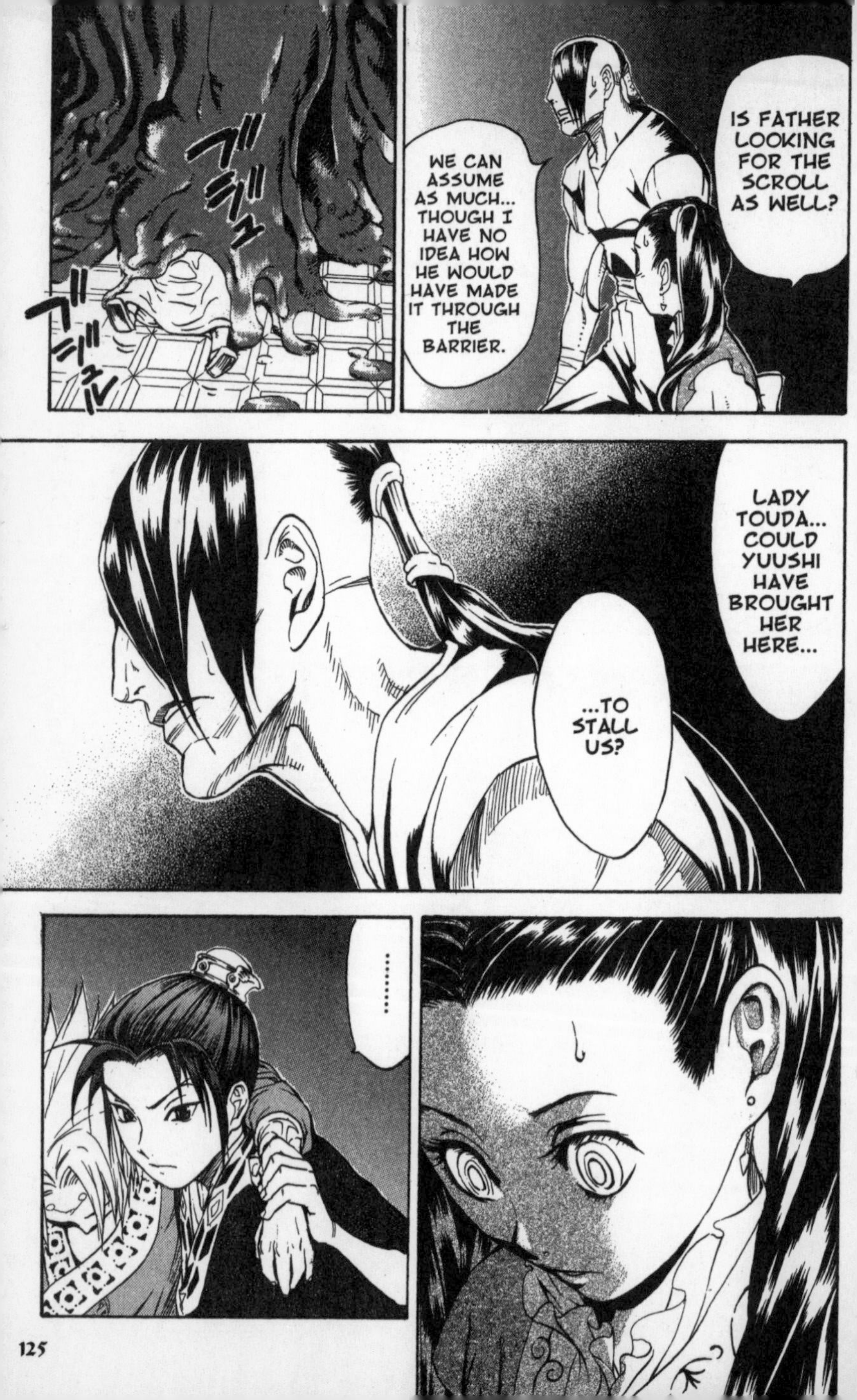
IS FATHER LOOKING FOR THE SCROLL AS WELL?
WE CAN ASSUME AS MUCH... THOUGH I HAVE NO IDEA HOW HE WOULD HAVE MADE IT THROUGH THE BARRIER.
LADY TOUDA... COULD YUUSHI HAVE BROUGHT HER HERE...
...TO STALL US?
......

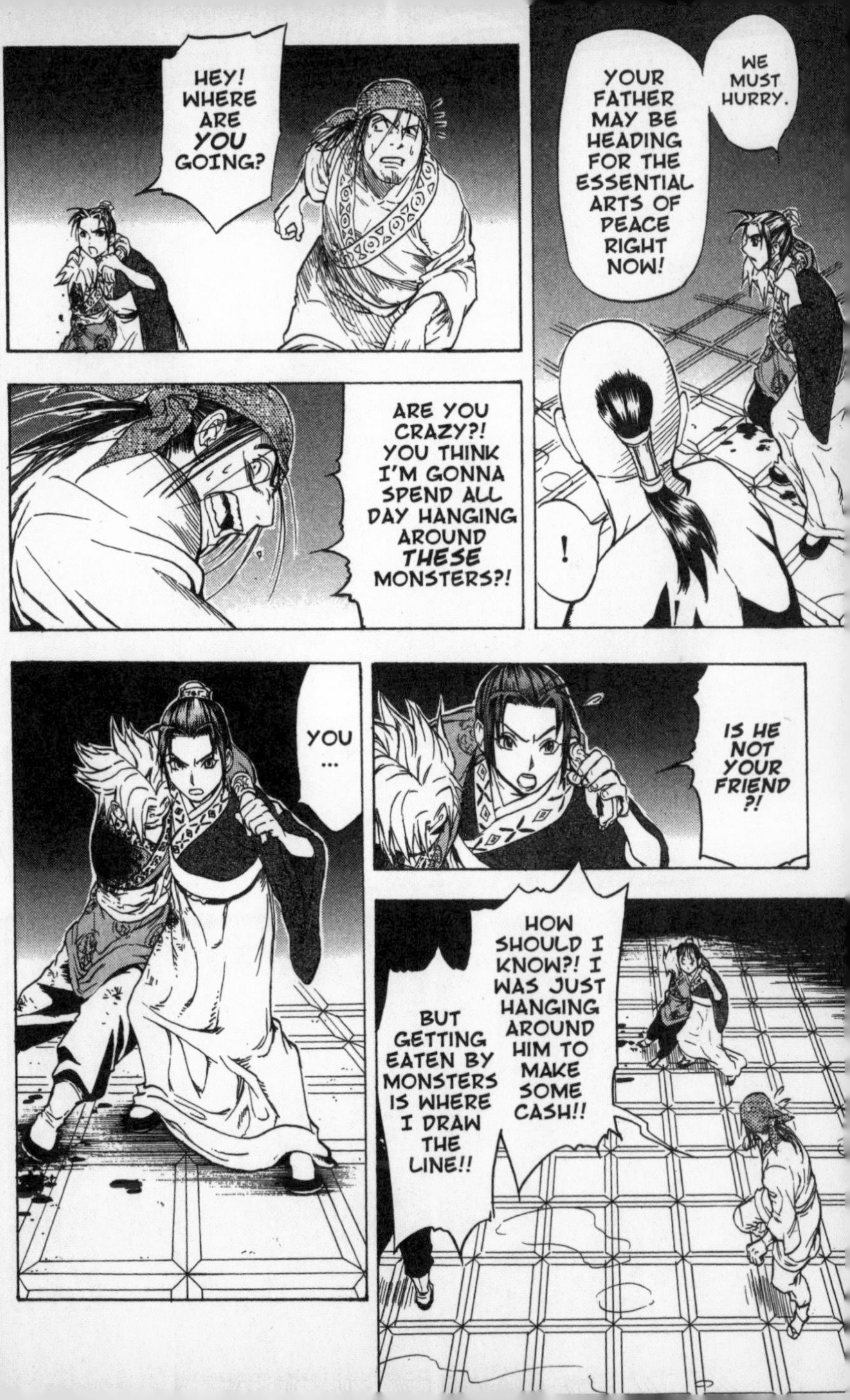
WE MUST HURRY.
YOUR FATHER MAY BE HEADING FOR THE ESSENTIAL ARTS OF PEACE RIGHT NOW!
!
HEY! WHERE ARE YOU GOING?
ARE YOU CRAZY?! YOU THINK I'M GONNA SPEND ALL DAY HANGING AROUND THESE MONSTERS?!
IS HE NOT YOUR FRIEND ?!
HOW SHOULD I KNOW?! I WAS JUST HANGING AROUND HIM TO MAKE SOME CASH!!
BUT GETTING EATEN BY MONSTERS IS WHERE I DRAW THE LINE!!
YOU ...

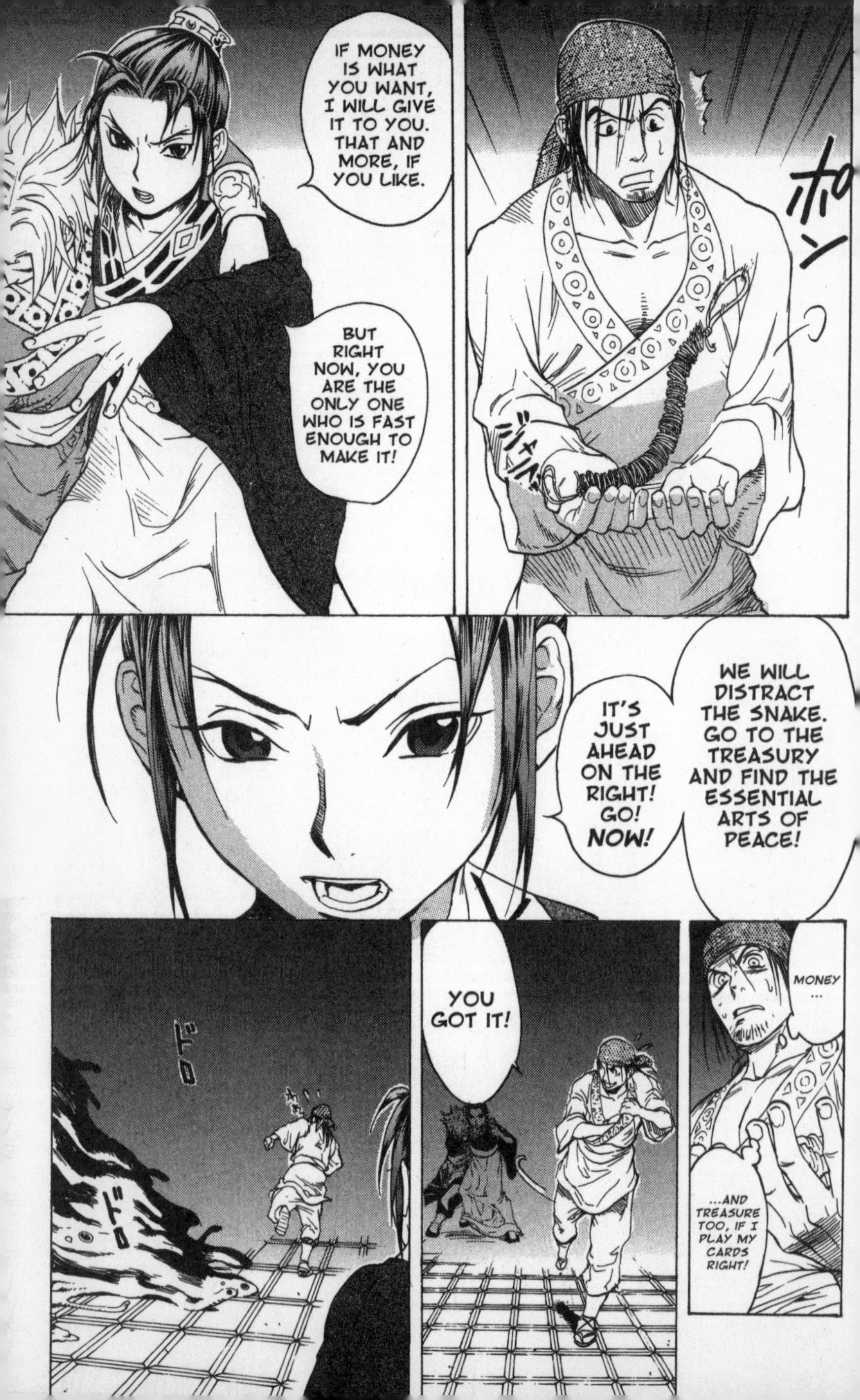
IF MONEY IS WHAT YOU WANT, I WILL GIVE IT TO YOU. THAT AND MORE, IF YOU LIKE.
BUT RIGHT NOW, YOU ARE THE ONLY ONE WHO IS FAST ENOUGH TO MAKE IT!
WE WILL DISTRACT THE SNAKE. GO TO THE TREASURY AND FIND THE ESSENTIAL ARTS OF PEACE!
IT'S JUST AHEAD ON THE RIGHT! GO! NOW!
MONEY ...
...AND TREASURE TOO, IF I PLAY MY CARDS RIGHT!
YOU GOT IT!

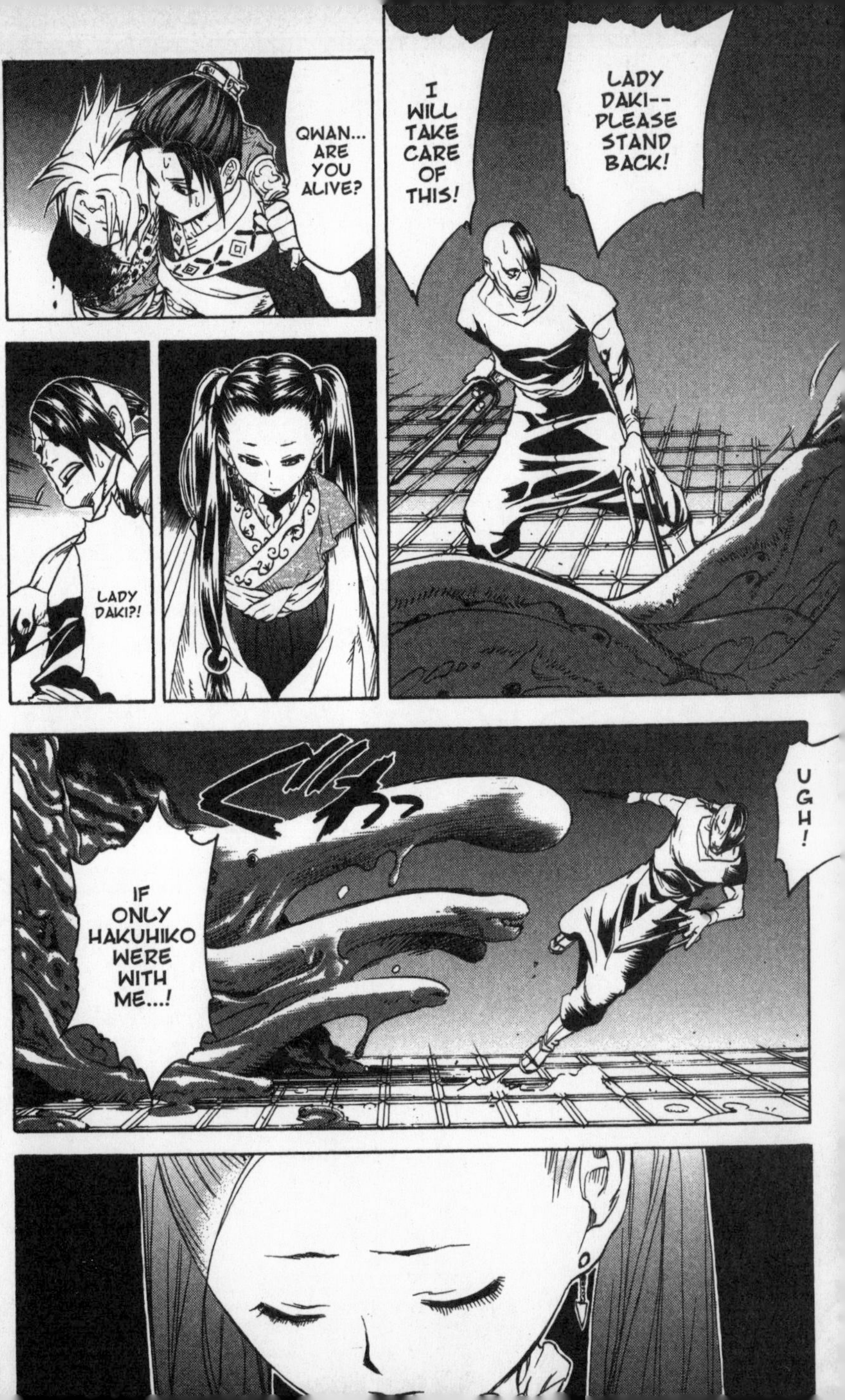
LADY DAKI-- PLEASE STAND BACK!
I WILL TAKE CARE OF THIS!
QWAN... ARE YOU ALIVE?
LADY DAKI?!
UGH!
IF ONLY HAKUHIKO WERE WITH ME...!

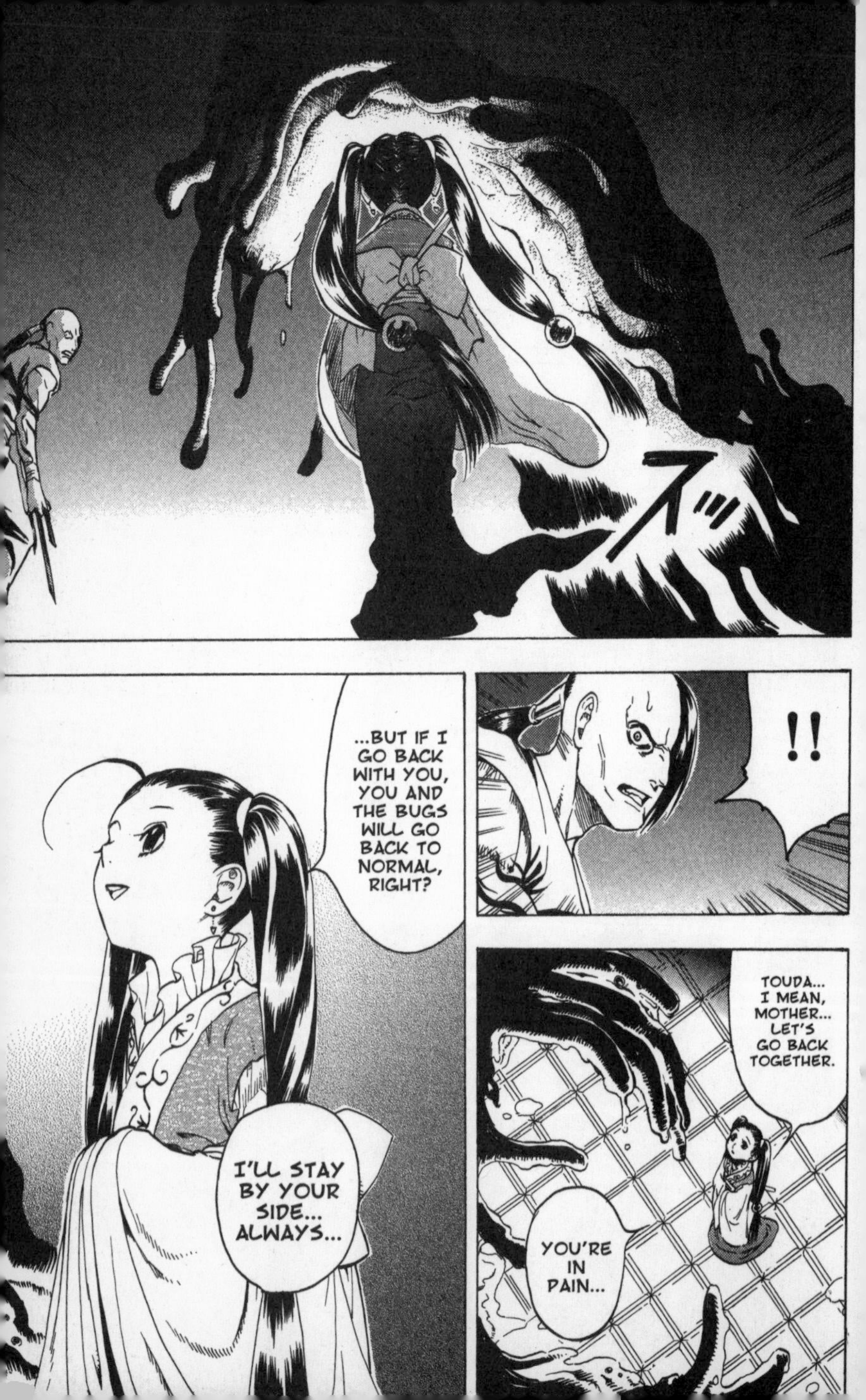
!!
TOUDA... I MEAN, MOTHER... LET'S GO BACK TOGETHER.
YOU'RE IN PAIN...
...BUT IF I GO BACK WITH YOU, YOU AND THE BUGS WILL GO BACK TO NORMAL, RIGHT?
I'LL STAY BY YOUR SIDE... ALWAYS...

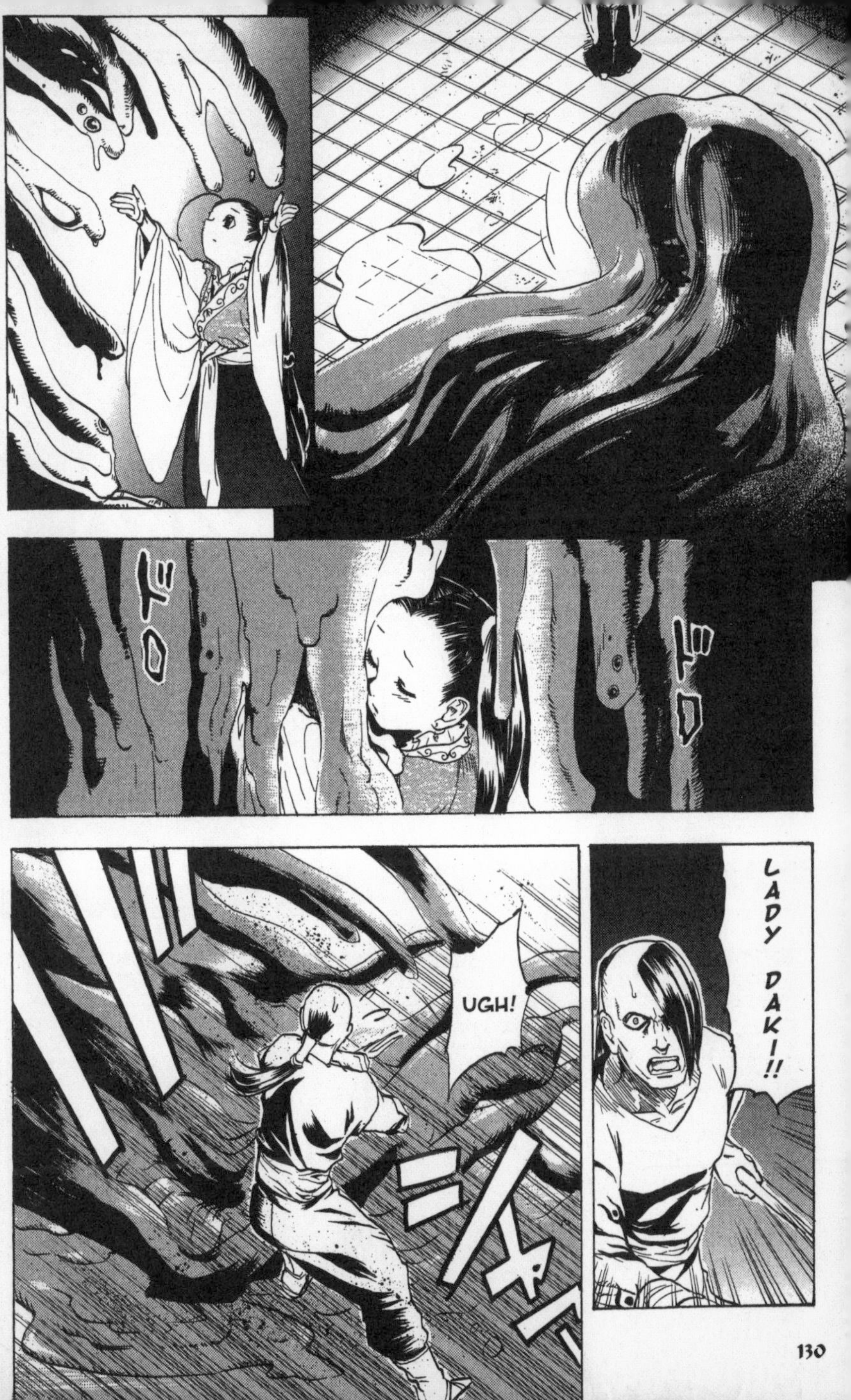
ドロ
ドロ
LADY DAKI!!
UGH!

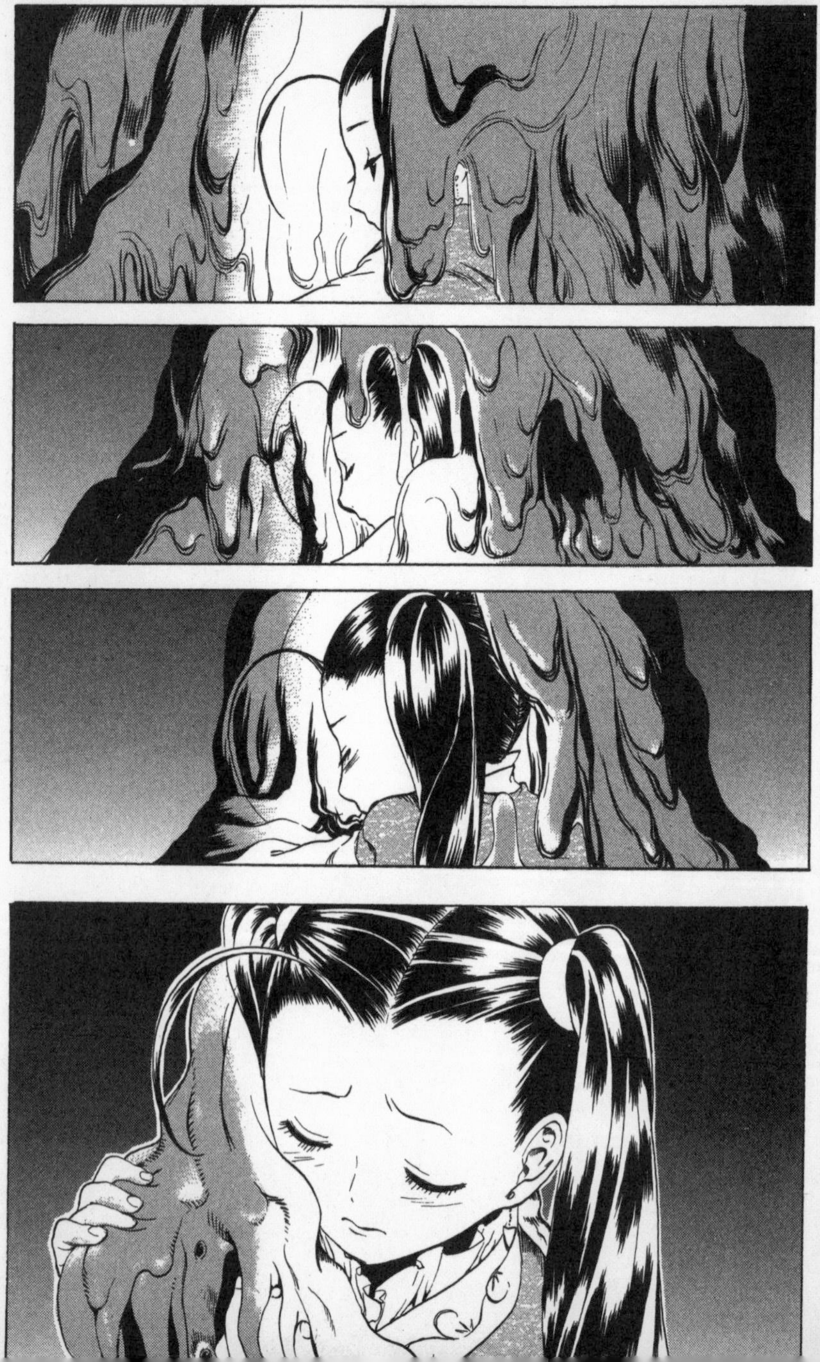

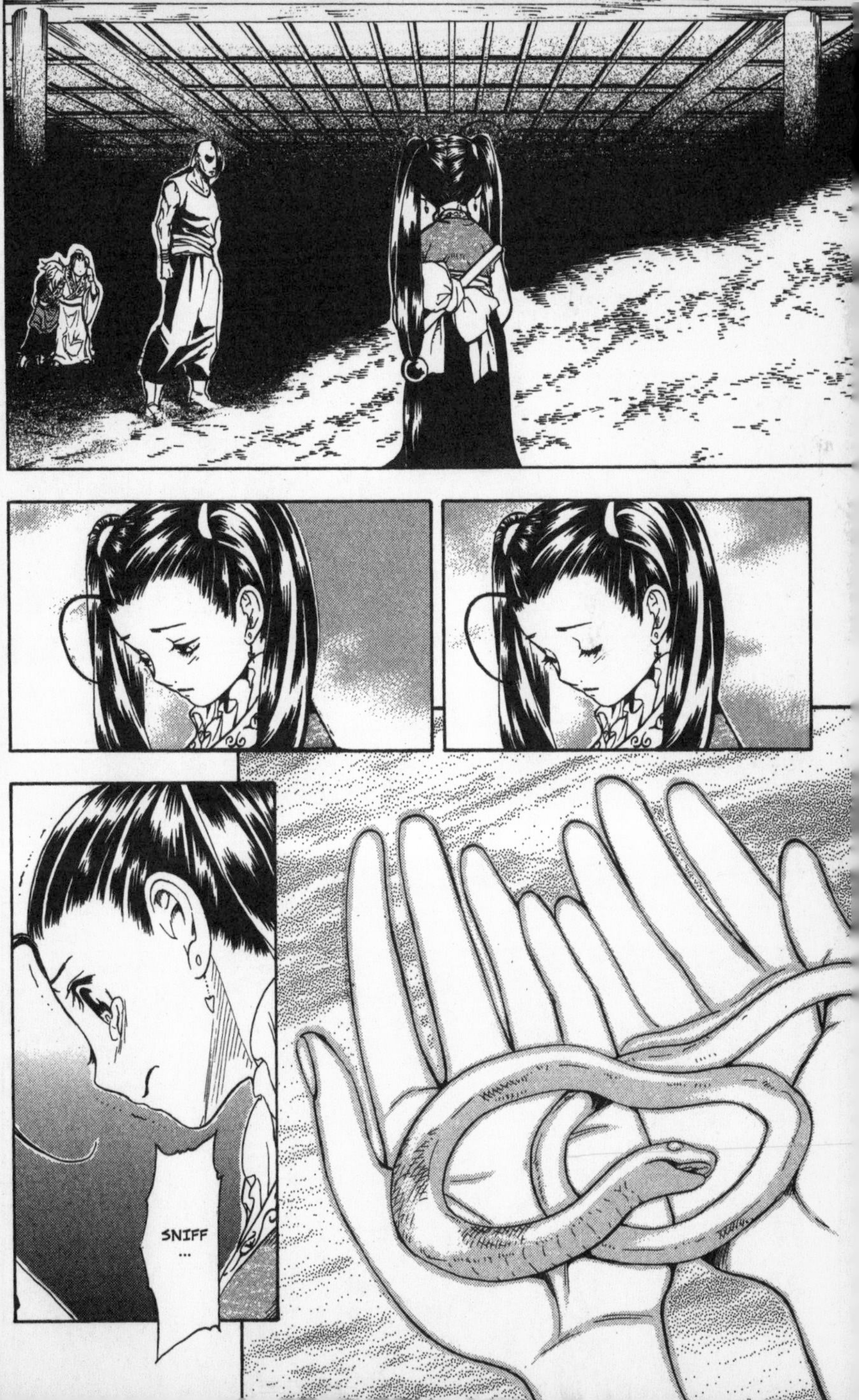
SNIFF
...

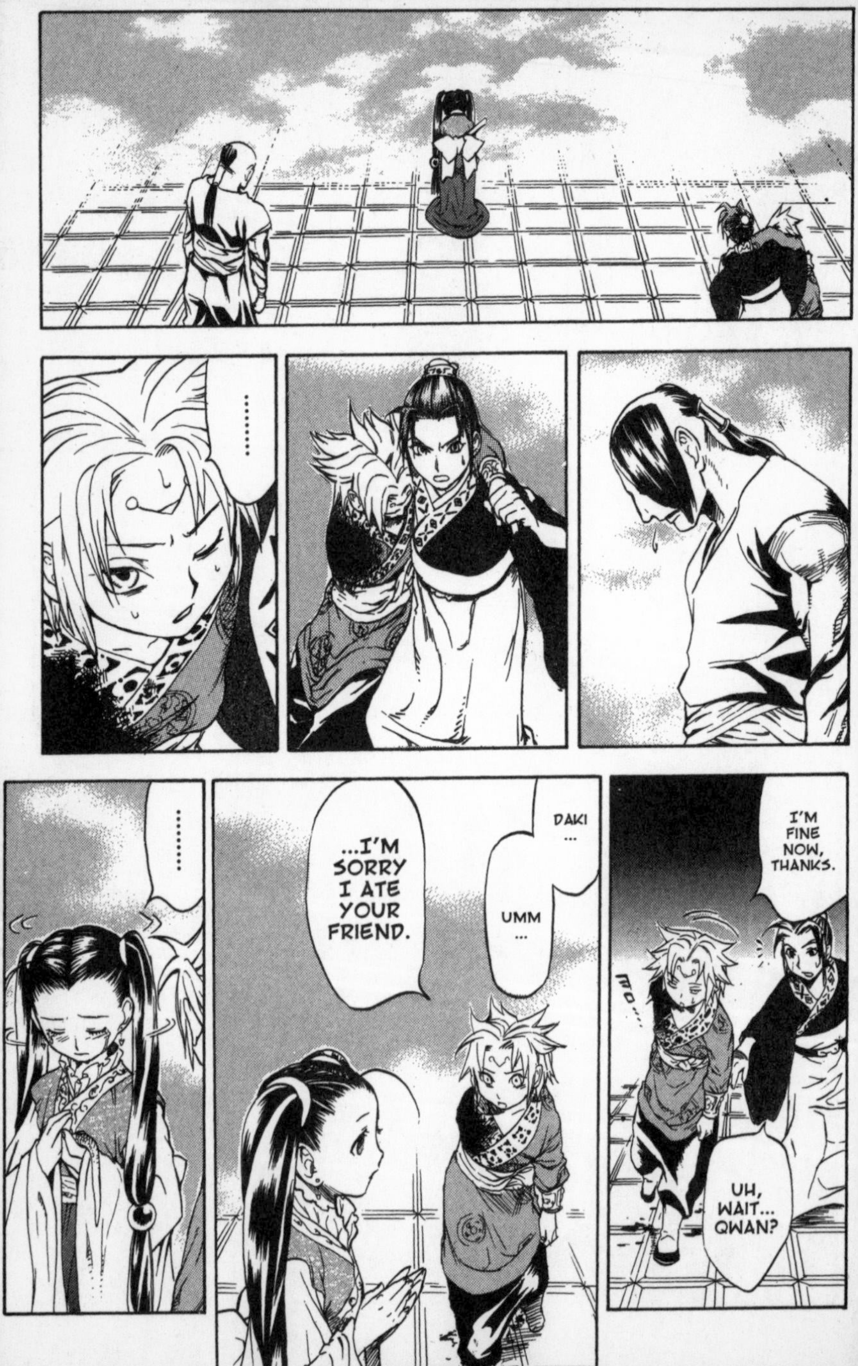
....
I'M FINE NOW, THANKS.
UH, WAIT... QWAN?
DAKI ...
UMM ...
...I'M SORRY I ATE YOUR FRIEND.
....

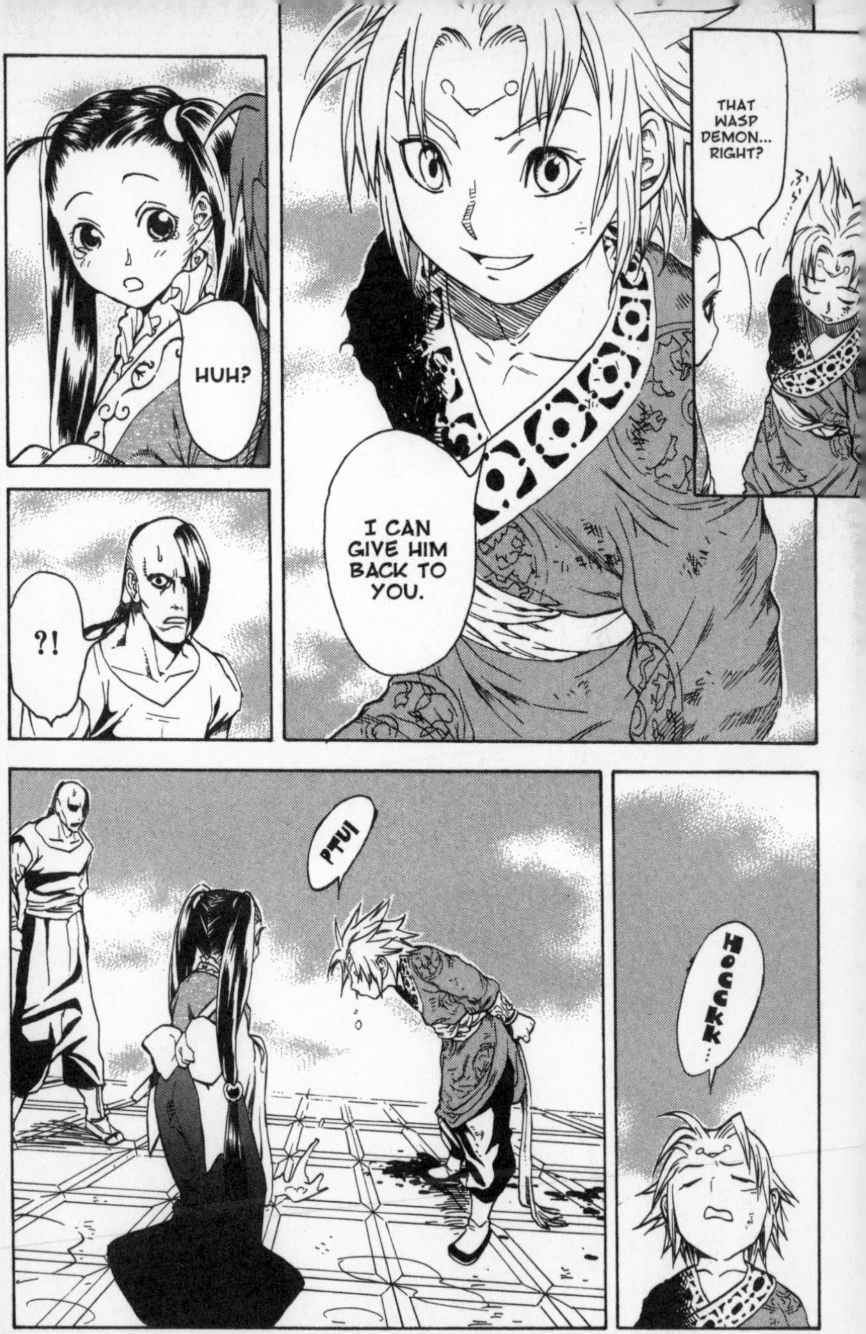
THAT WASP DEMON... RIGHT?
I CAN GIVE HIM BACK TO YOU.
HUH?
?!
HOCCKK...
PTUI

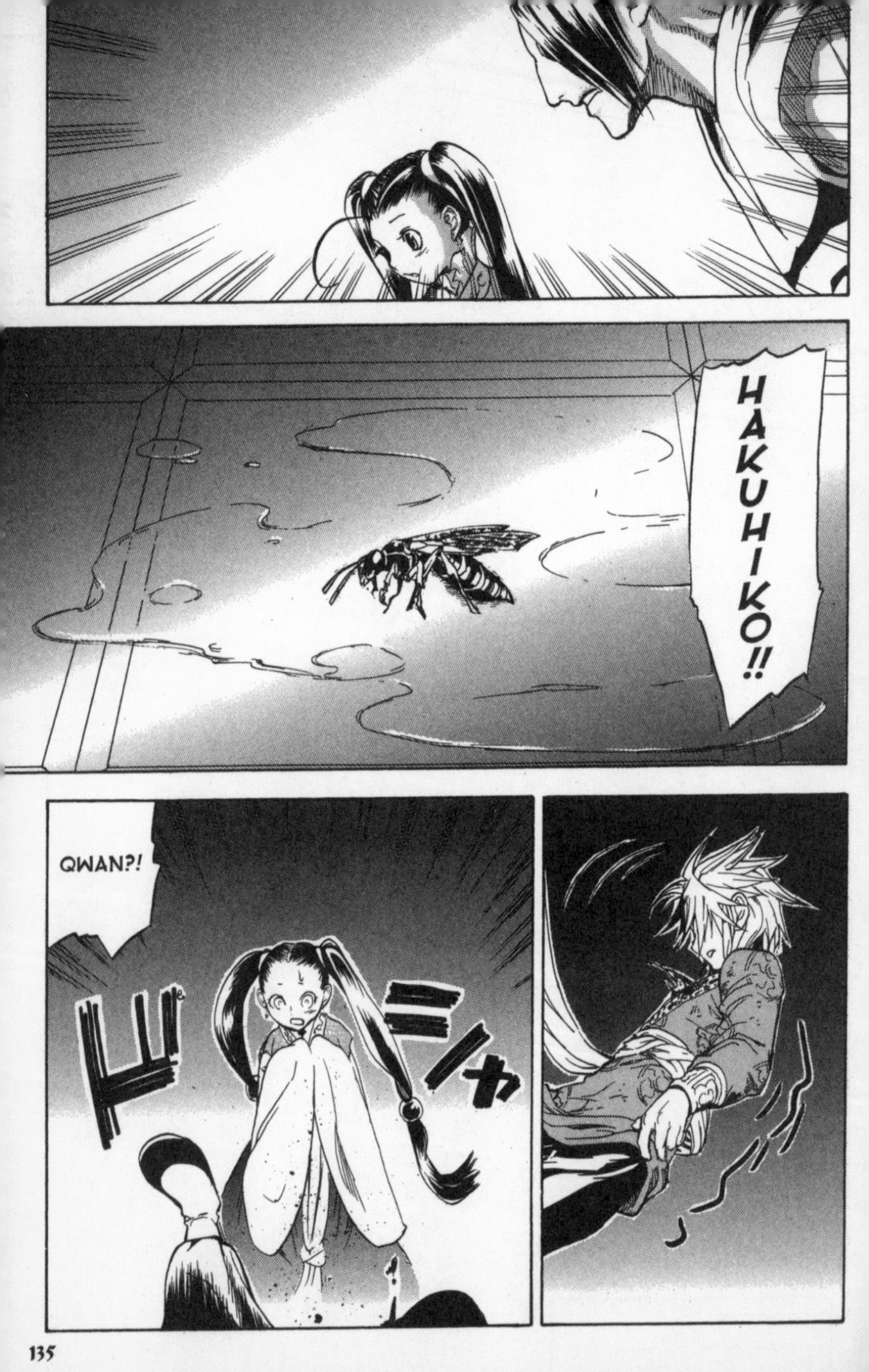
HAKUHIKO!!
QWAN?!

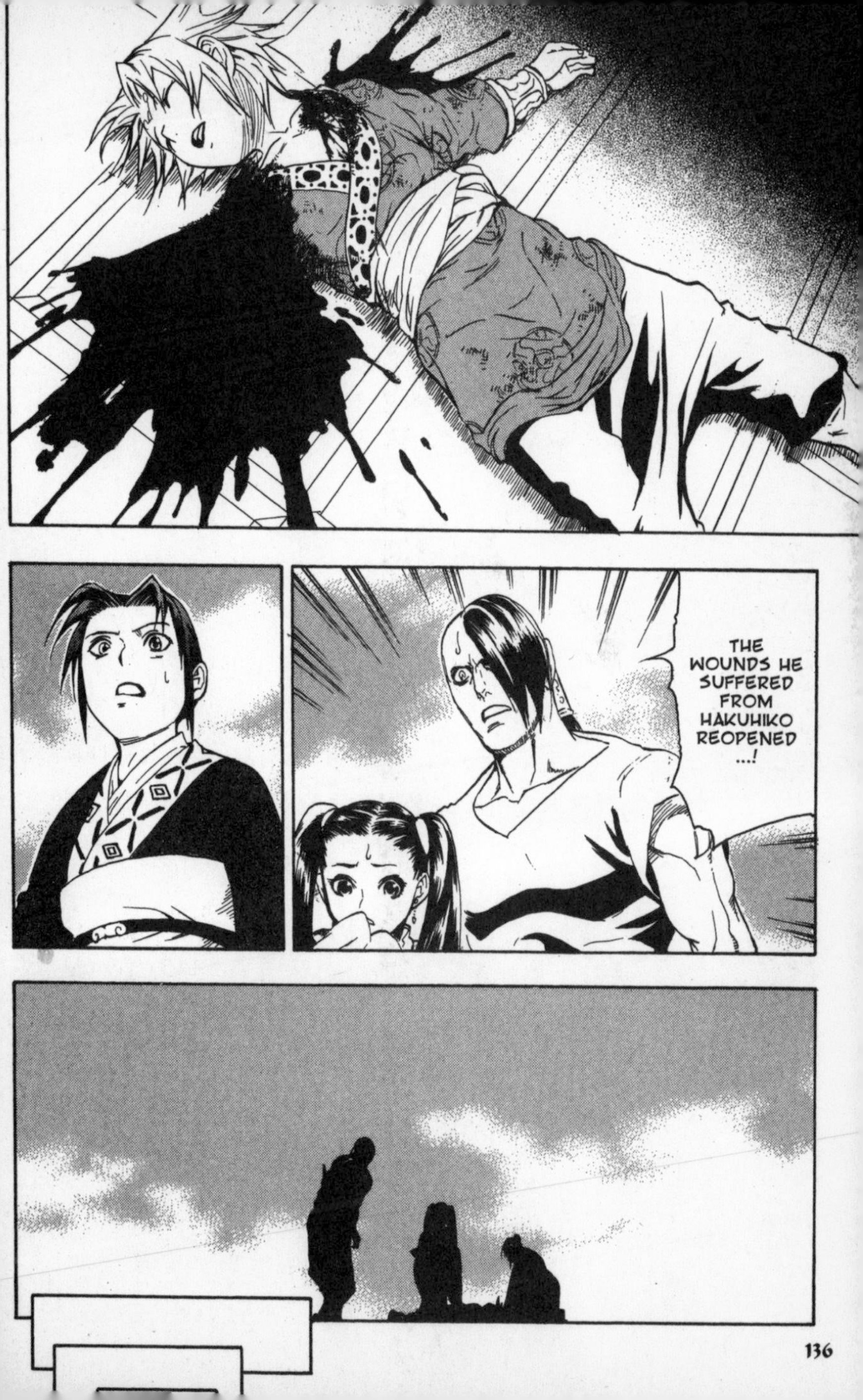
THE WOUNDS HE SUFFERED FROM HAKUHIKO REOPENED ...!

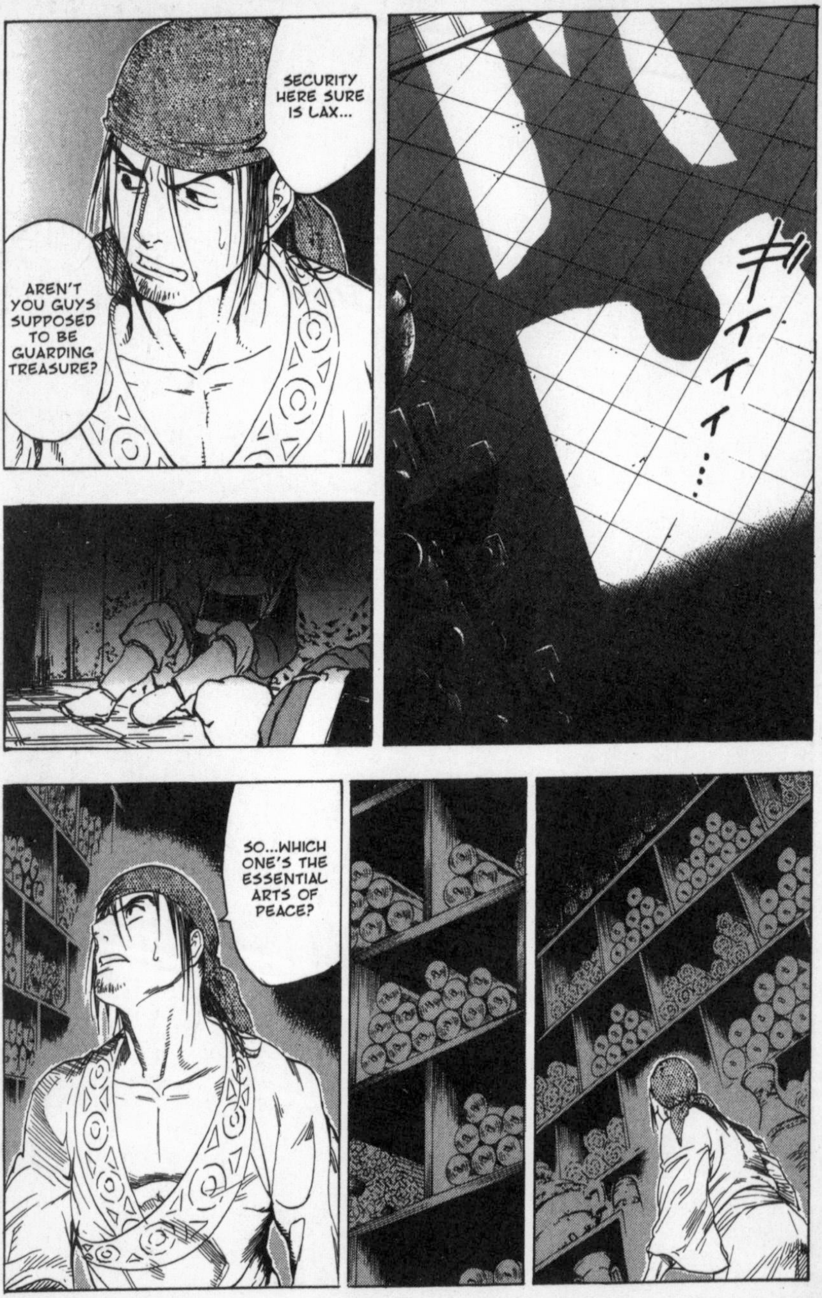
ギイイイ…
SECURITY HERE SURE IS LAX...
AREN'T YOU GUYS SUPPOSED TO BE GUARDING TREASURE?
SO...WHICH ONE'S THE ESSENTIAL ARTS OF PEACE?

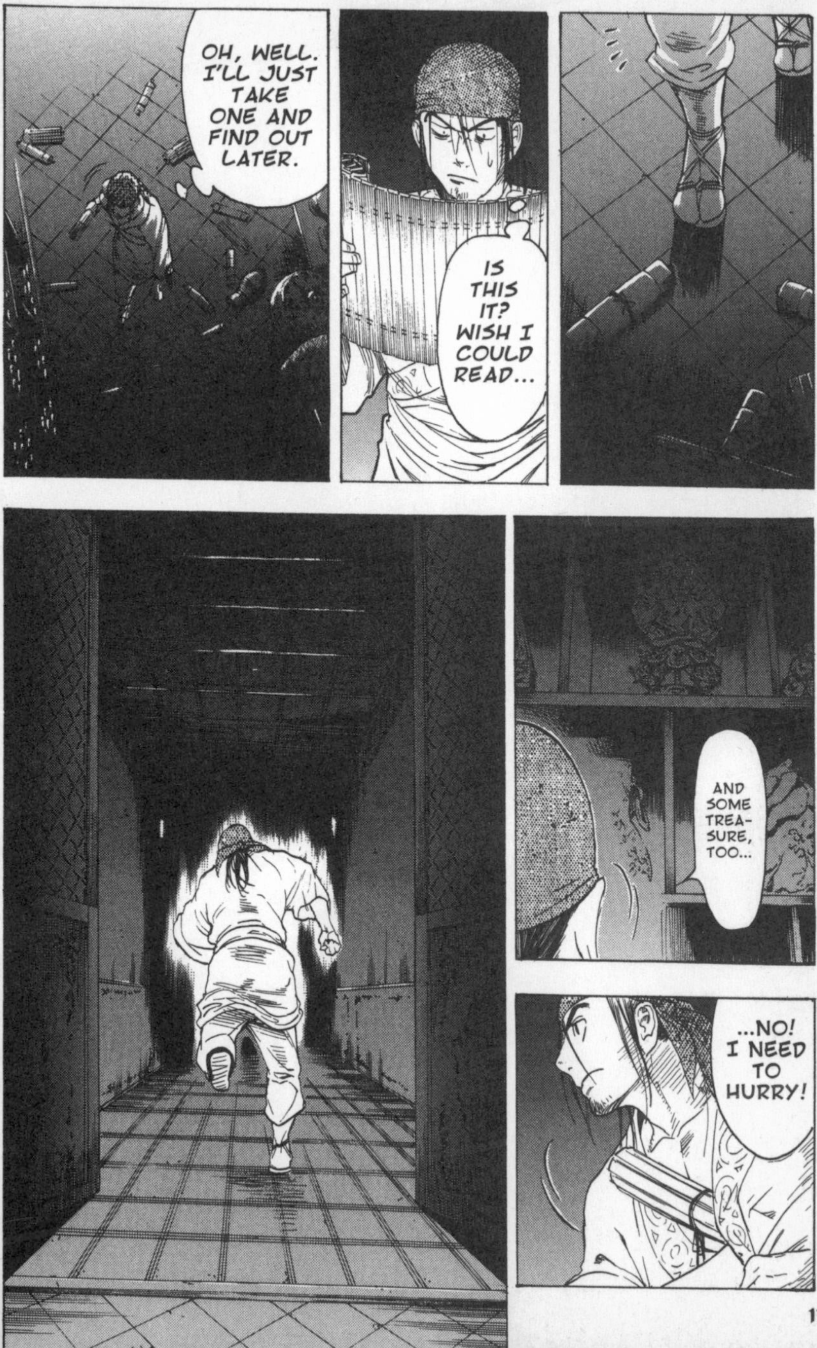
IS THIS IT? WISH I COULD READ...
OH, WELL. I'LL JUST TAKE ONE AND FIND OUT LATER.
AND SOME TREA-SURE, TOO...
...NO! I NEED TO HURRY!

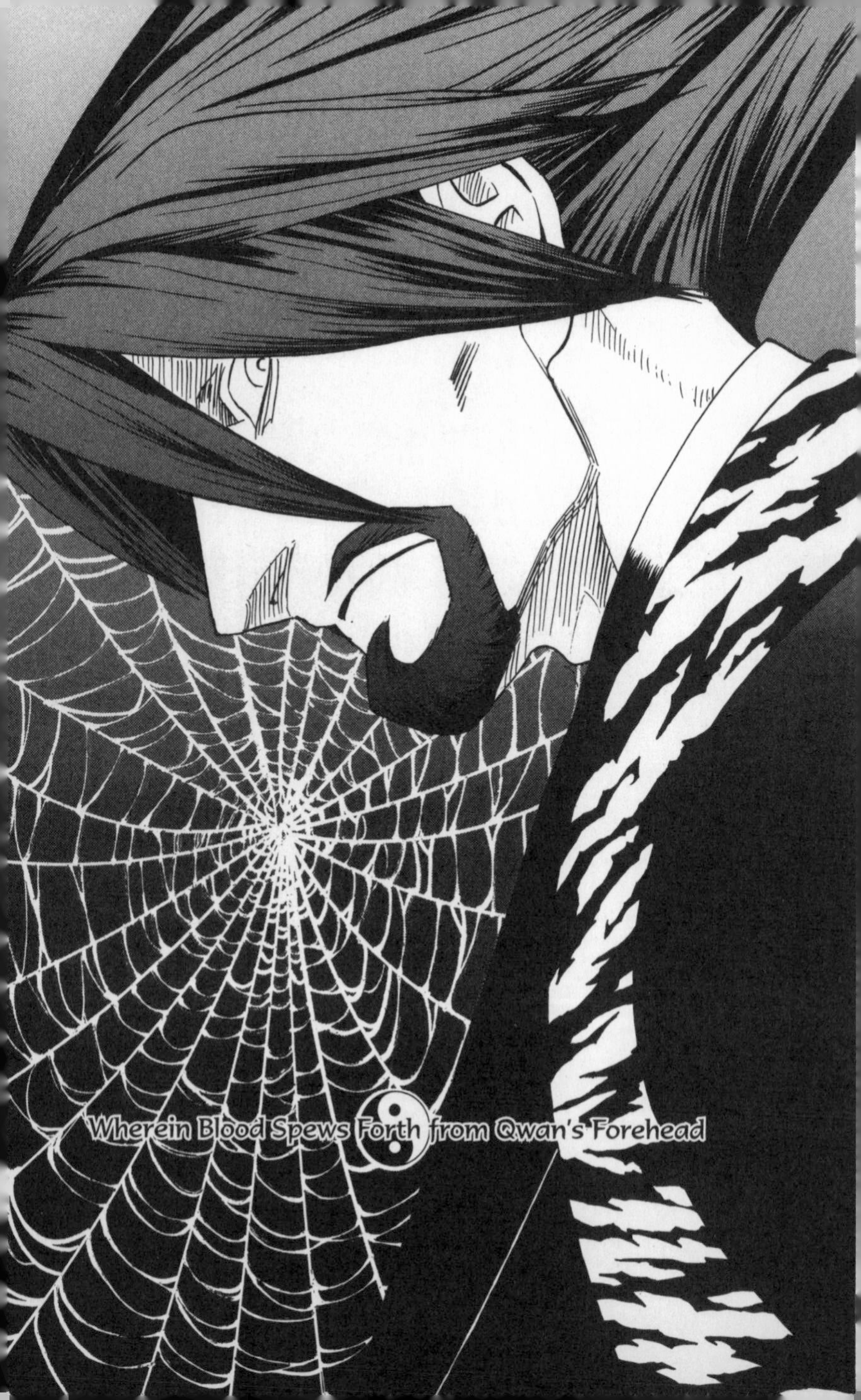
Wherein Blood Spews Forth from Qwan's Forehead

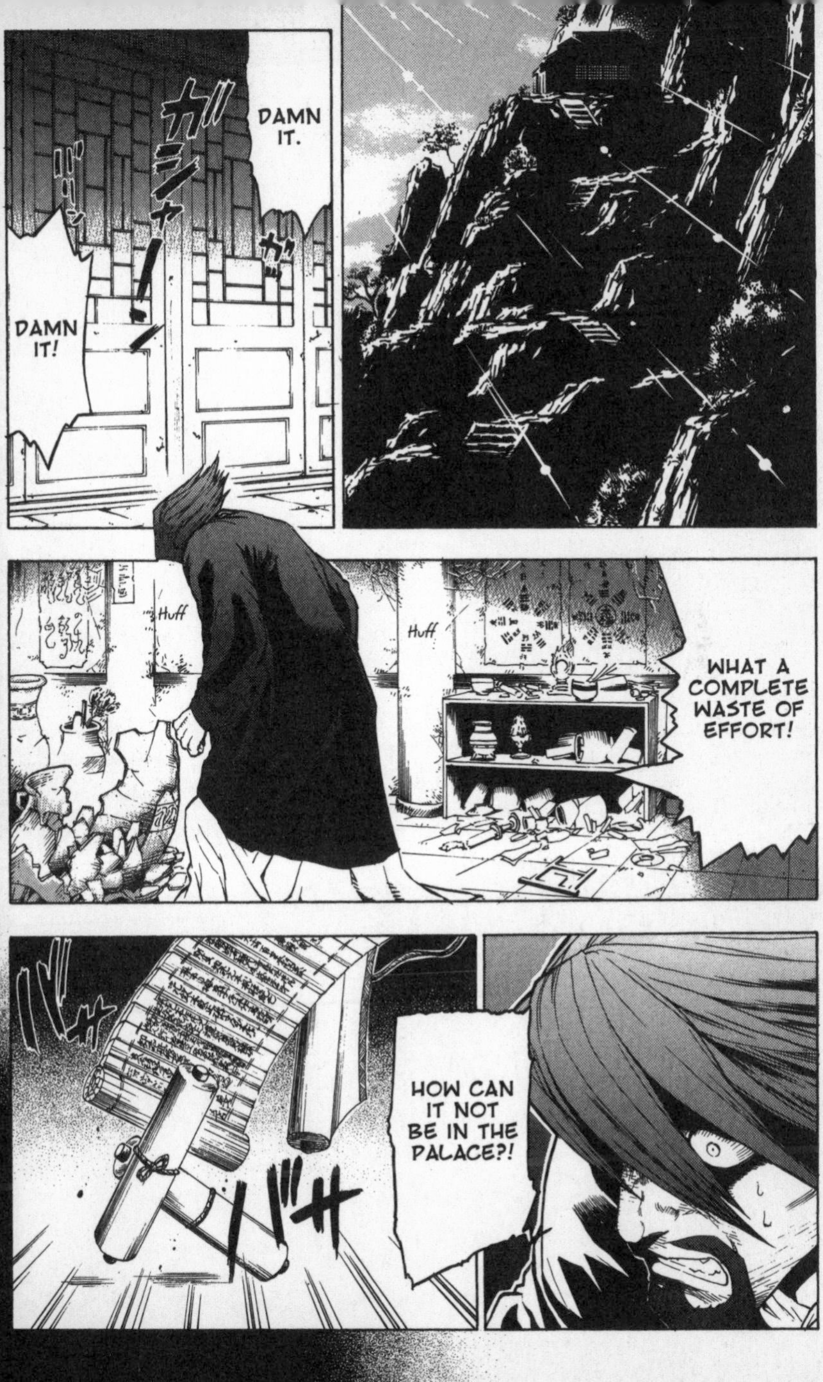
DAMN IT.
DAMN IT!
Huff
Huff
WHAT A COMPLETE WASTE OF EFFORT!
HOW CAN IT NOT BE IN THE PALACE?!

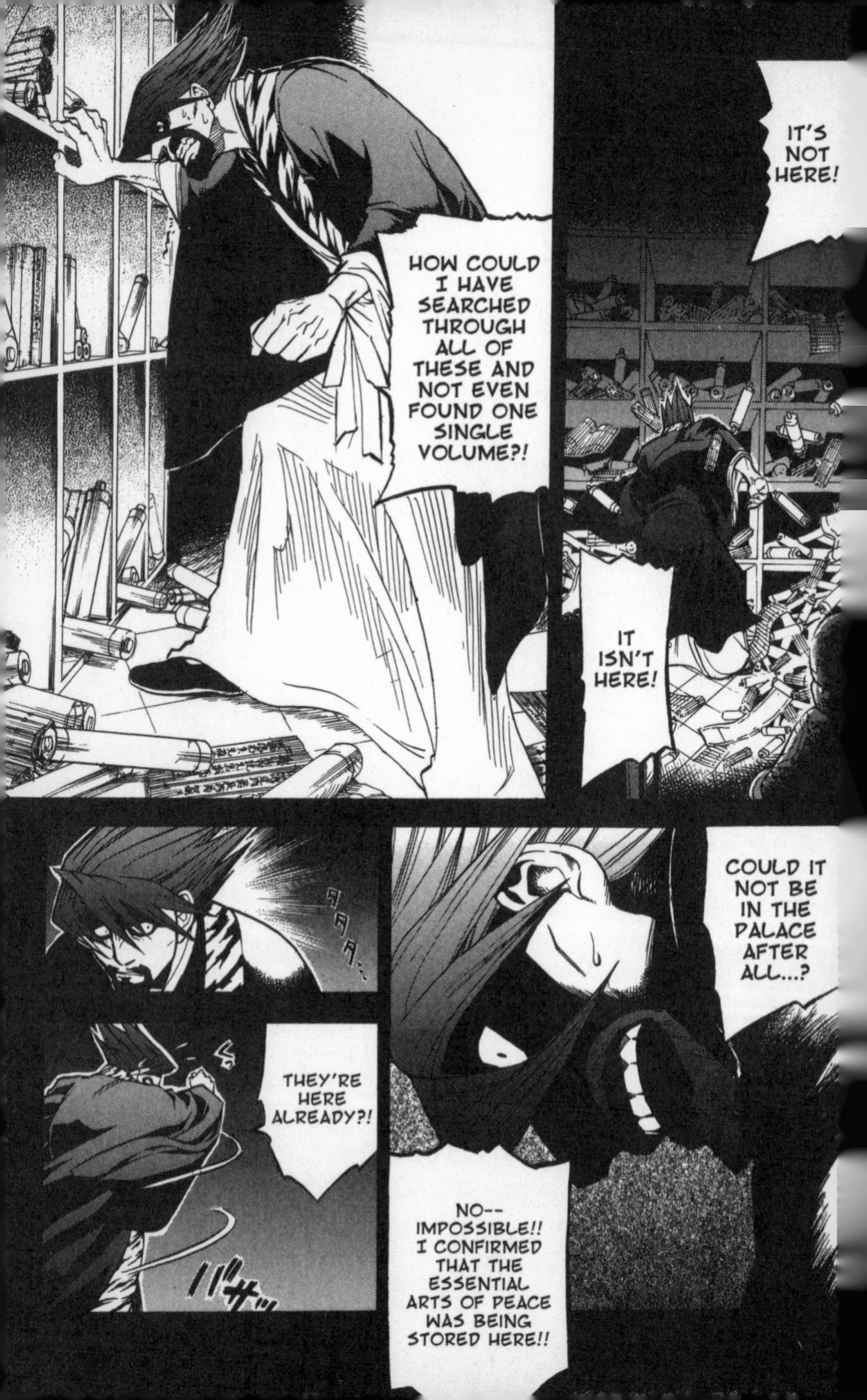
IT'S NOT HERE!
IT ISN'T HERE!
HOW COULD I HAVE SEARCHED THROUGH ALL OF THESE AND NOT EVEN FOUND ONE SINGLE VOLUME?!
COULD IT NOT BE IN THE PALACE AFTER ALL...?
NO-- IMPOSSIBLE!! I CONFIRMED THAT THE ESSENTIAL ARTS OF PEACE WAS BEING STORED HERE!!
THEY'RE HERE ALREADY?!

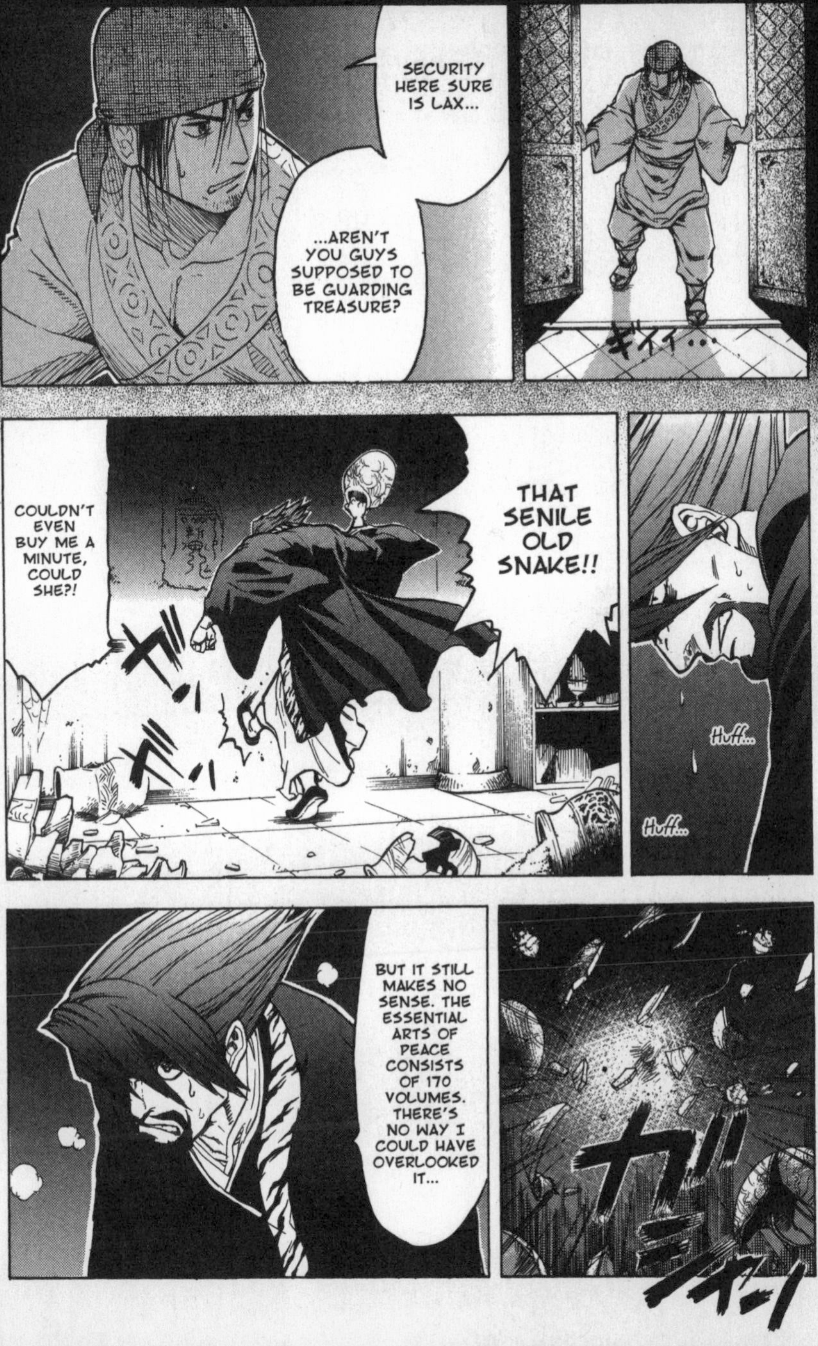
ギィィ…
SECURITY HERE SURE IS LAX...
...AREN'T YOU GUYS SUPPOSED TO BE GUARDING TREASURE?
Huff...
Huff...
THAT SENILE OLD SNAKE!!
COULDN'T EVEN BUY ME A MINUTE, COULD SHE?!
BUT IT STILL MAKES NO SENSE. THE ESSENTIAL ARTS OF PEACE CONSISTS OF 170 VOLUMES. THERE'S NO WAY I COULD HAVE OVERLOOKED IT...

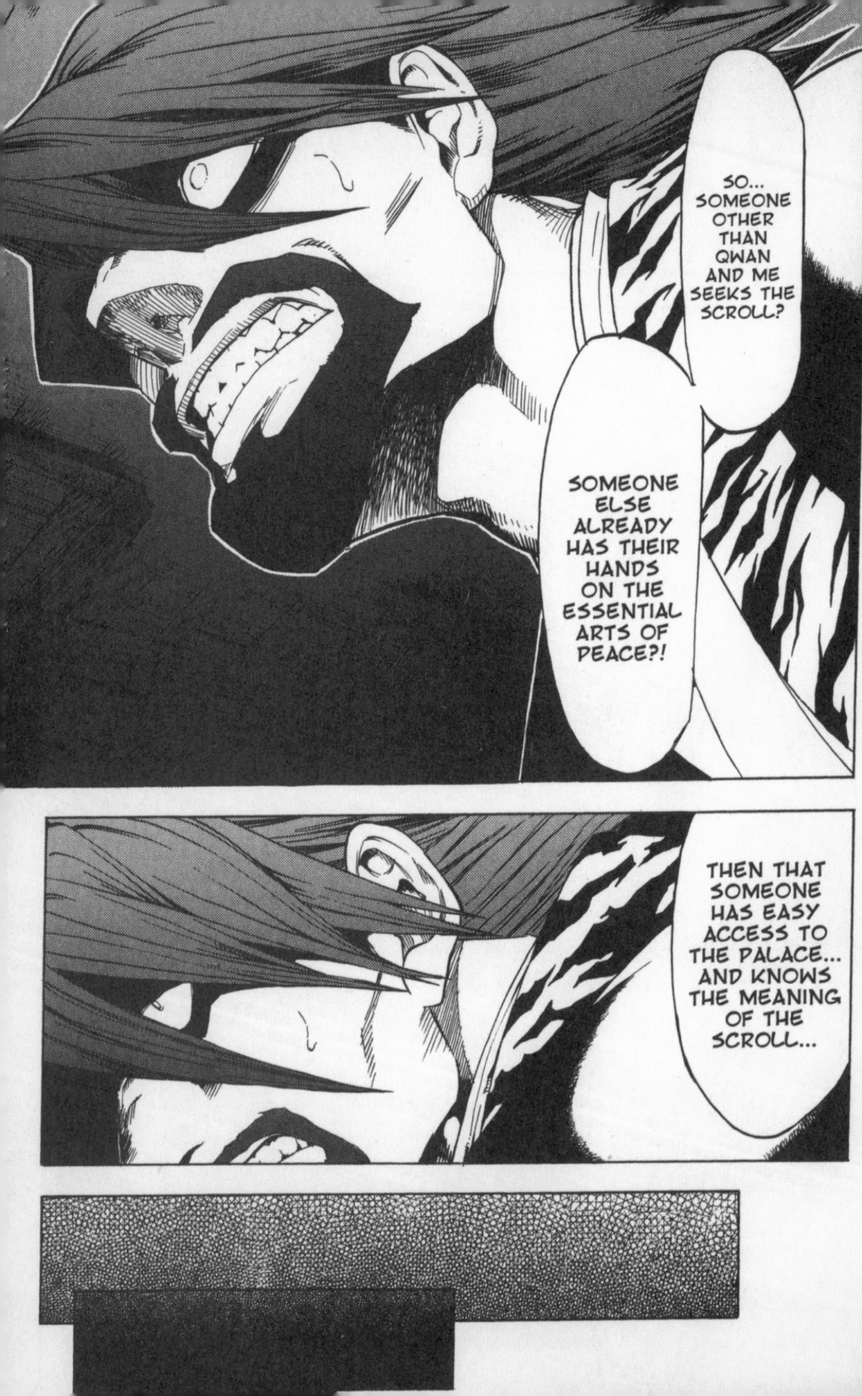
SO... SOMEONE OTHER THAN QWAN AND ME SEEKS THE SCROLL?
SOMEONE ELSE ALREADY HAS THEIR HANDS ON THE ESSENTIAL ARTS OF PEACE?!
THEN THAT SOMEONE HAS EASY ACCESS TO THE PALACE... AND KNOWS THE MEANING OF THE SCROLL...

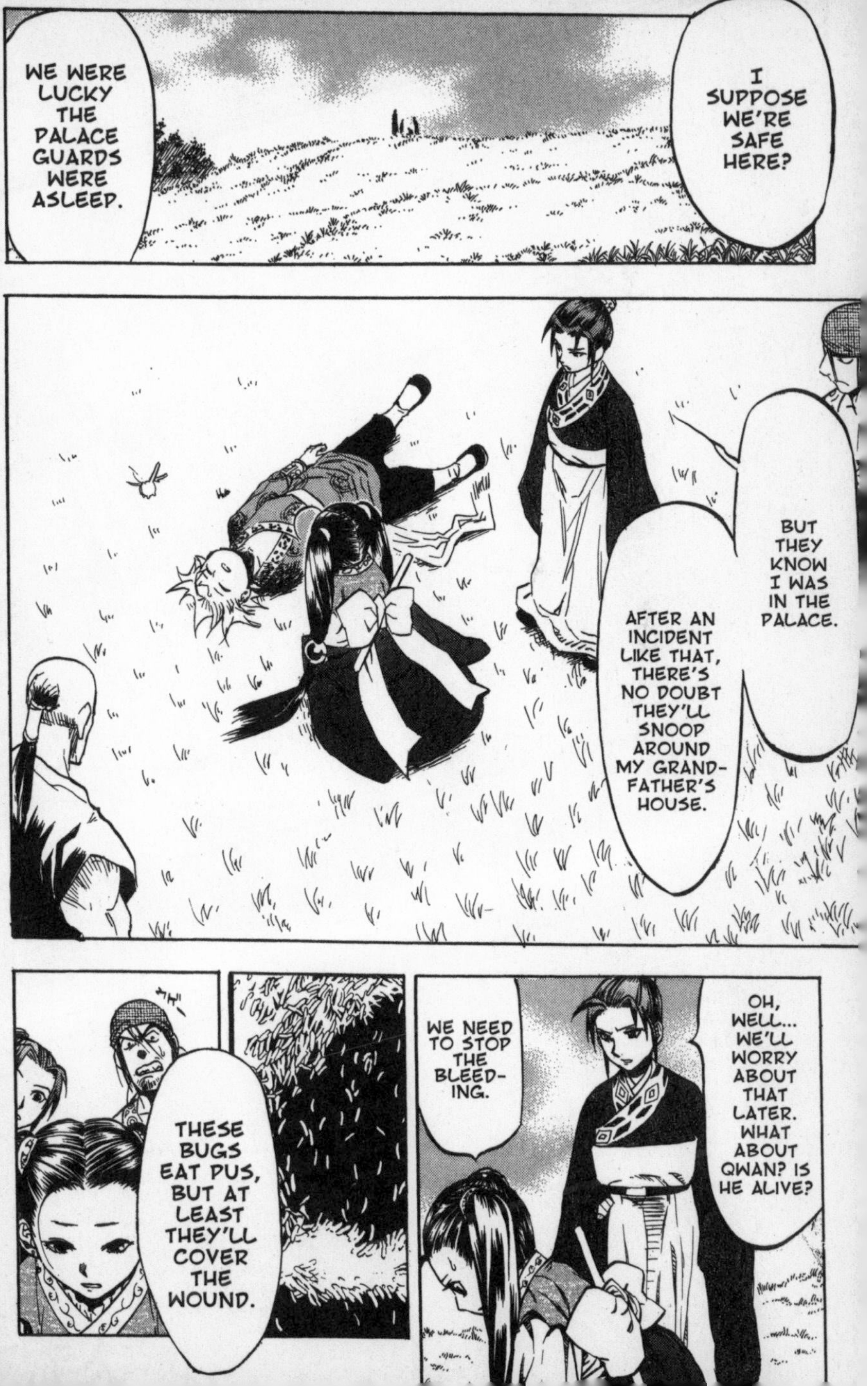
I SUPPOSE WE'RE SAFE HERE?
WE WERE LUCKY THE PALACE GUARDS WERE ASLEEP.
BUT THEY KNOW I WAS IN THE PALACE.
AFTER AN INCIDENT LIKE THAT, THERE'S NO DOUBT THEY'LL SNOOP AROUND MY GRAND-FATHER'S HOUSE.
OH, WELL... WE'LL WORRY ABOUT THAT LATER. WHAT ABOUT QWAN? IS HE ALIVE?
WE NEED TO STOP THE BLEED-ING.
THESE BUGS EAT PUS, BUT AT LEAST THEY'LL COVER THE WOUND.

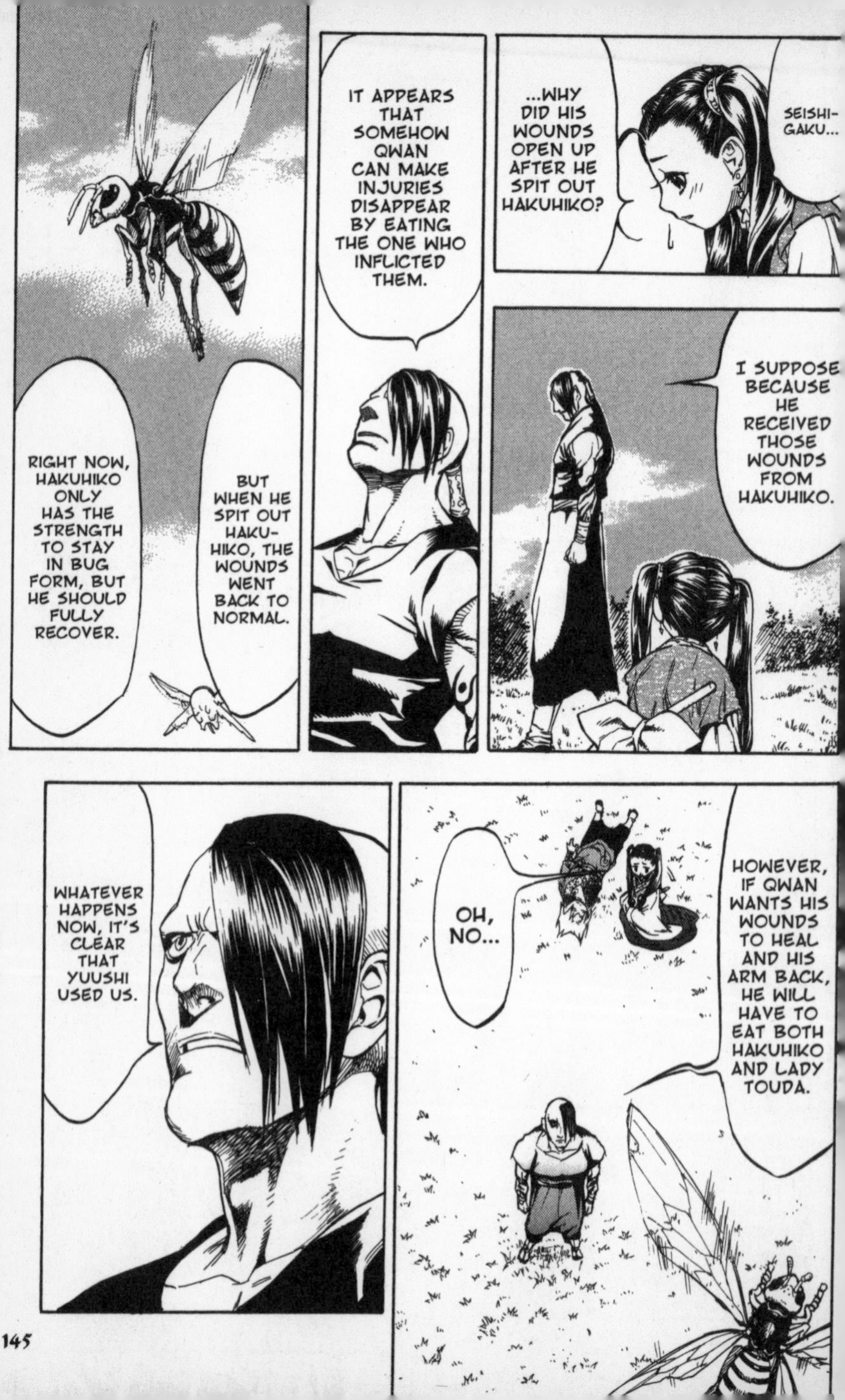
SEISHI-GAKU...
...WHY DID HIS WOUNDS OPEN UP AFTER HE SPIT OUT HAKUHIKO?
I SUPPOSE BECAUSE HE RECEIVED THOSE WOUNDS FROM HAKUHIKO.
IT APPEARS THAT SOMEHOW QWAN CAN MAKE INJURIES DISAPPEAR BY EATING THE ONE WHO INFLICTED THEM.
BUT WHEN HE SPIT OUT HAKU-HIKO, THE WOUNDS WENT BACK TO NORMAL.
RIGHT NOW, HAKUHIKO ONLY HAS THE STRENGTH TO STAY IN BUG FORM, BUT HE SHOULD FULLY RECOVER.
HOWEVER, IF QWAN WANTS HIS WOUNDS TO HEAL AND HIS ARM BACK, HE WILL HAVE TO EAT BOTH HAKUHIKO AND LADY TOUDA.
OH, NO...
WHATEVER HAPPENS NOW, IT'S CLEAR THAT YUUSHI USED US.

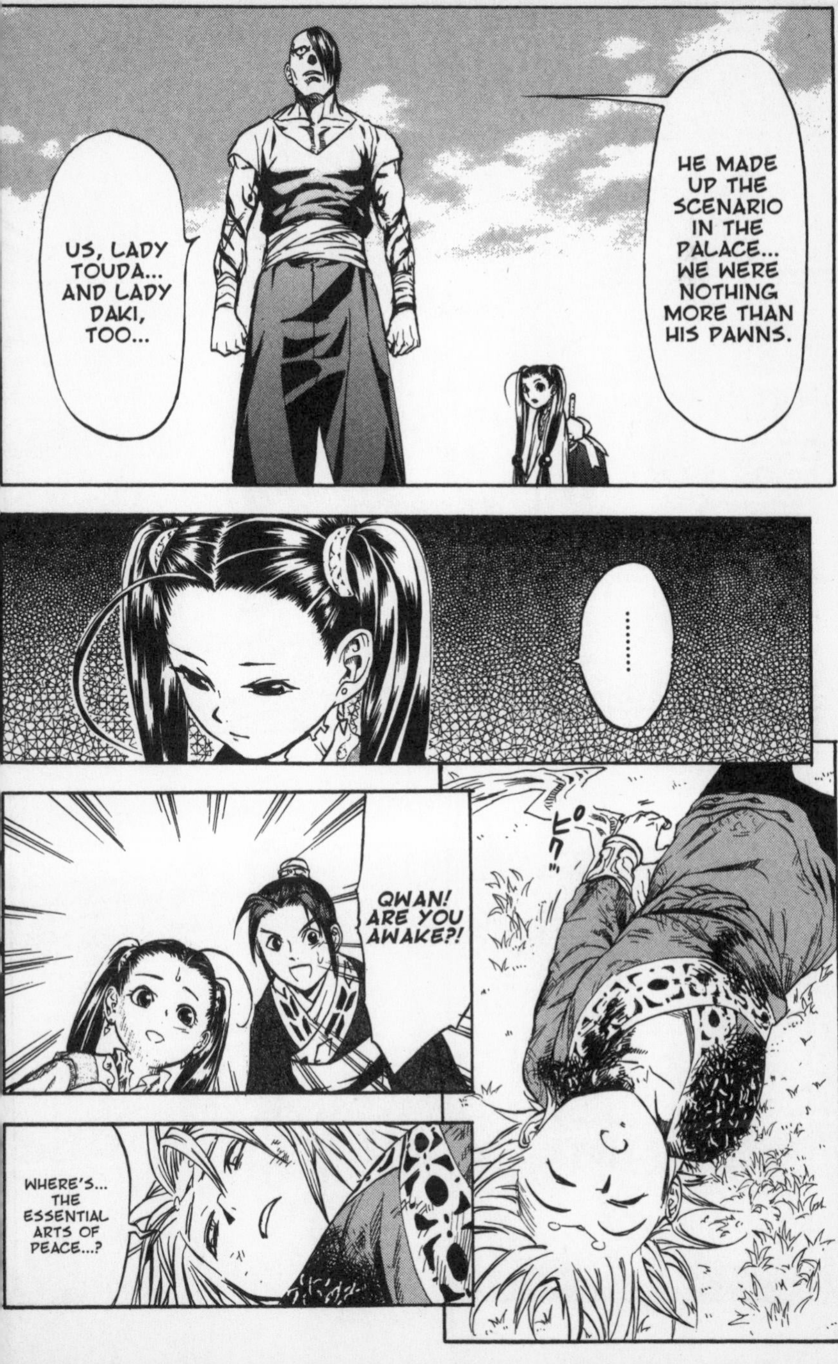
HE MADE UP THE SCENARIO IN THE PALACE... WE WERE NOTHING MORE THAN HIS PAWNS.
US, LADY TOUDA... AND LADY DAKI, TOO...
……
ピク
QWAN! ARE YOU AWAKE?!
WHERE'S... THE ESSENTIAL ARTS OF PEACE...?

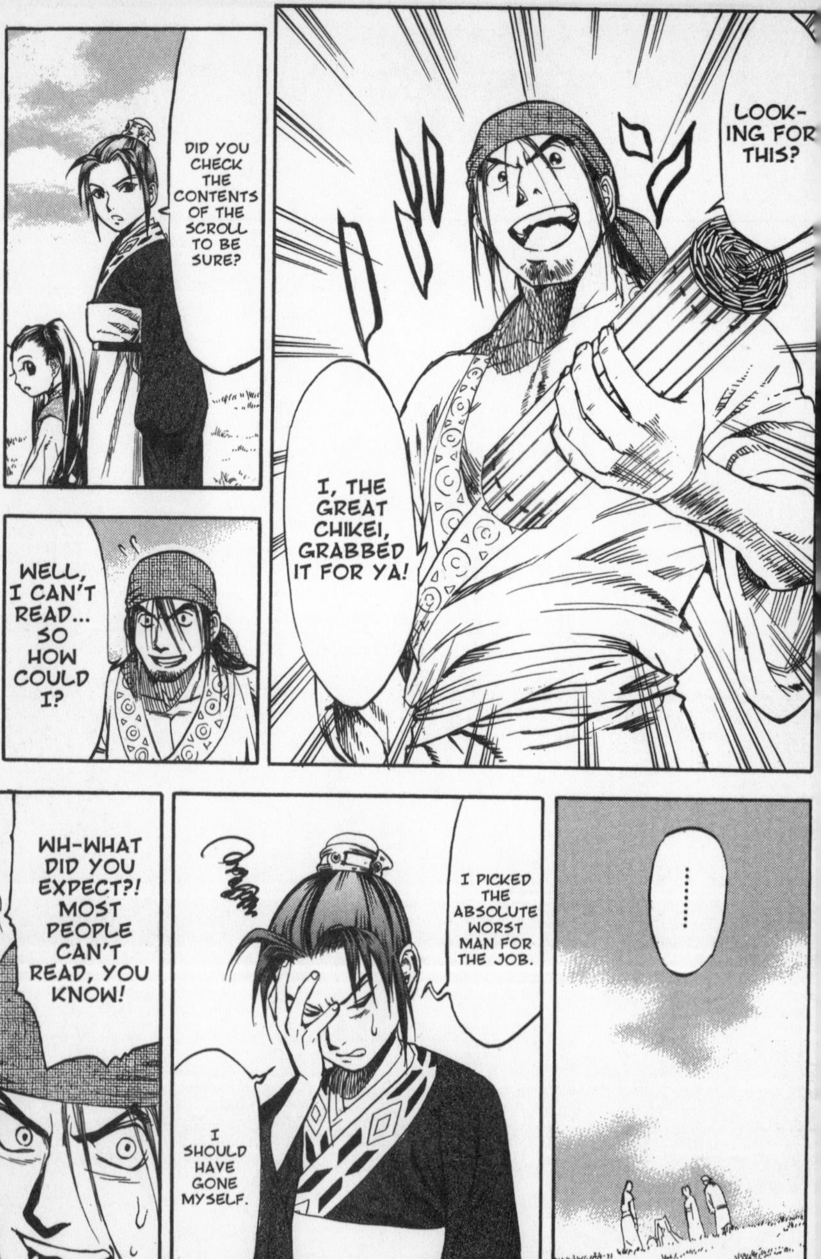
LOOKING FOR THIS?
I, THE GREAT CHIKEI, GRABBED IT FOR YA!
DID YOU CHECK THE CONTENTS OF THE SCROLL TO BE SURE?
WELL, I CAN'T READ... SO HOW COULD I?
......
I PICKED THE ABSOLUTE WORST MAN FOR THE JOB.
I SHOULD HAVE GONE MYSELF.
WH-WHAT DID YOU EXPECT?! MOST PEOPLE CAN'T READ, YOU KNOW!

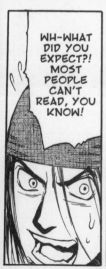

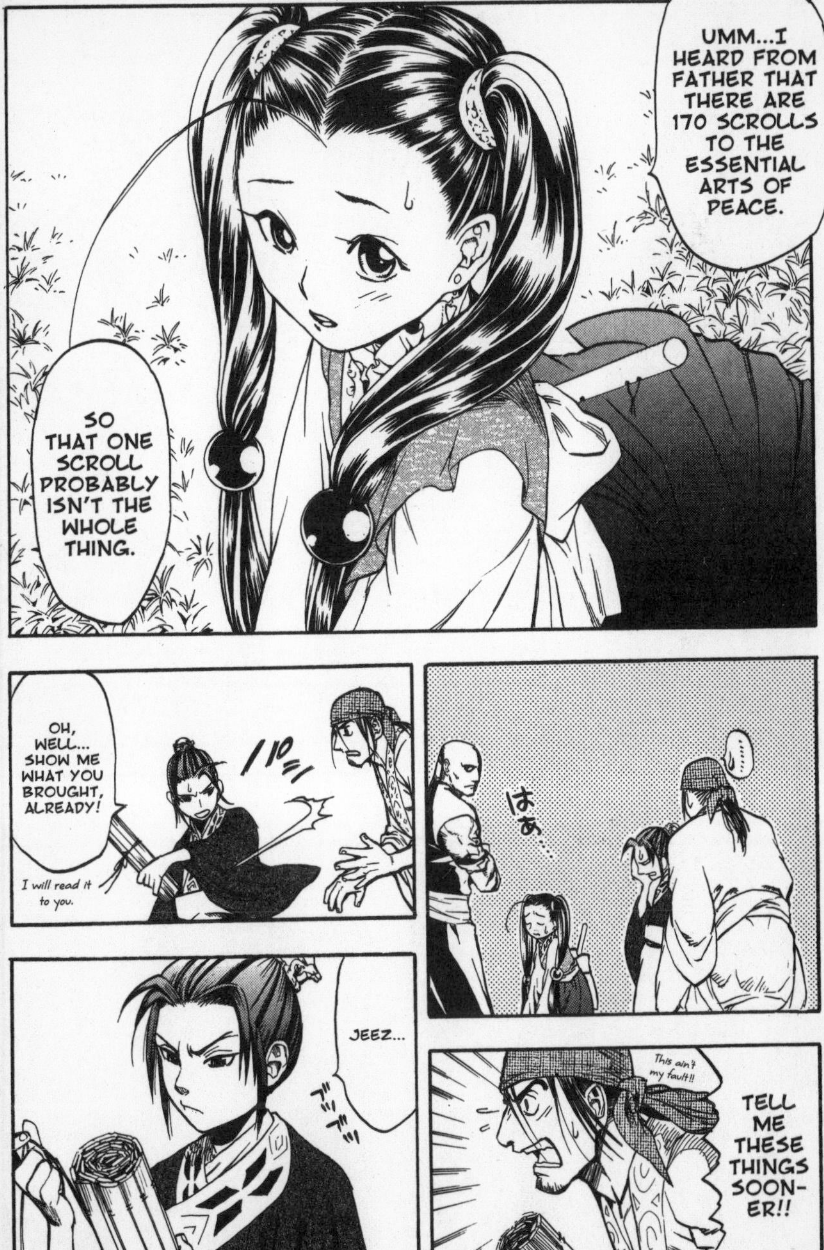
UMM...I HEARD FROM FATHER THAT THERE ARE 170 SCROLLS TO THE ESSENTIAL ARTS OF PEACE.
SO THAT ONE SCROLL PROBABLY ISN'T THE WHOLE THING.
......
はぁ...
OH, WELL... SHOW ME WHAT YOU BROUGHT, ALREADY!
I will read it to you.
This ain't my fault!!
TELL ME THESE THINGS SOONER!!
JEEZ...

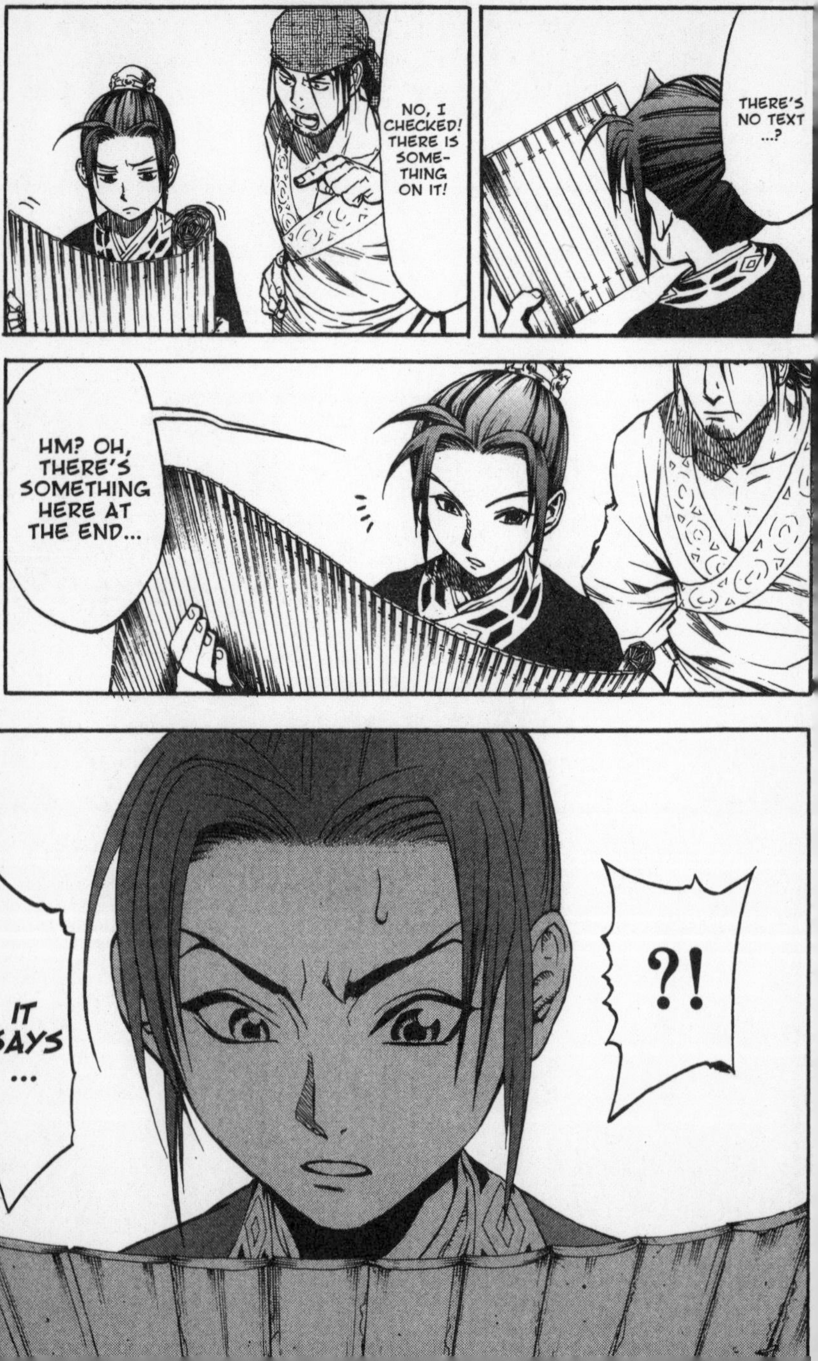
THERE'S NO TEXT ...?
NO, I CHECKED! THERE IS SOME-THING ON IT!
HM? OH, THERE'S SOMETHING HERE AT THE END...
?!
IT SAYS ...

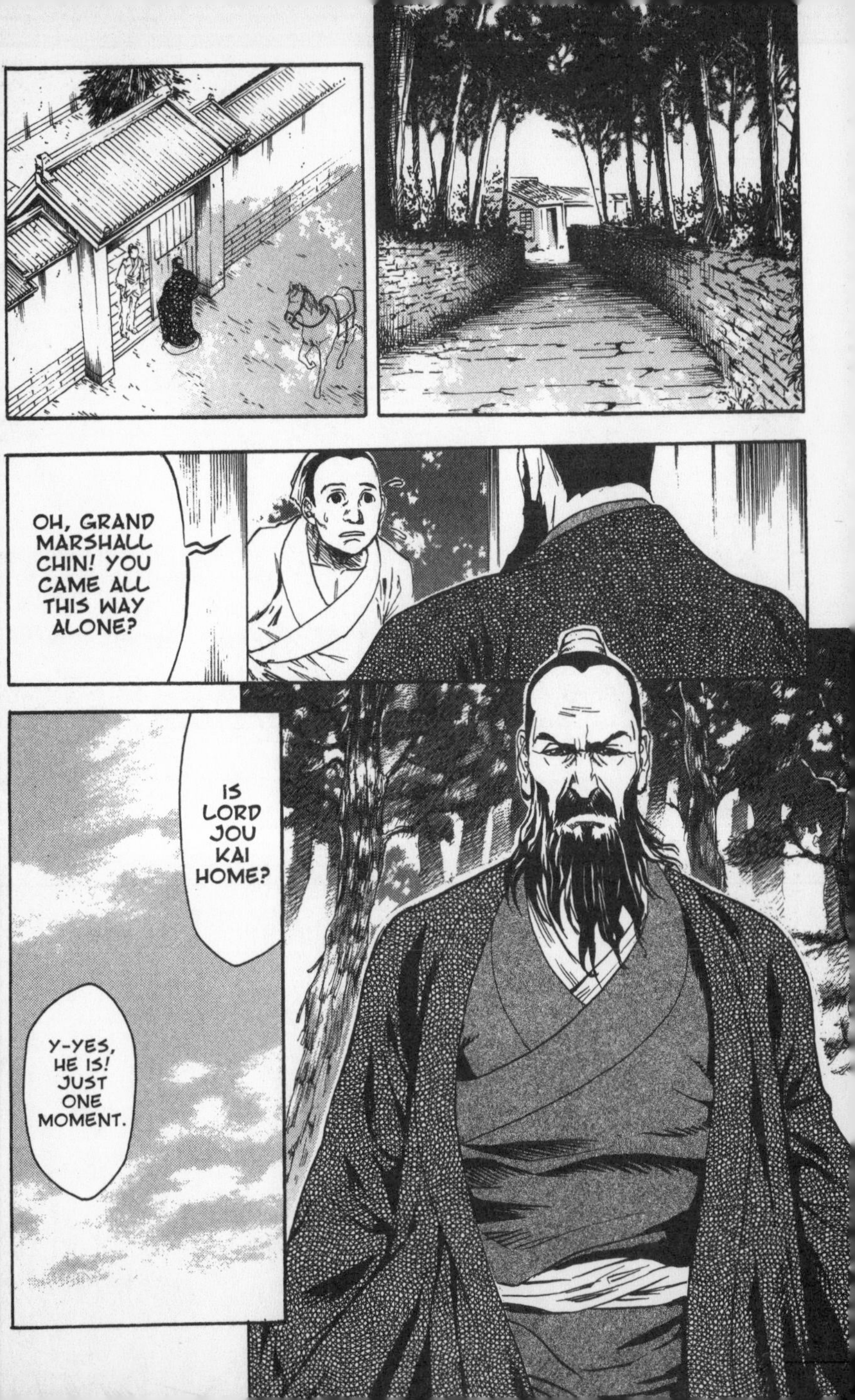
OH, GRAND MARSHALL CHIN! YOU CAME ALL THIS WAY ALONE?
IS LORD JOU KAI HOME?
Y-YES, HE IS! JUST ONE MOMENT.

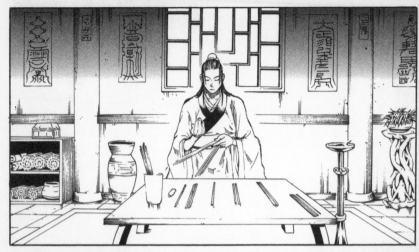

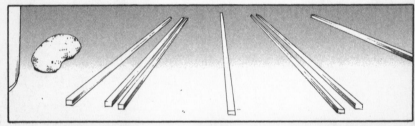

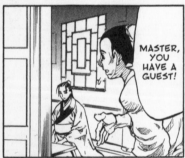

MASTER, YOU HAVE A GUEST!

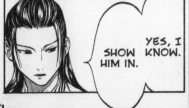

YES, I KNOW. SHOW HIM IN.

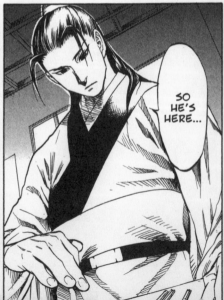

SO HE'S HERE...

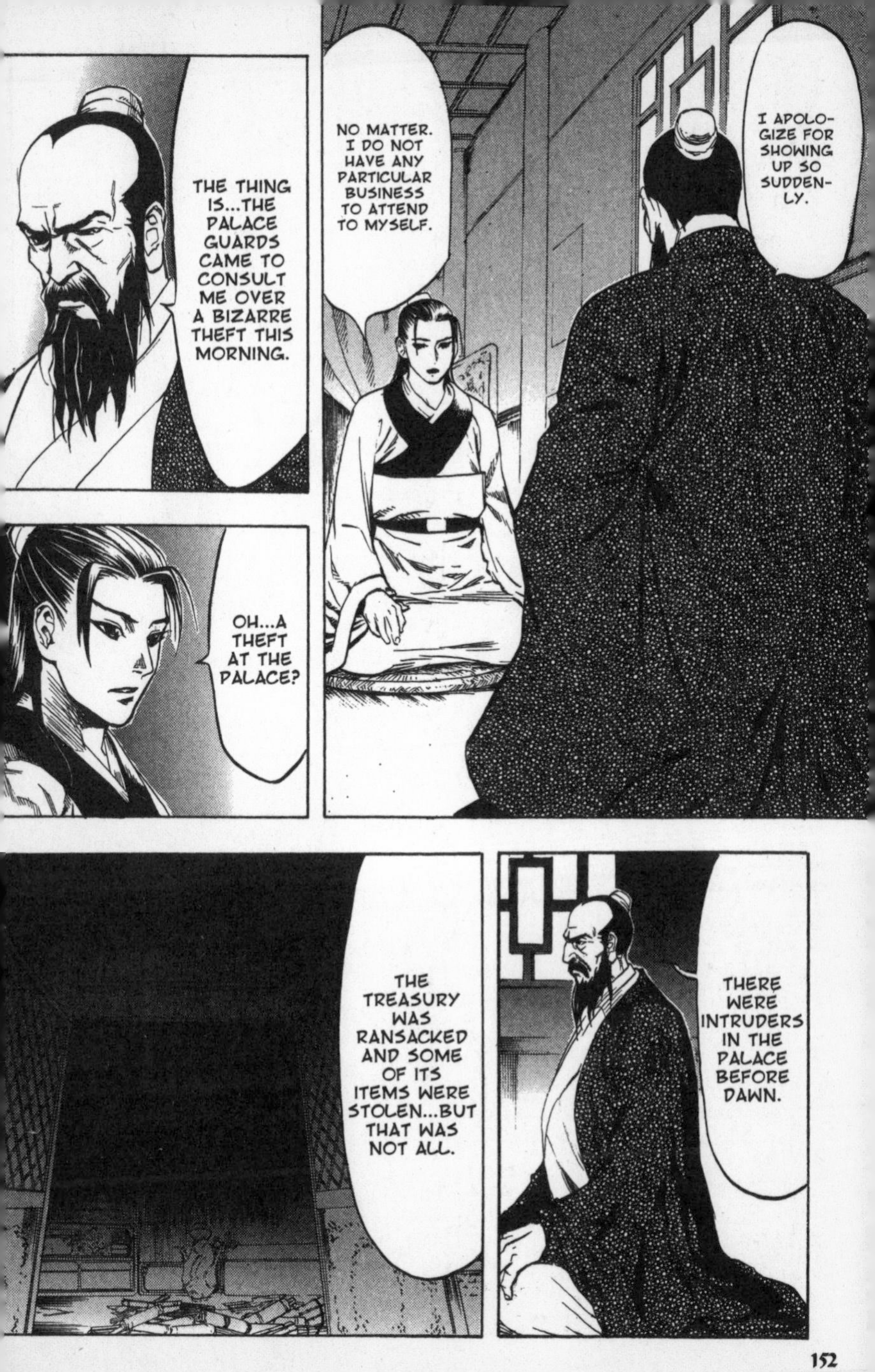
I APOLOGIZE FOR SHOWING UP SO SUDDENLY.
NO MATTER. I DO NOT HAVE ANY PARTICULAR BUSINESS TO ATTEND TO MYSELF.
THE THING IS...THE PALACE GUARDS CAME TO CONSULT ME OVER A BIZARRE THEFT THIS MORNING.
OH...A THEFT AT THE PALACE?
THERE WERE INTRUDERS IN THE PALACE BEFORE DAWN.
THE TREASURY WAS RANSACKED AND SOME OF ITS ITEMS WERE STOLEN...BUT THAT WAS NOT ALL.

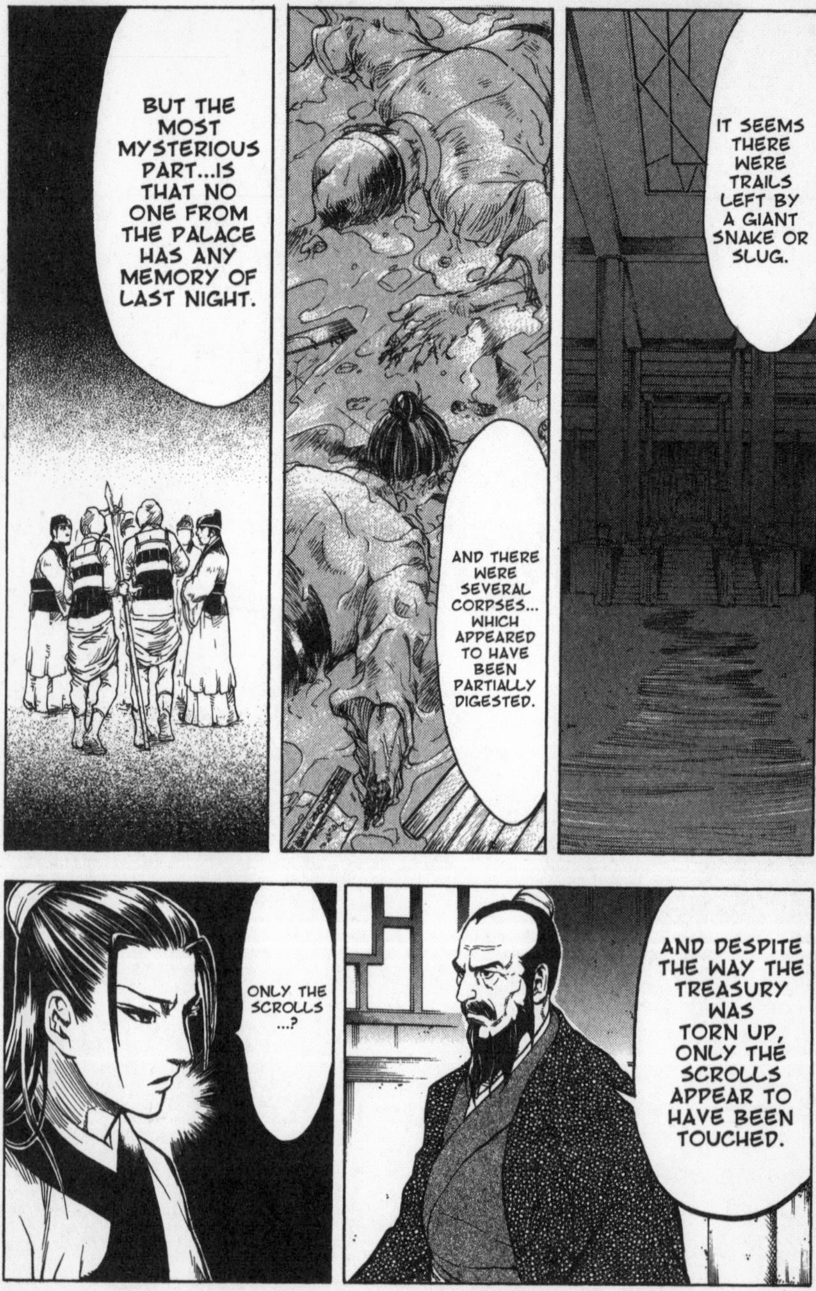
IT SEEMS THERE WERE TRAILS LEFT BY A GIANT SNAKE OR SLUG.
AND THERE WERE SEVERAL CORPSES... WHICH APPEARED TO HAVE BEEN PARTIALLY DIGESTED.
BUT THE MOST MYSTERIOUS PART...IS THAT NO ONE FROM THE PALACE HAS ANY MEMORY OF LAST NIGHT.
AND DESPITE THE WAY THE TREASURY WAS TORN UP, ONLY THE SCROLLS APPEAR TO HAVE BEEN TOUCHED.
ONLY THE SCROLLS ...?

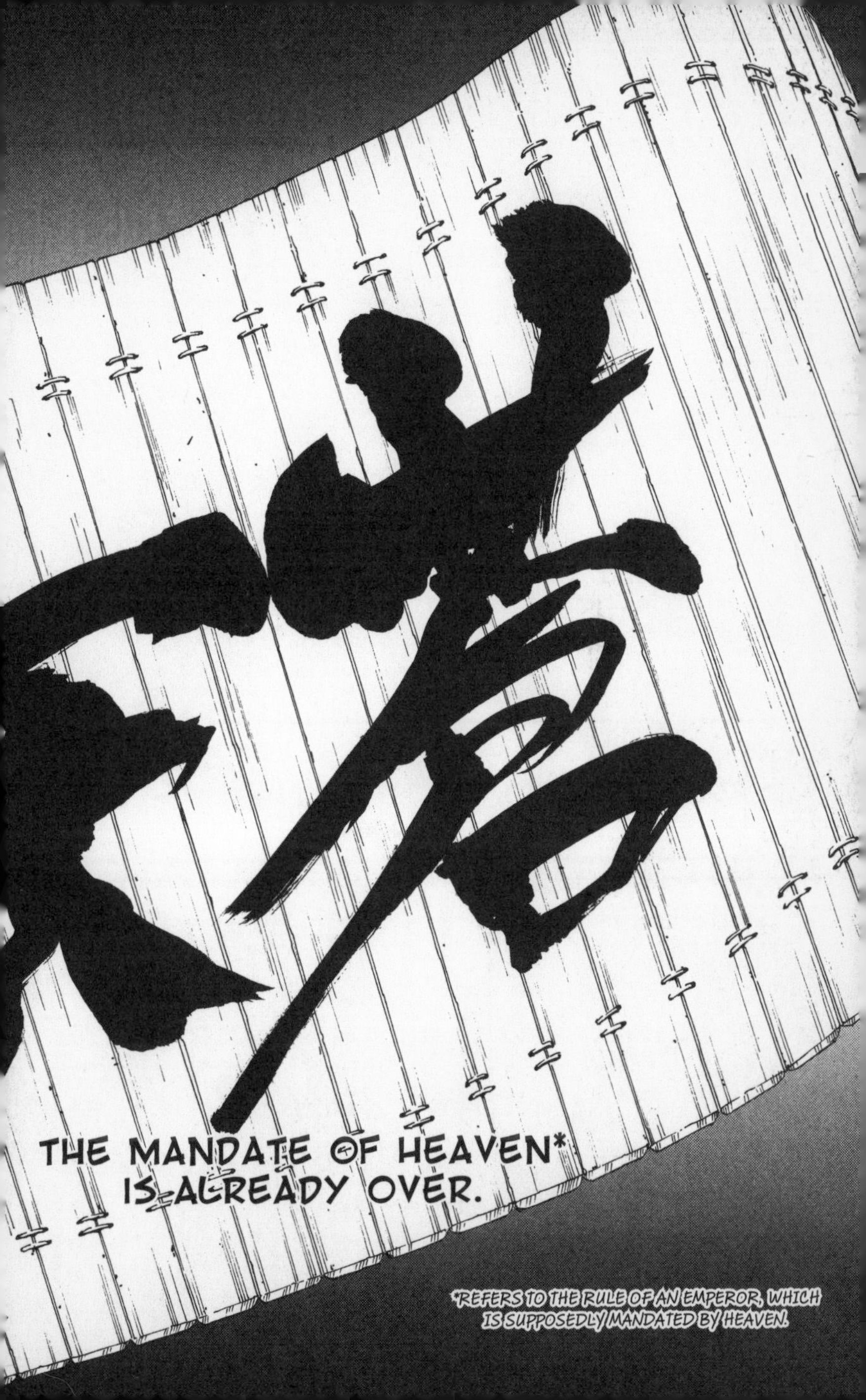
THE MANDATE OF HEAVEN* IS ALREADY OVER.
*REFERS TO THE RULE OF AN EMPEROR, WHICH IS SUPPOSEDLY MANDATED BY HEAVEN.

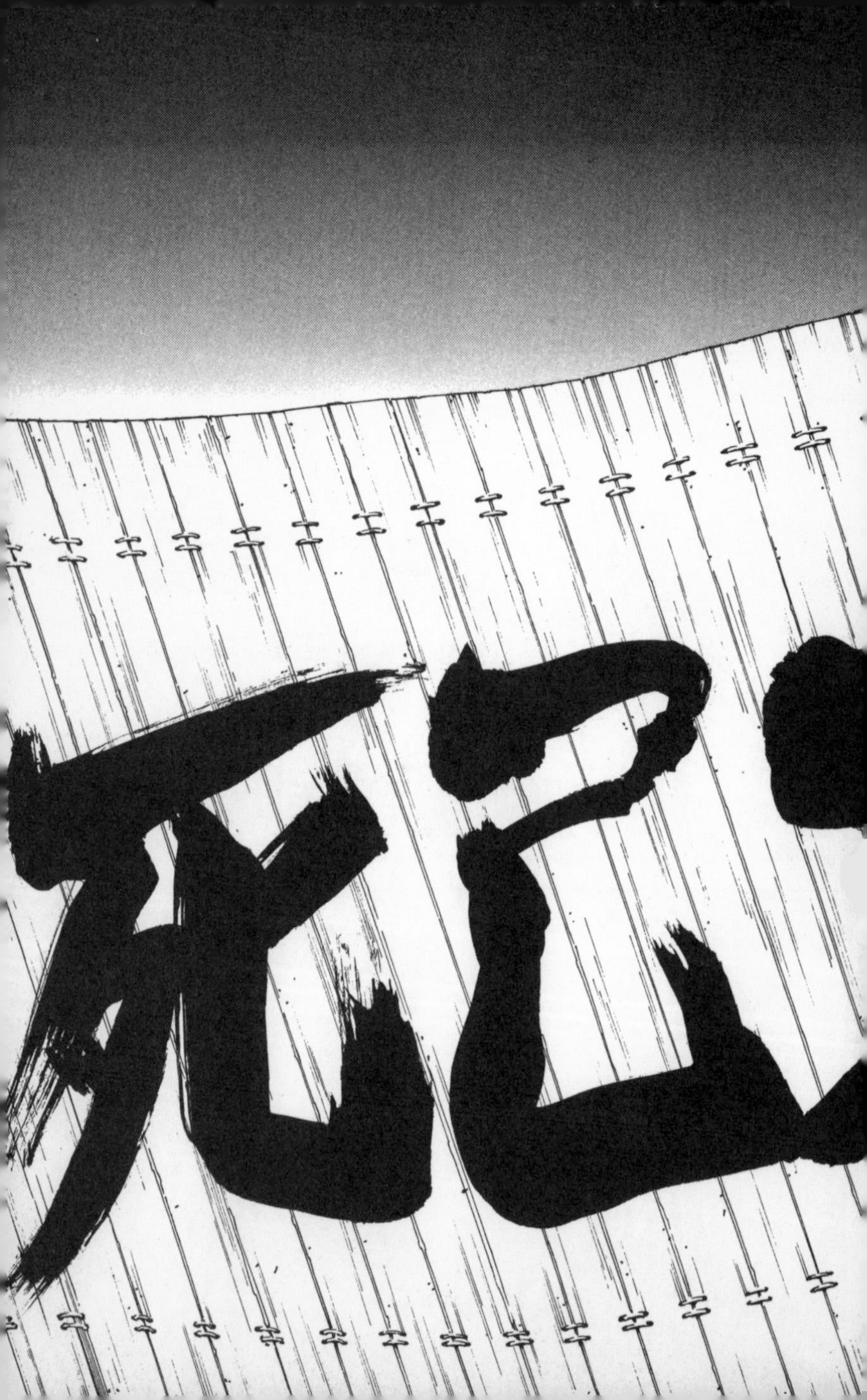
死

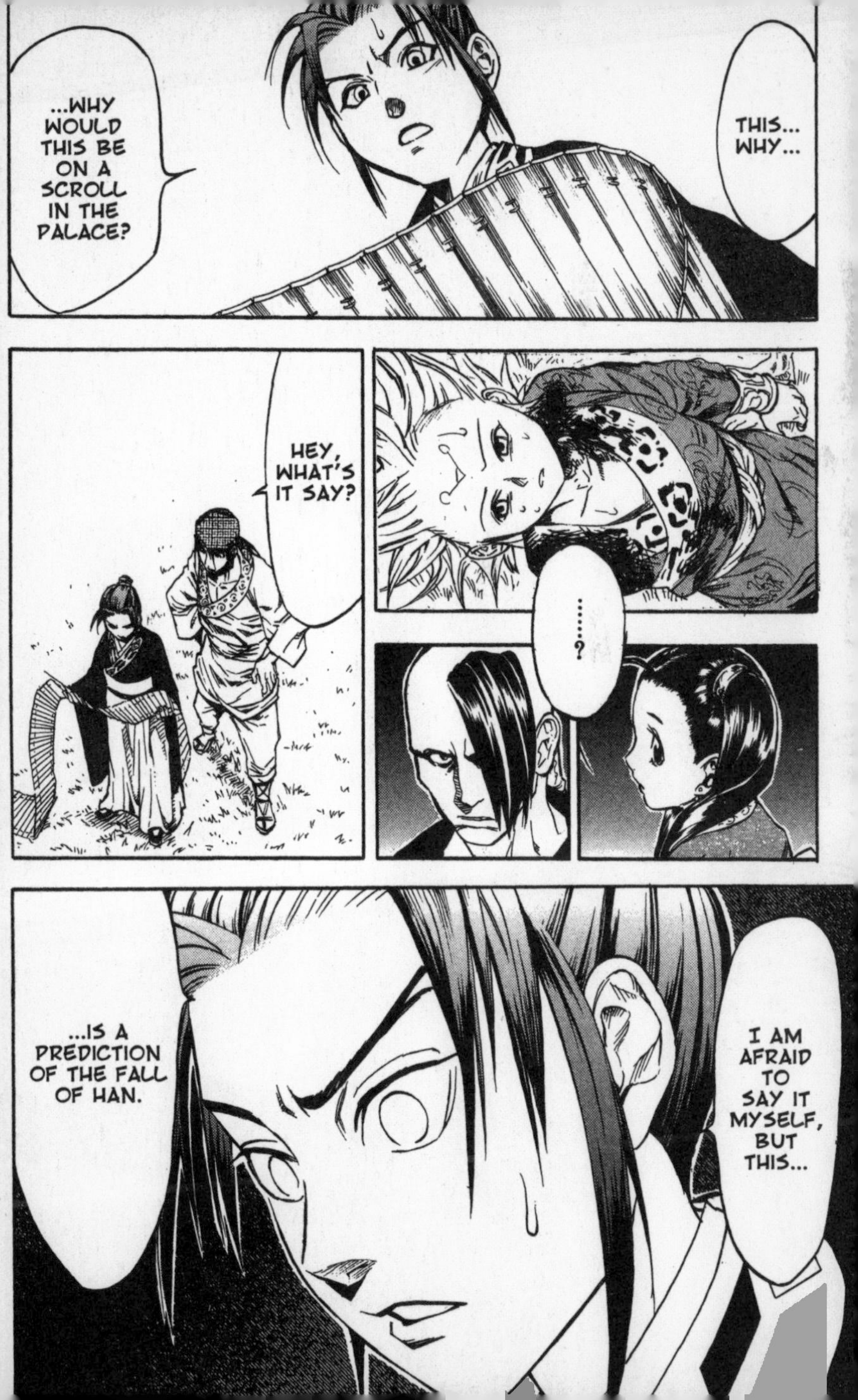
THIS... WHY...
...WHY WOULD THIS BE ON A SCROLL IN THE PALACE?
......?
HEY, WHAT'S IT SAY?
I AM AFRAID TO SAY IT MYSELF, BUT THIS...
...IS A PREDICTION OF THE FALL OF HAN.

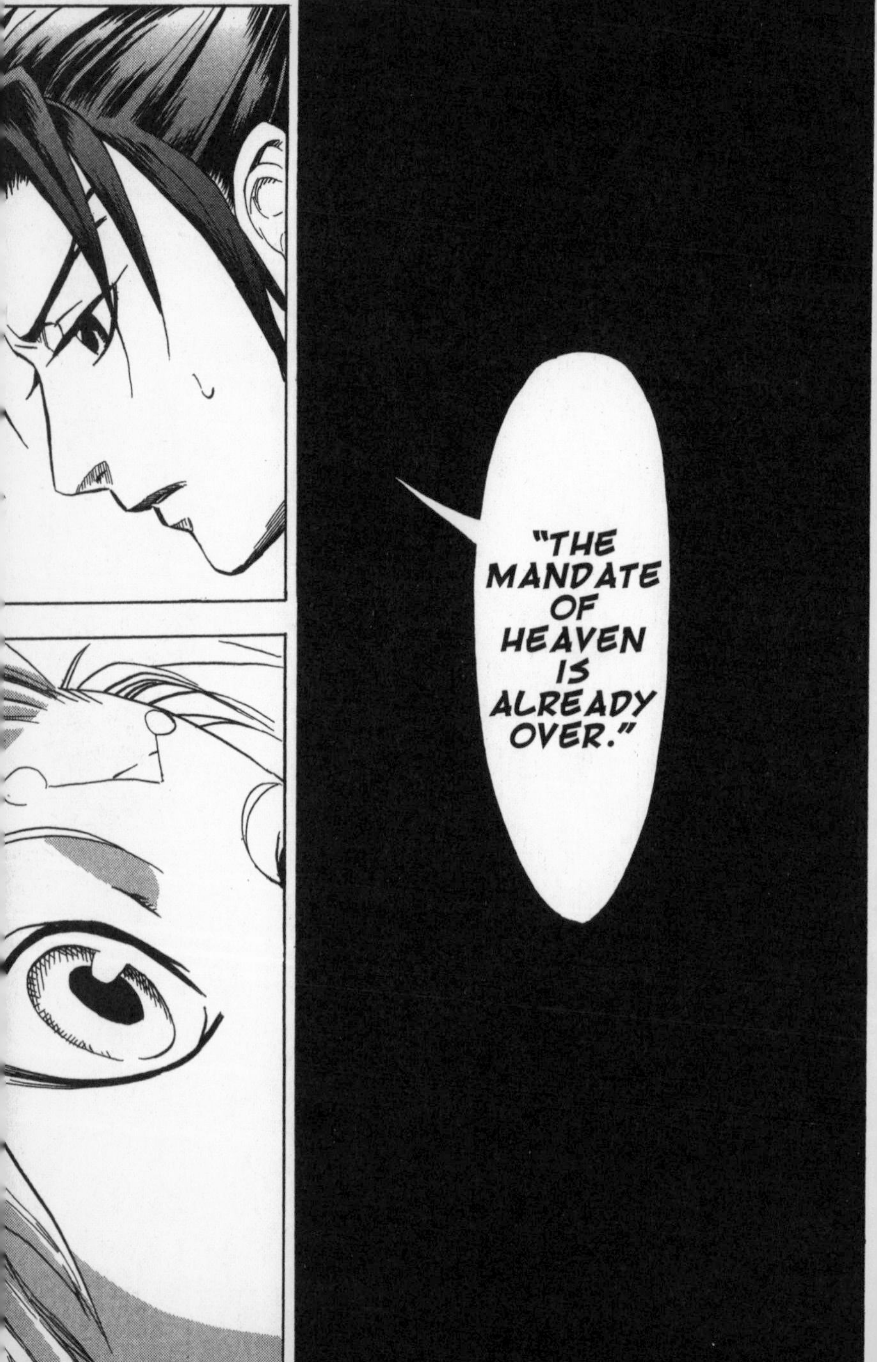
"THE MANDATE OF HEAVEN IS ALREADY OVER."

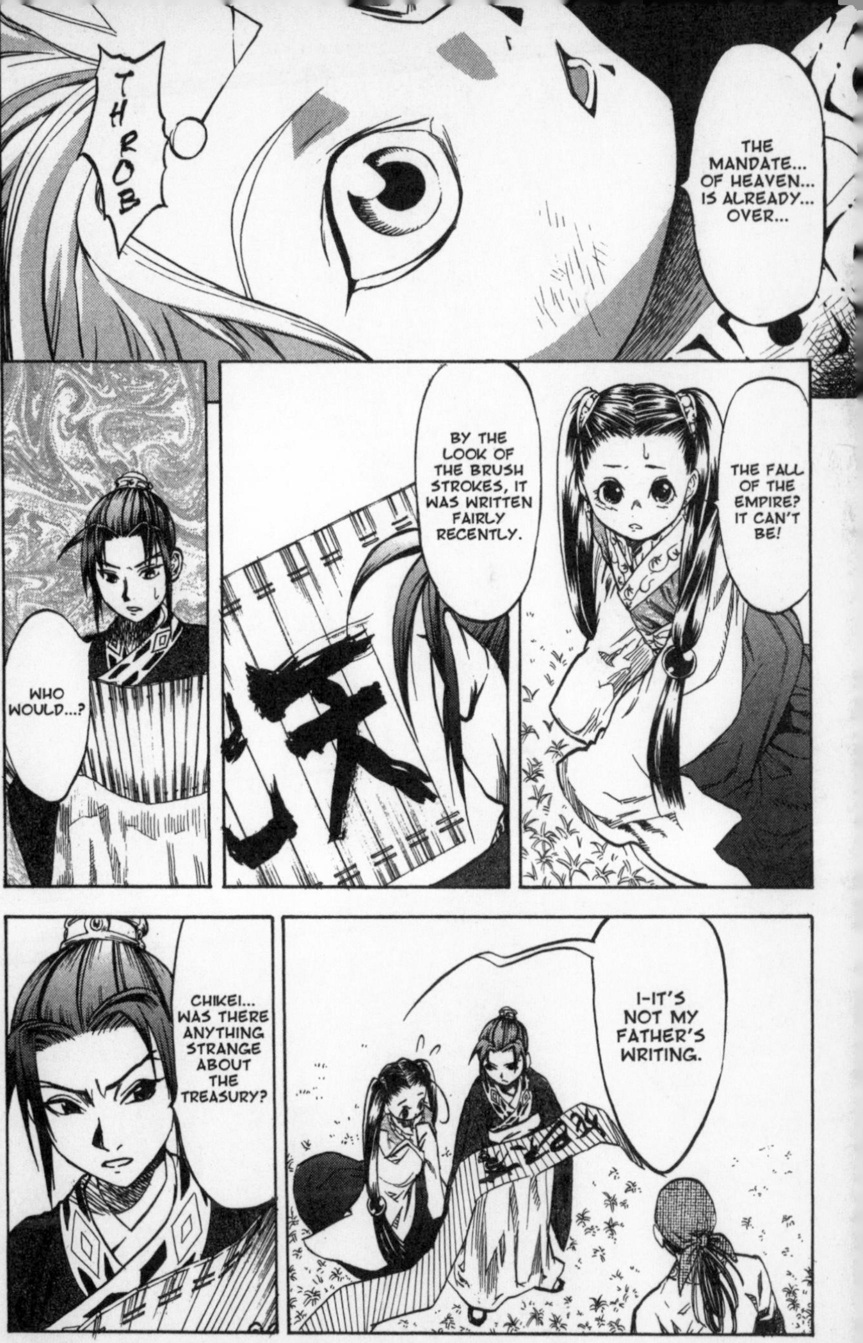
THE MANDATE... OF HEAVEN... IS ALREADY... OVER...
THROB
THE FALL OF THE EMPIRE? IT CAN'T BE!
BY THE LOOK OF THE BRUSH STROKES, IT WAS WRITTEN FAIRLY RECENTLY.
WHO WOULD...?
I-IT'S NOT MY FATHER'S WRITING.
CHIKEI... WAS THERE ANYTHING STRANGE ABOUT THE TREASURY?

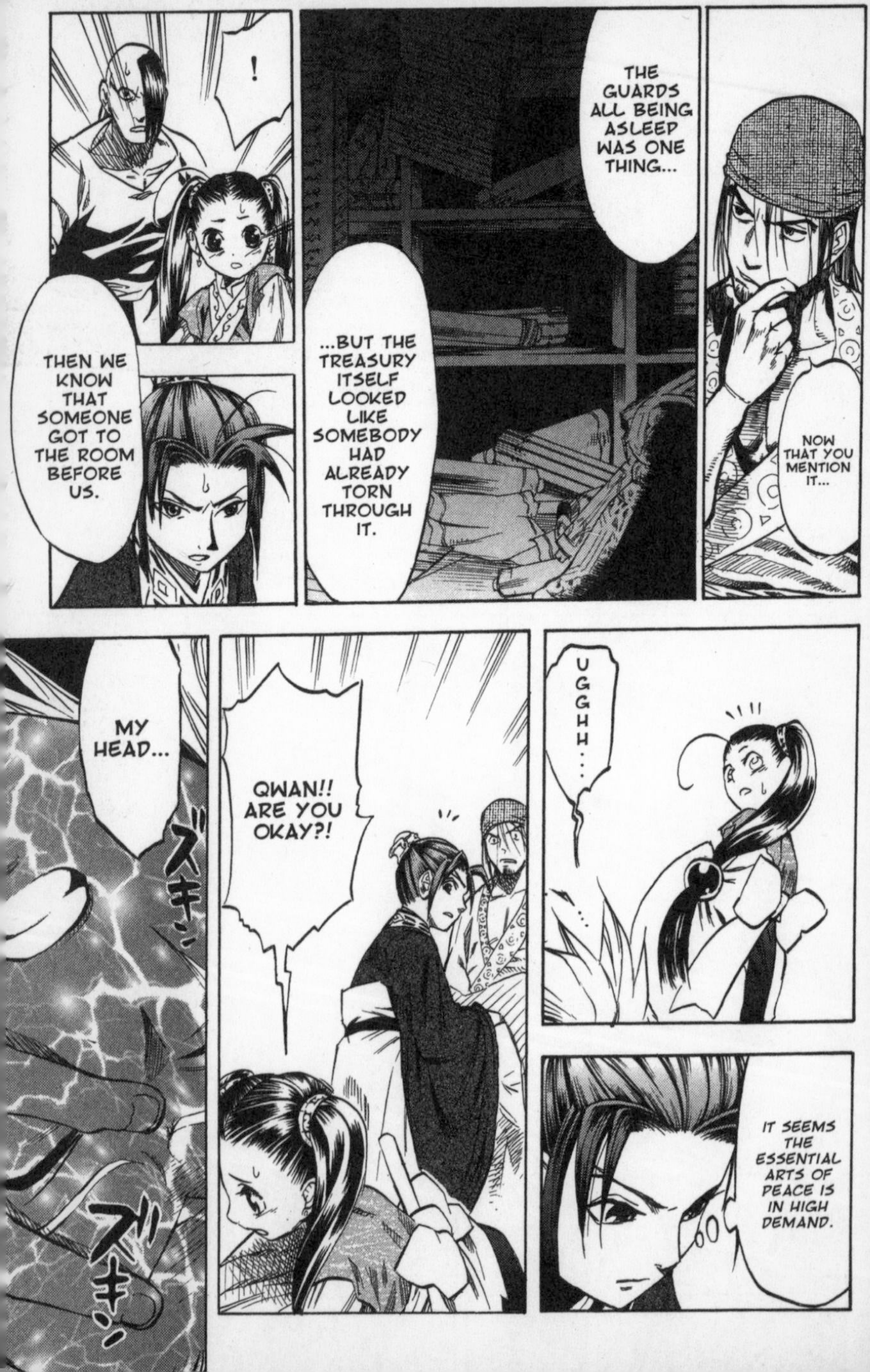
THE GUARDS ALL BEING ASLEEP WAS ONE THING...
...BUT THE TREASURY ITSELF LOOKED LIKE SOMEBODY HAD ALREADY TORN THROUGH IT.
NOW THAT YOU MENTION IT...
!
THEN WE KNOW THAT SOMEONE GOT TO THE ROOM BEFORE US.
UGGHH...
IT SEEMS THE ESSENTIAL ARTS OF PEACE IS IN HIGH DEMAND.
QWAN!! ARE YOU OKAY?!
MY HEAD...
ズキン
ズキン

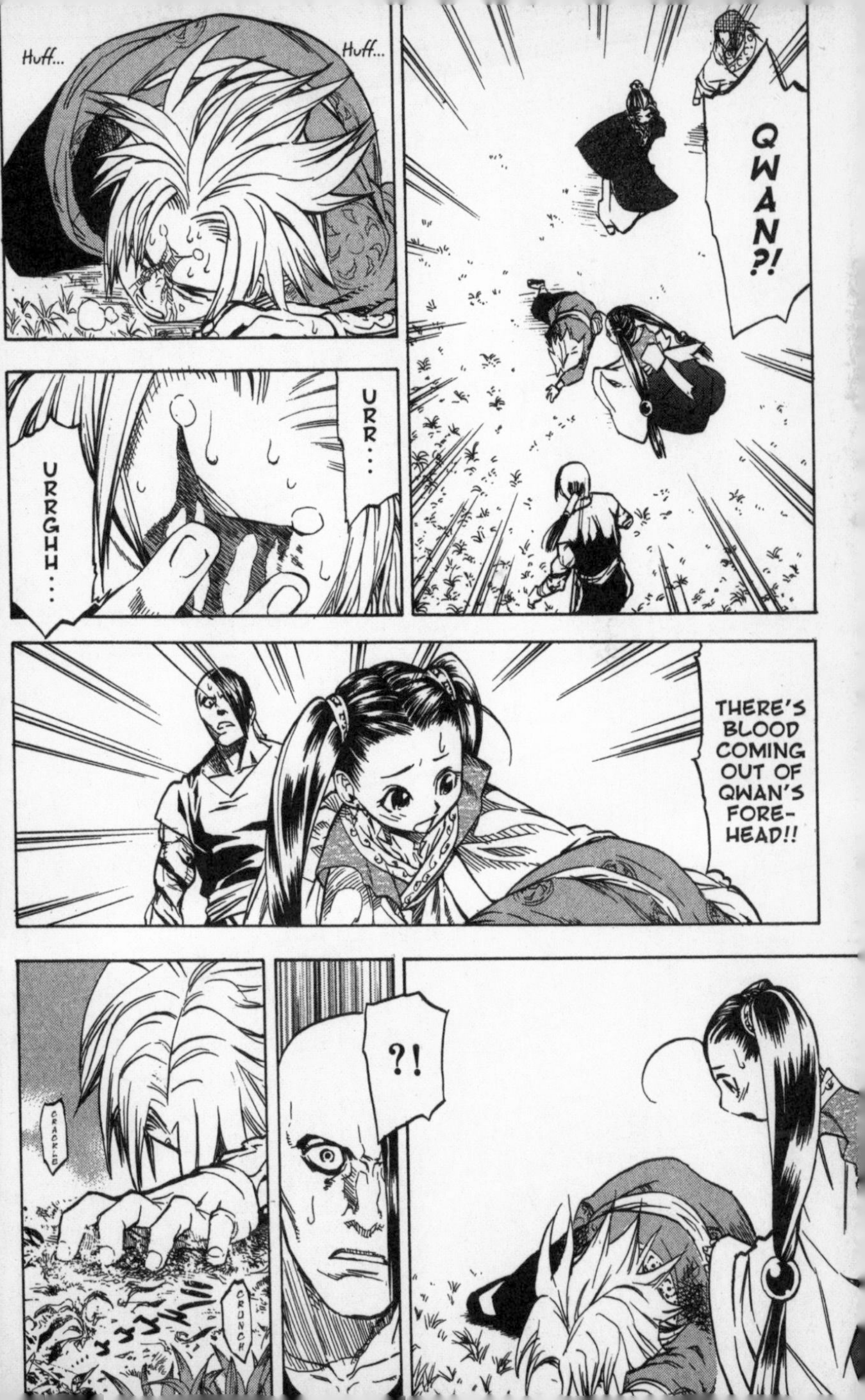
QWAN?!
Huff...
Huff...
URR...
URRGHH...
THERE'S BLOOD COMING OUT OF QWAN'S FORE-HEAD!!
?!
CRACKLE
CRUNCH

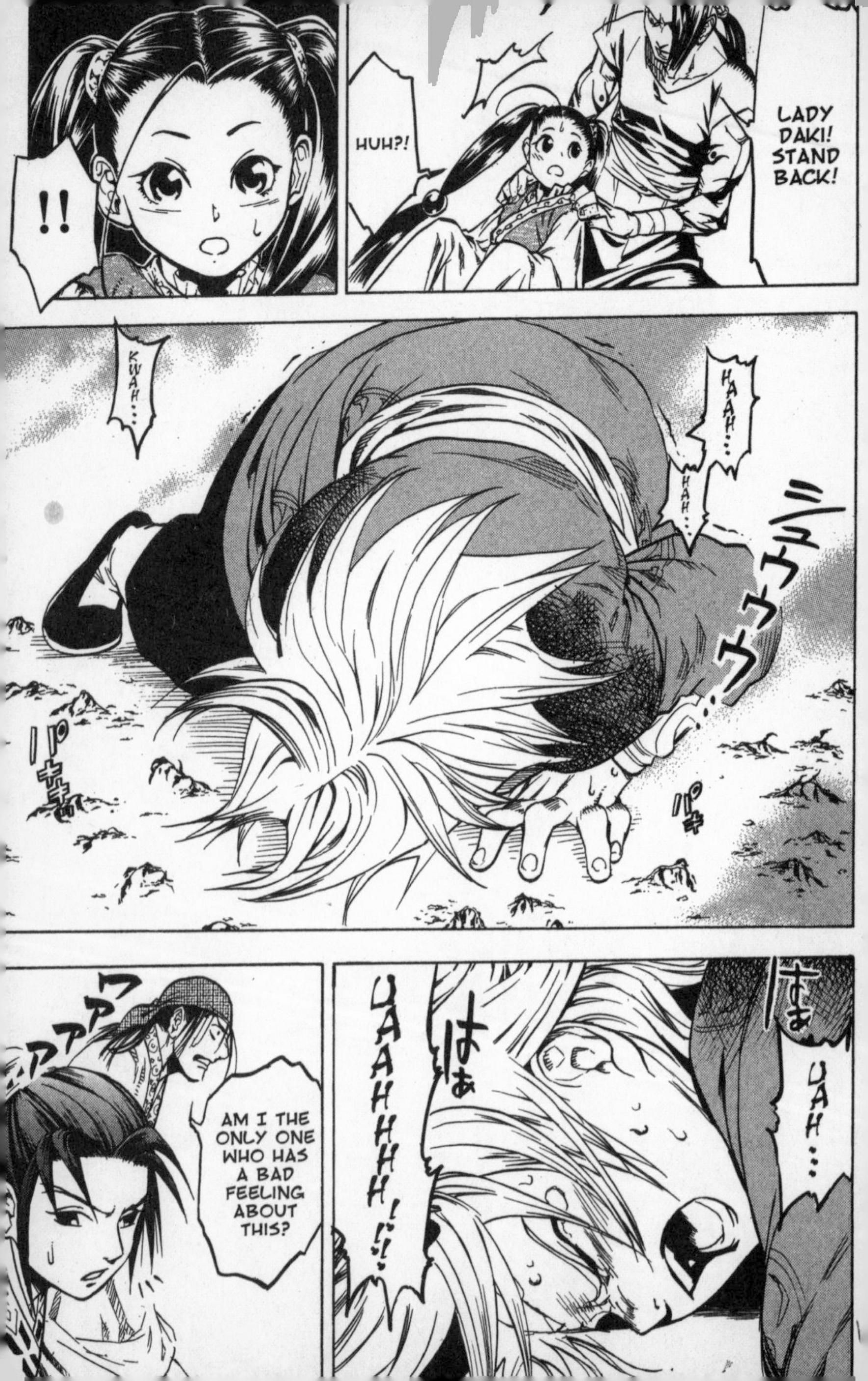
LADY DAKI! STAND BACK!
HUH?!
!!
HAAH...
HAH...
シュウウウ…
パキ
KWAH...
はぁ
UAH...
UAAHHHHH!!!!
はぁ
AM I THE ONLY ONE WHO HAS A BAD FEELING ABOUT THIS?

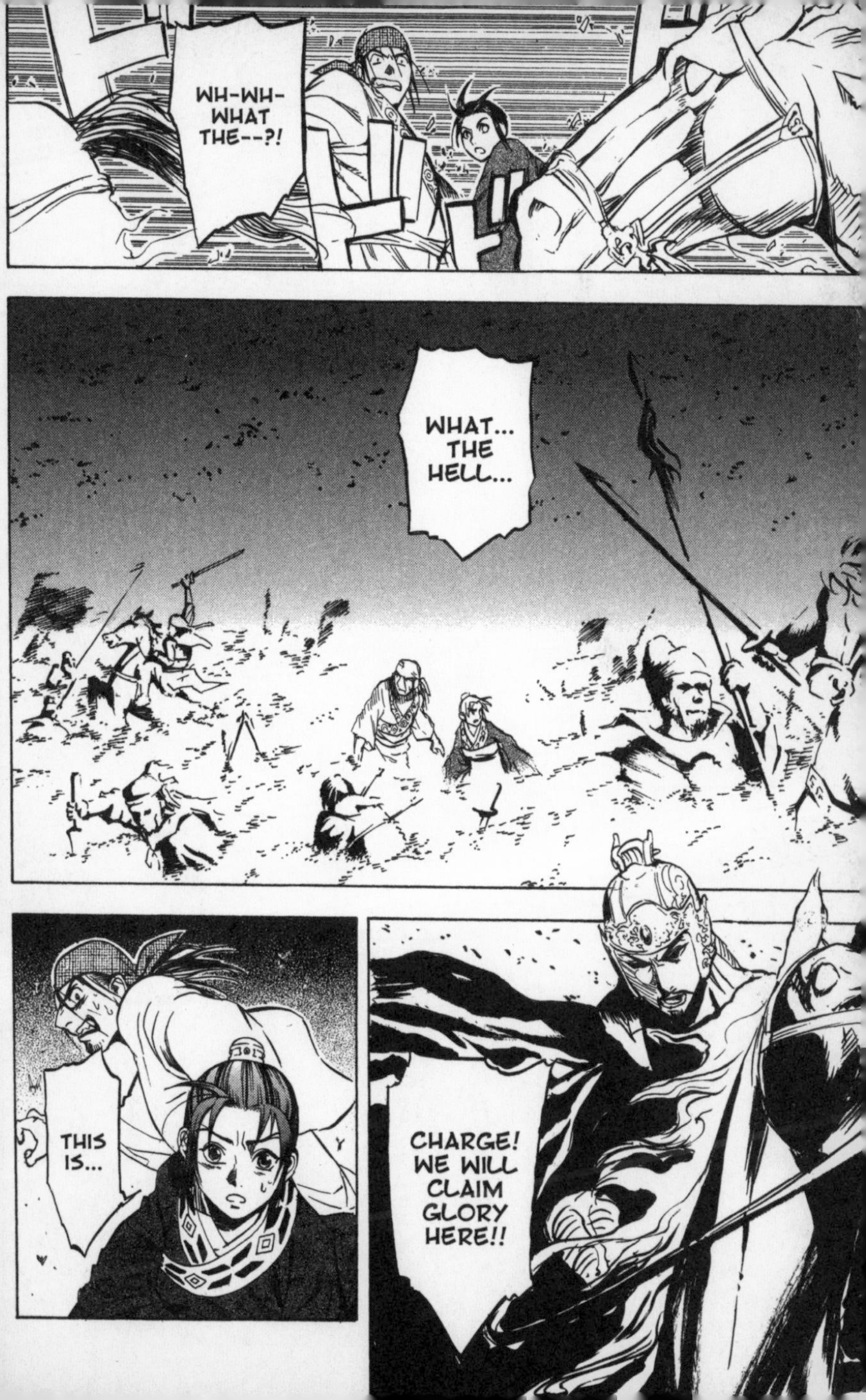
WH-WH-WHAT THE--?!
WHAT... THE HELL...
CHARGE! WE WILL CLAIM GLORY HERE!!
THIS IS...

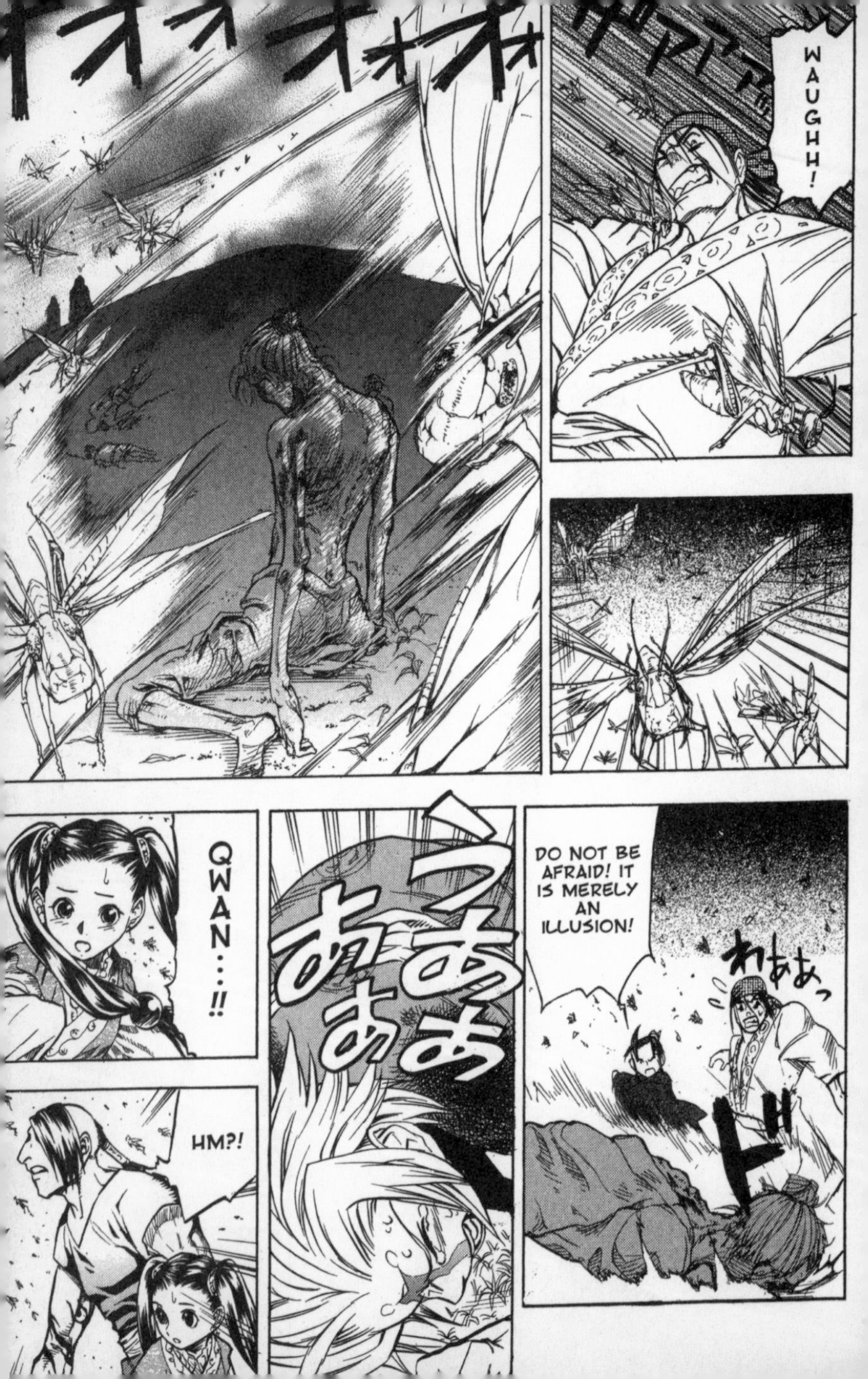
ザァァァ
WAUGHH!
オォォ オォォォ
DO NOT BE AFRAID! IT IS MERELY AN ILLUSION!
わあぁっ
ド
うあぁぁ
QWAN...!!
HM?!

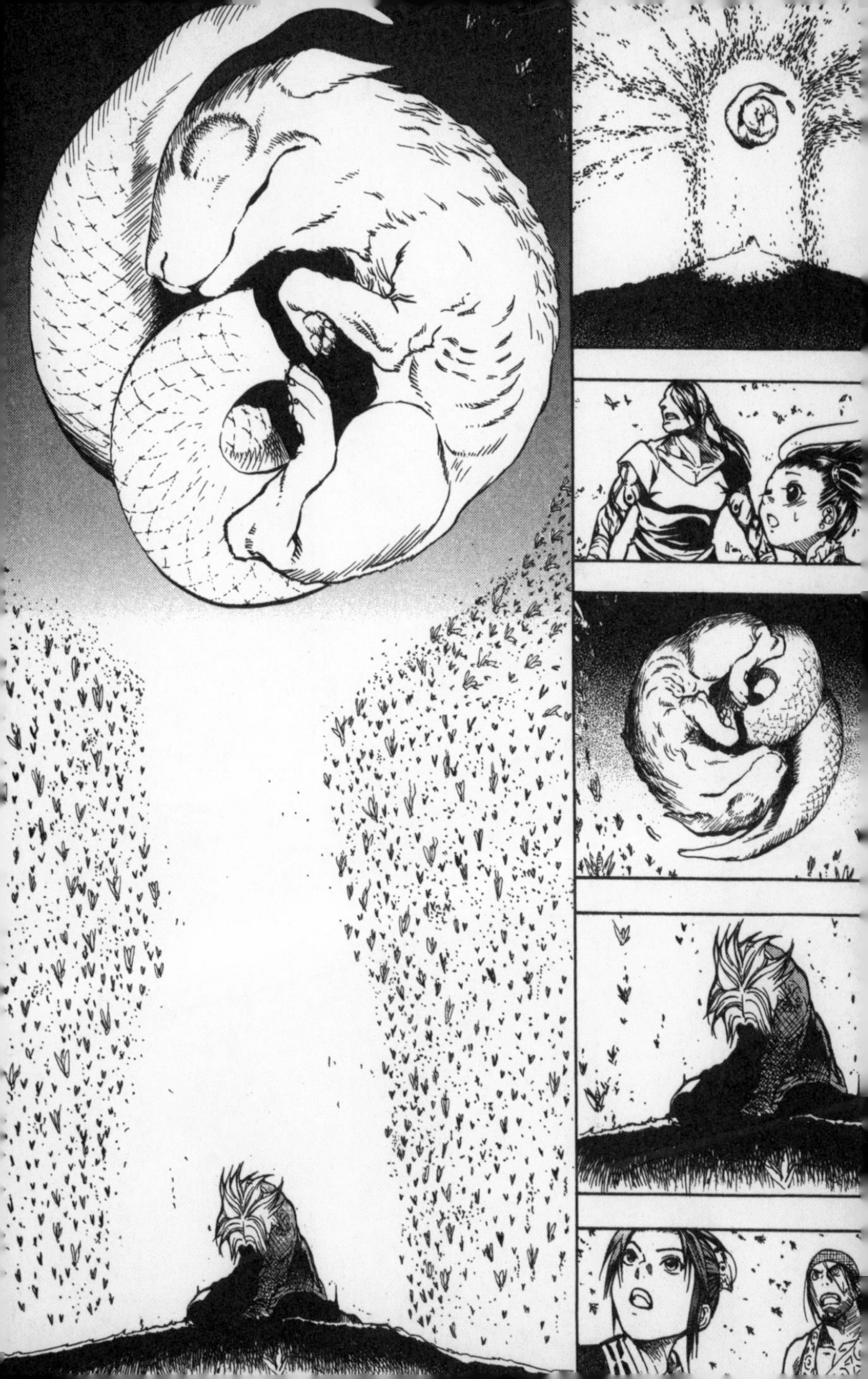

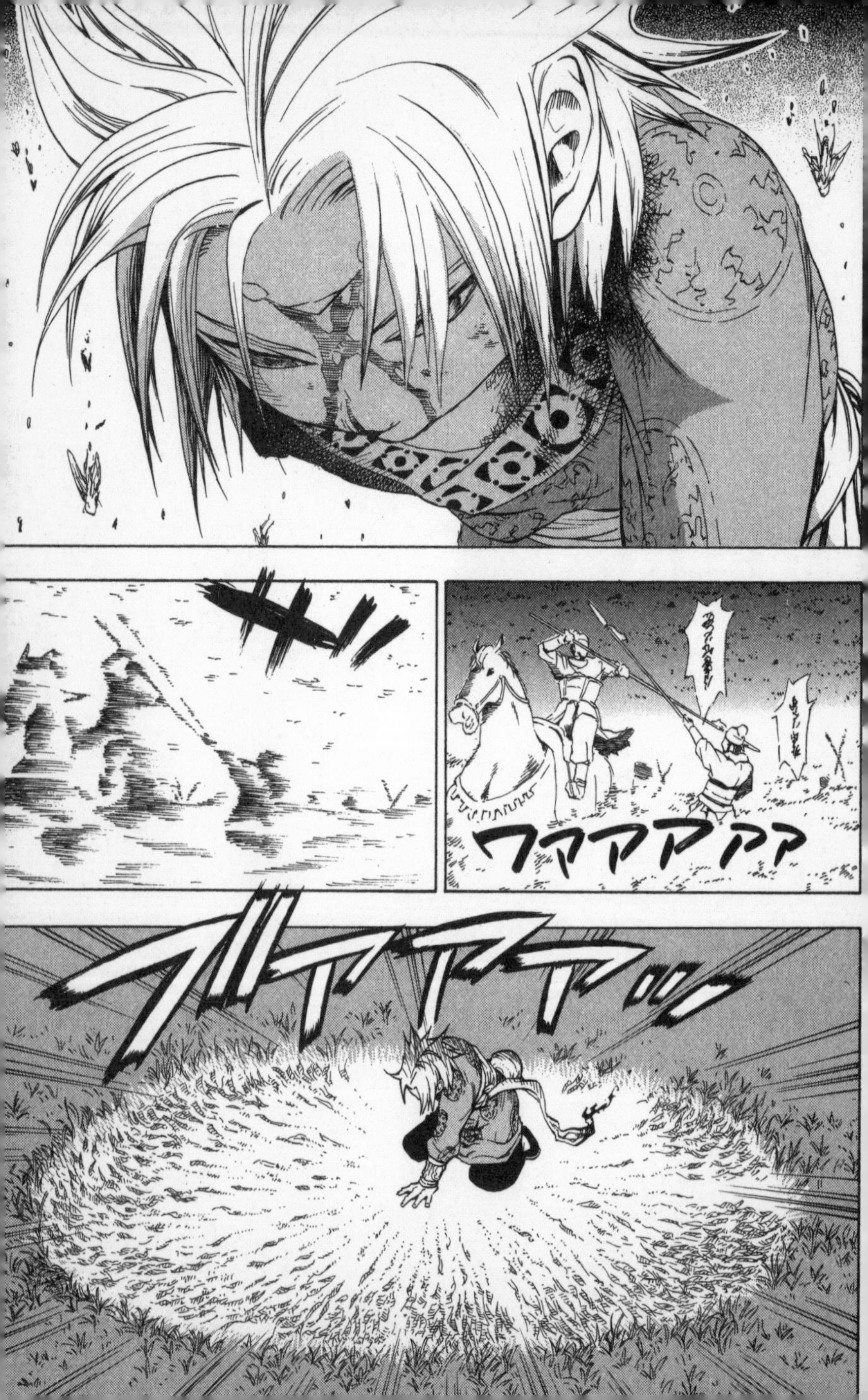
ワァアアアア
ザッ
ブワァァァッ

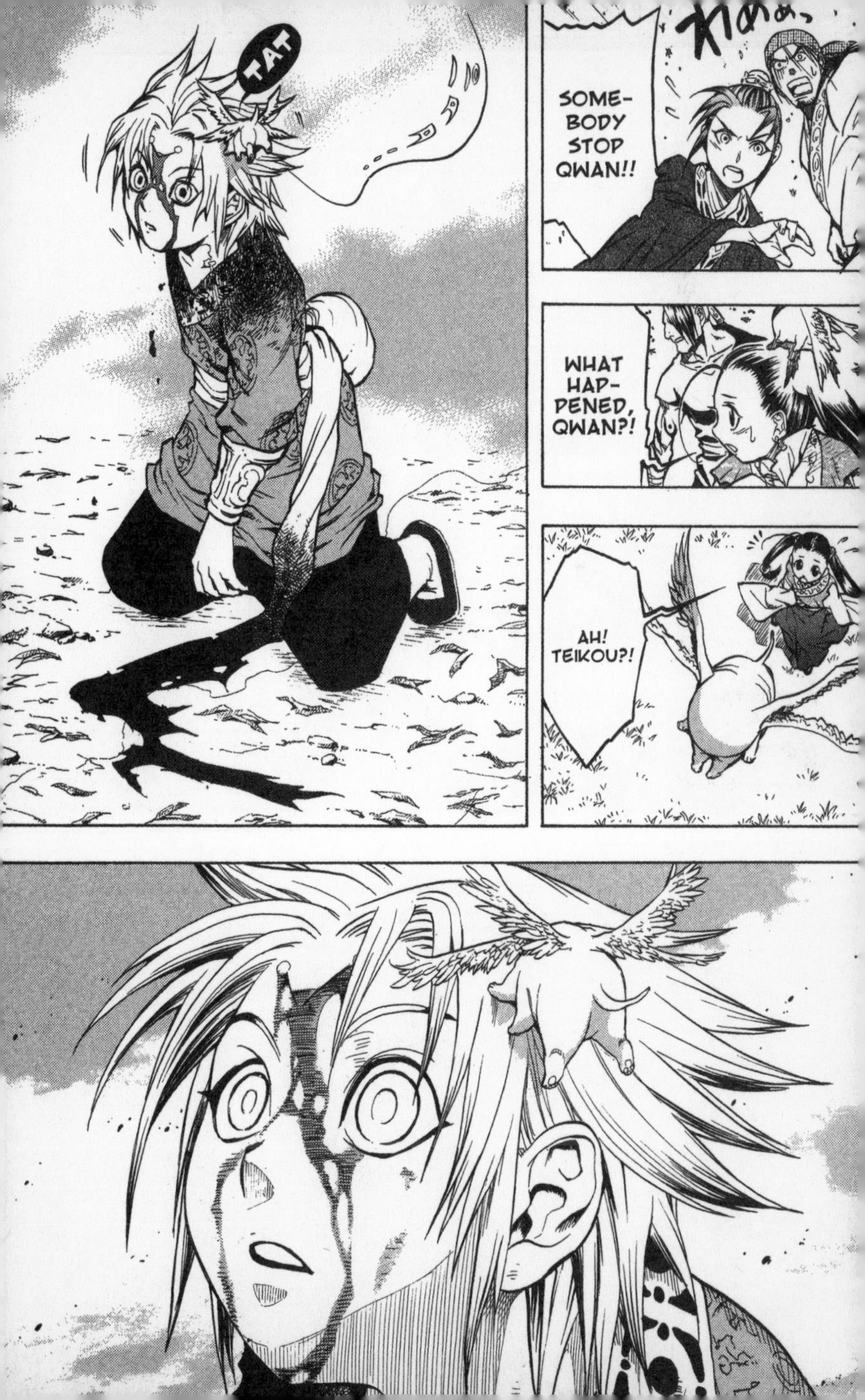
SOME-BODY STOP QWAN!!
WHAT HAP-PENED, QWAN?!
AH! TEIKOU?!
TAT

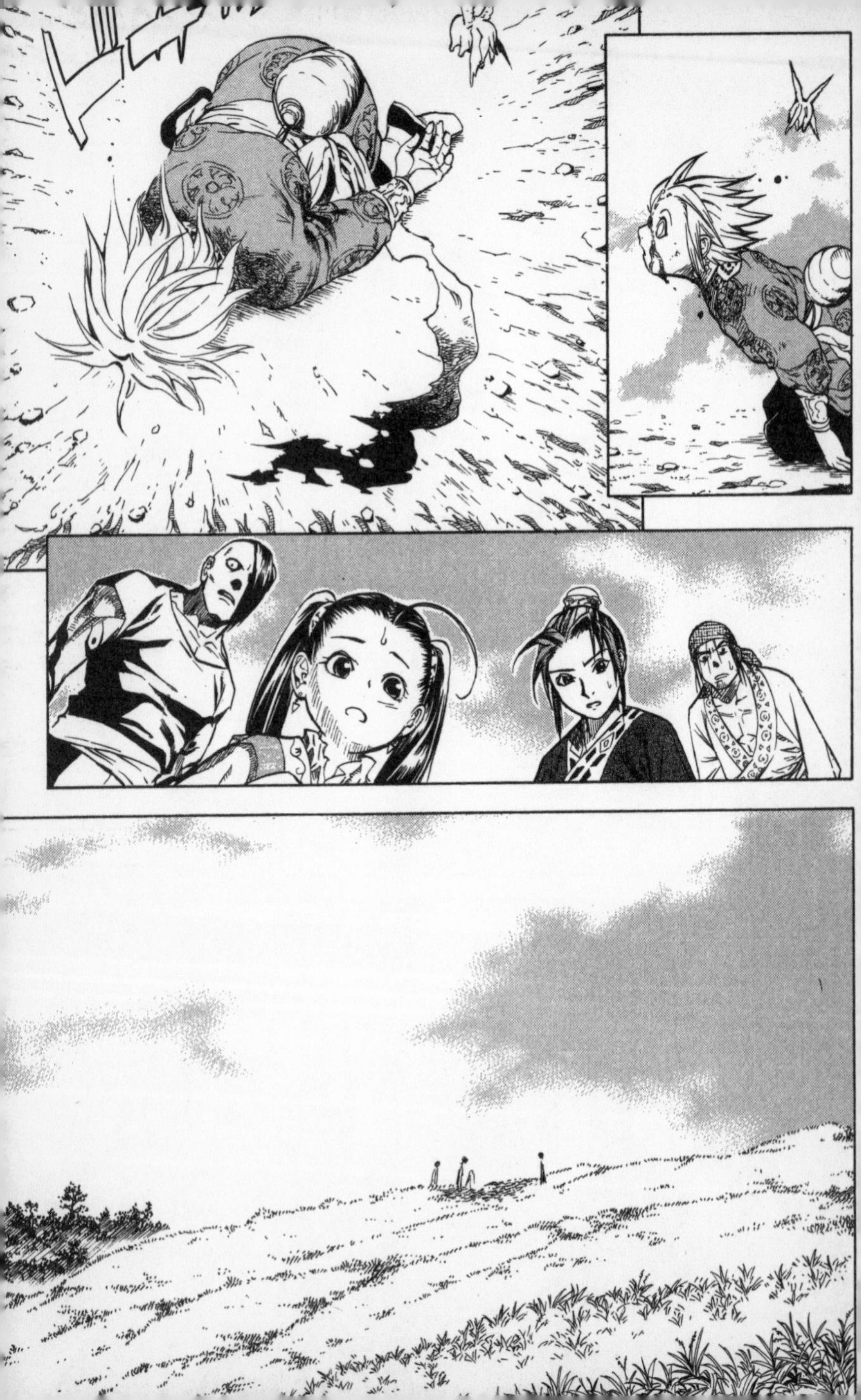

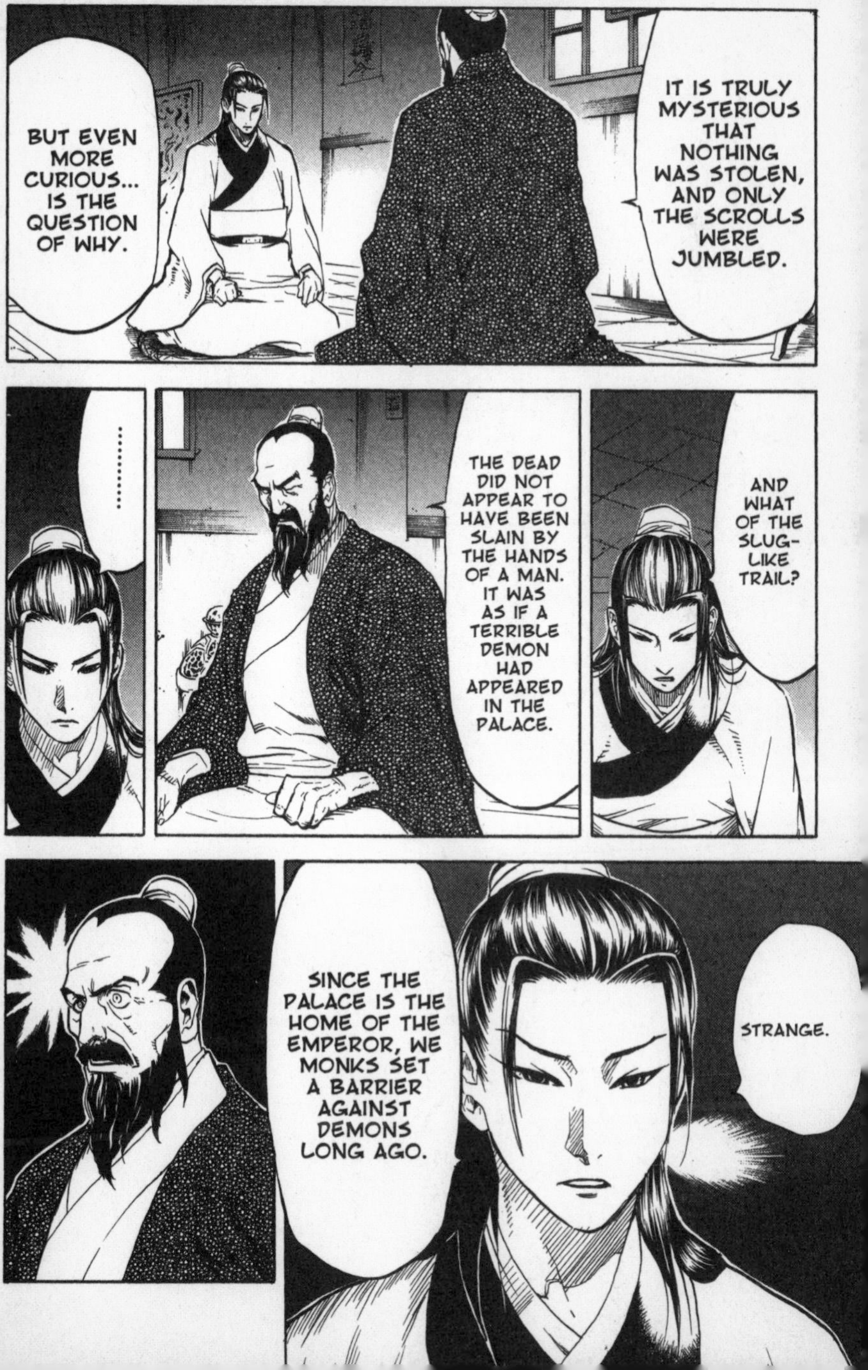
IT IS TRULY MYSTERIOUS THAT NOTHING WAS STOLEN, AND ONLY THE SCROLLS WERE JUMBLED.
BUT EVEN MORE CURIOUS... IS THE QUESTION OF WHY.
AND WHAT OF THE SLUG-LIKE TRAIL?
THE DEAD DID NOT APPEAR TO HAVE BEEN SLAIN BY THE HANDS OF A MAN. IT WAS AS IF A TERRIBLE DEMON HAD APPEARED IN THE PALACE.
....
STRANGE.
SINCE THE PALACE IS THE HOME OF THE EMPEROR, WE MONKS SET A BARRIER AGAINST DEMONS LONG AGO.

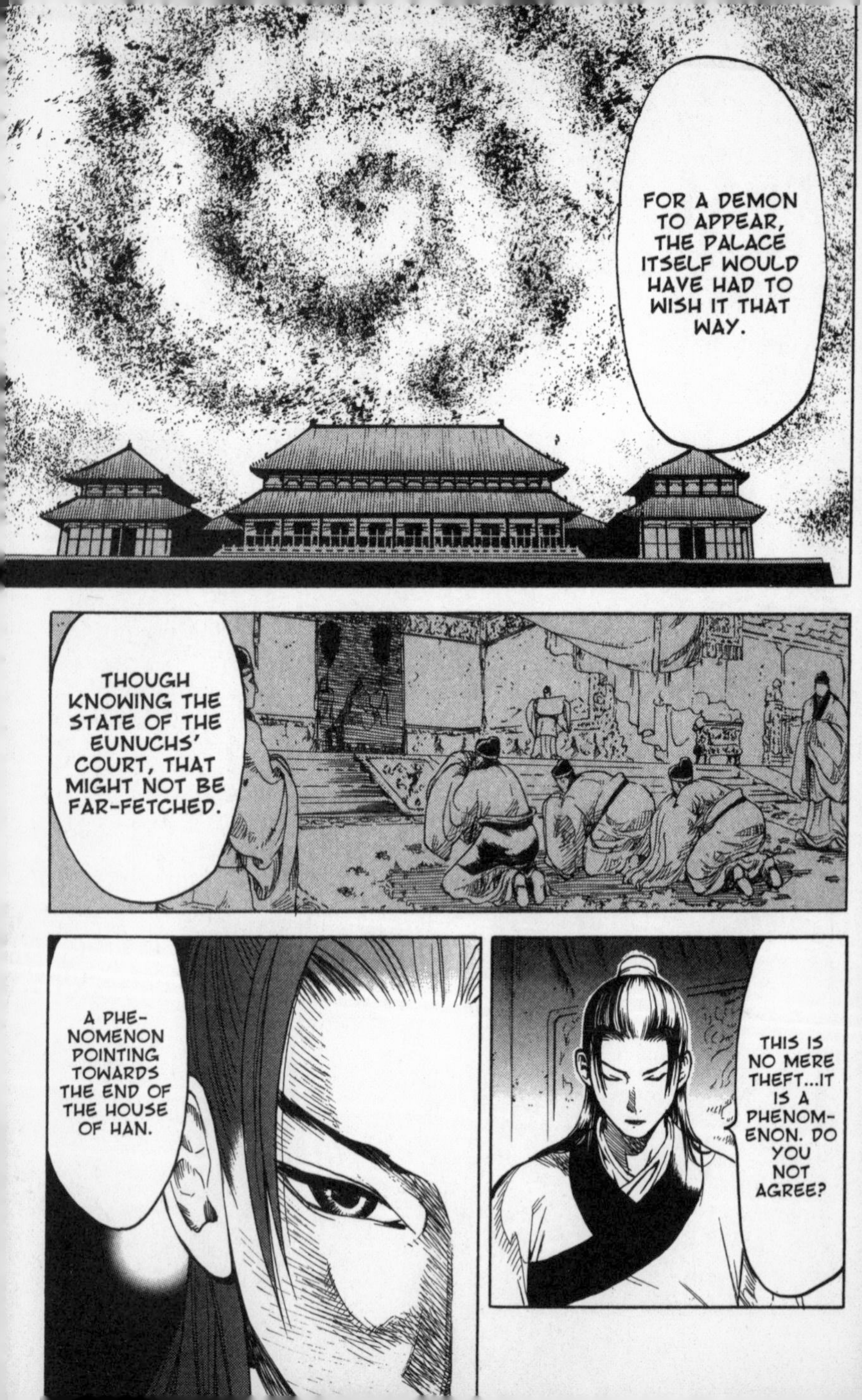
FOR A DEMON TO APPEAR, THE PALACE ITSELF WOULD HAVE HAD TO WISH IT THAT WAY.
THOUGH KNOWING THE STATE OF THE EUNUCHS' COURT, THAT MIGHT NOT BE FAR-FETCHED.
THIS IS NO MERE THEFT...IT IS A PHENOMENON. DO YOU NOT AGREE?
A PHENOMENON POINTING TOWARDS THE END OF THE HOUSE OF HAN.

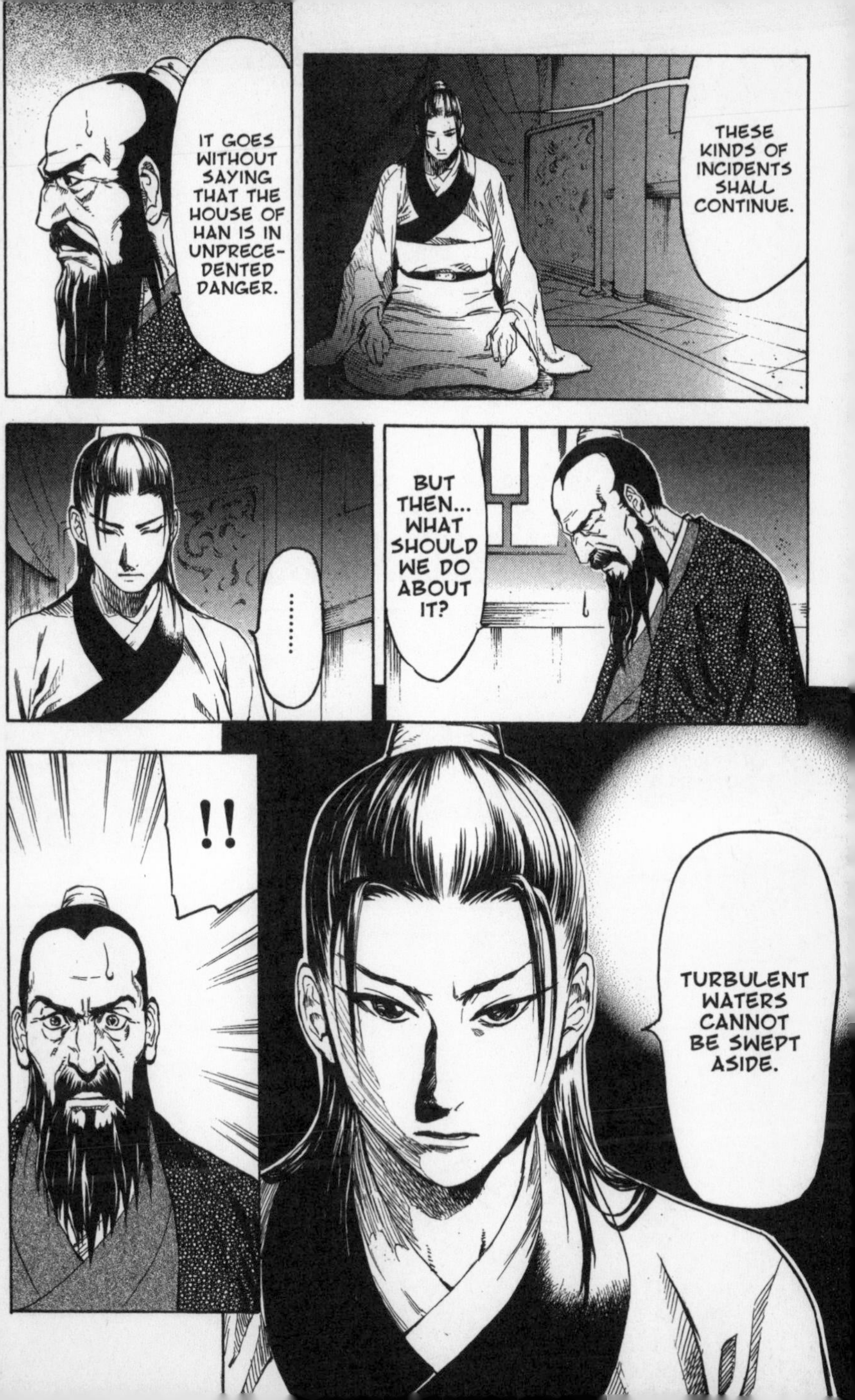
THESE KINDS OF INCIDENTS SHALL CONTINUE.
IT GOES WITHOUT SAYING THAT THE HOUSE OF HAN IS IN UNPRECEDENTED DANGER.
BUT THEN... WHAT SHOULD WE DO ABOUT IT?
....
TURBULENT WATERS CANNOT BE SWEPT ASIDE.
!!

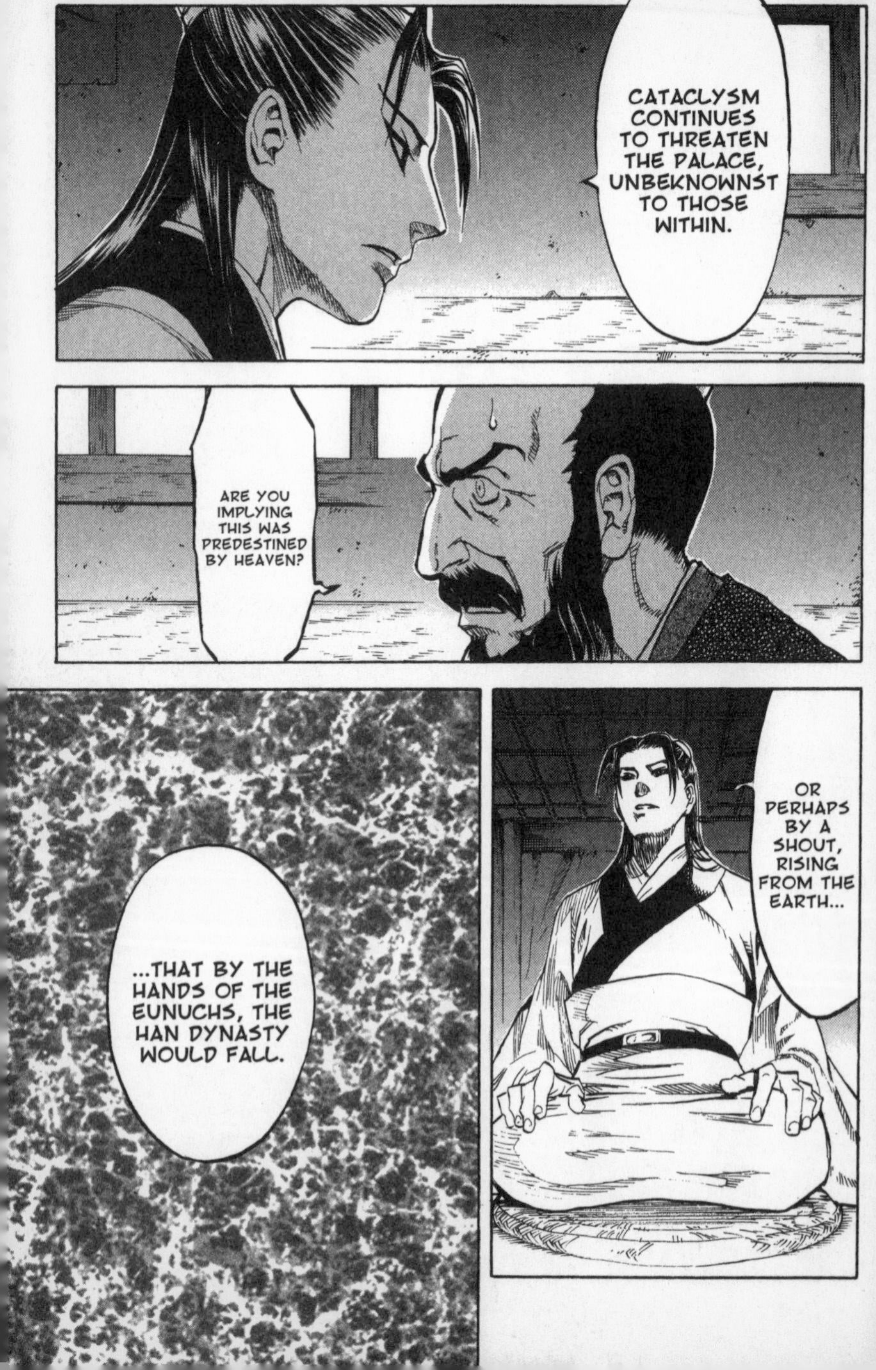
CATACLYSM CONTINUES TO THREATEN THE PALACE, UNBEKNOWNST TO THOSE WITHIN.
ARE YOU IMPLYING THIS WAS PREDESTINED BY HEAVEN?
OR PERHAPS BY A SHOUT, RISING FROM THE EARTH...
...THAT BY THE HANDS OF THE EUNUCHS, THE HAN DYNASTY WOULD FALL.

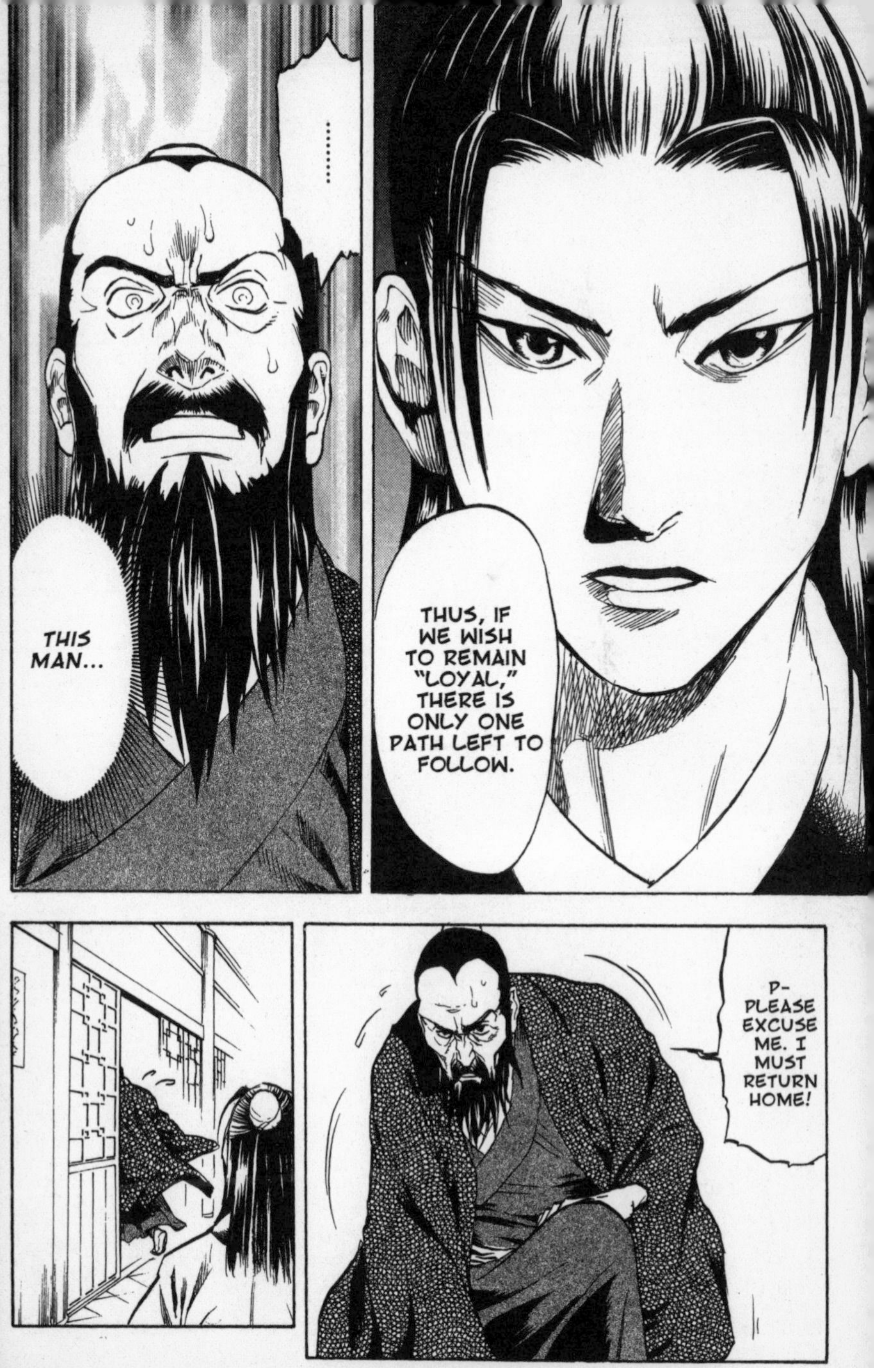
THUS, IF WE WISH TO REMAIN "LOYAL," THERE IS ONLY ONE PATH LEFT TO FOLLOW.
......
THIS MAN...
P-PLEASE EXCUSE ME. I MUST RETURN HOME!

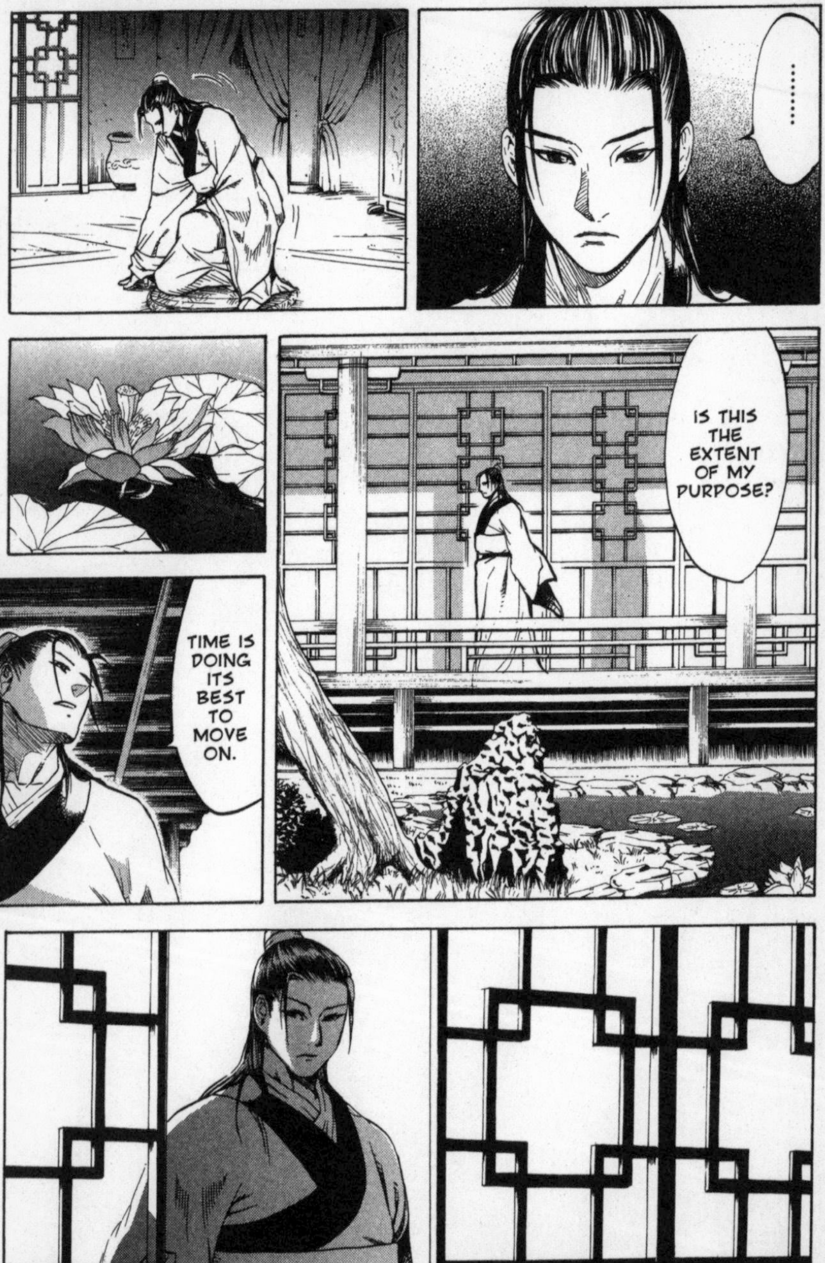
......
IS THIS THE EXTENT OF MY PURPOSE?
TIME IS DOING ITS BEST TO MOVE ON.

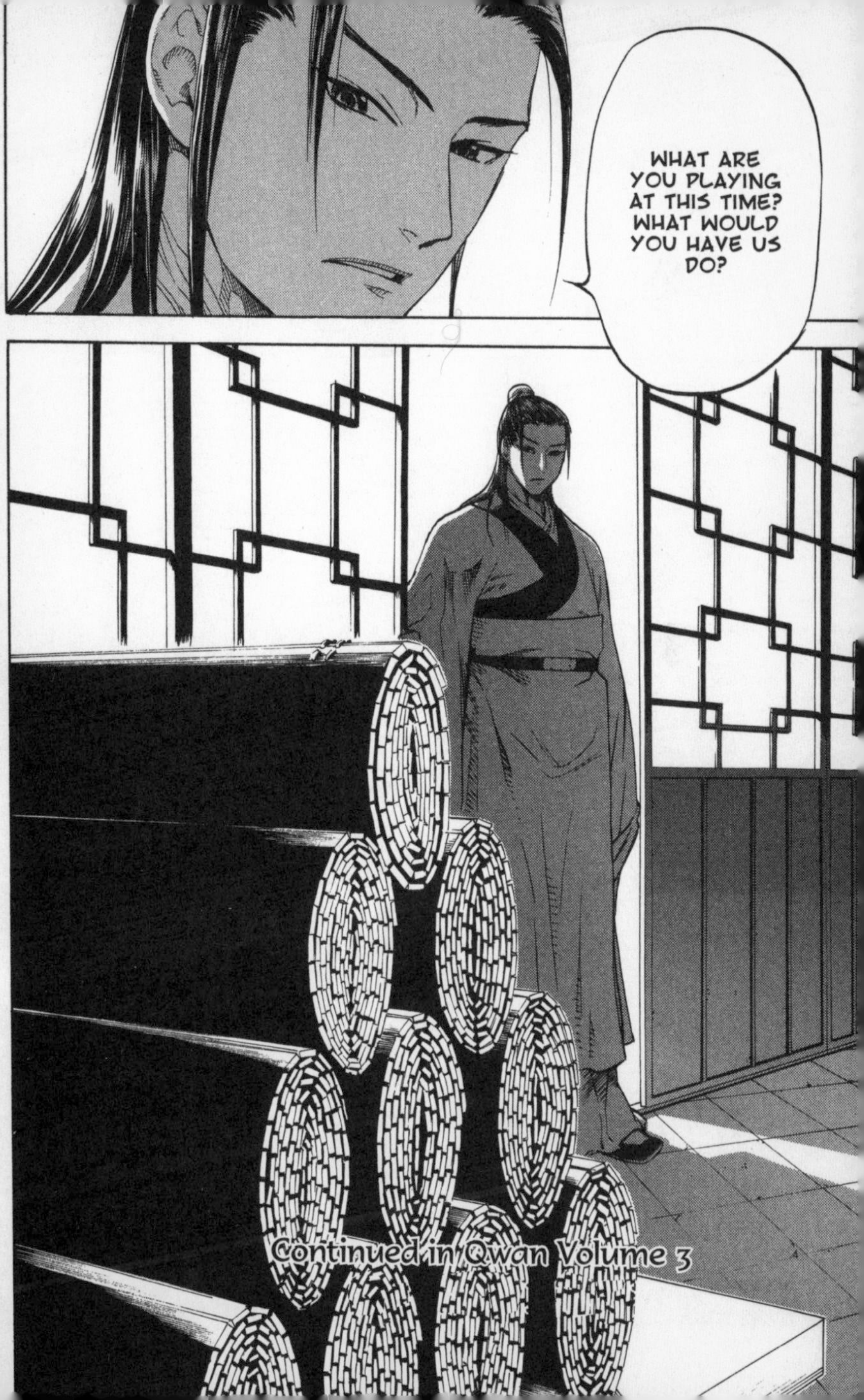
WHAT ARE YOU PLAYING AT THIS TIME? WHAT WOULD YOU HAVE US DO?
Continued in Qwan Volume 3

~Afterword~

Thank you very much for buying Qwan Volume 2! Several characters in this manga are actually real historical figures: for example, Aman, Cao Jie, Chin Ban and Jou Kai (among others). Those interested in Chinese history may enjoy reading up on them.

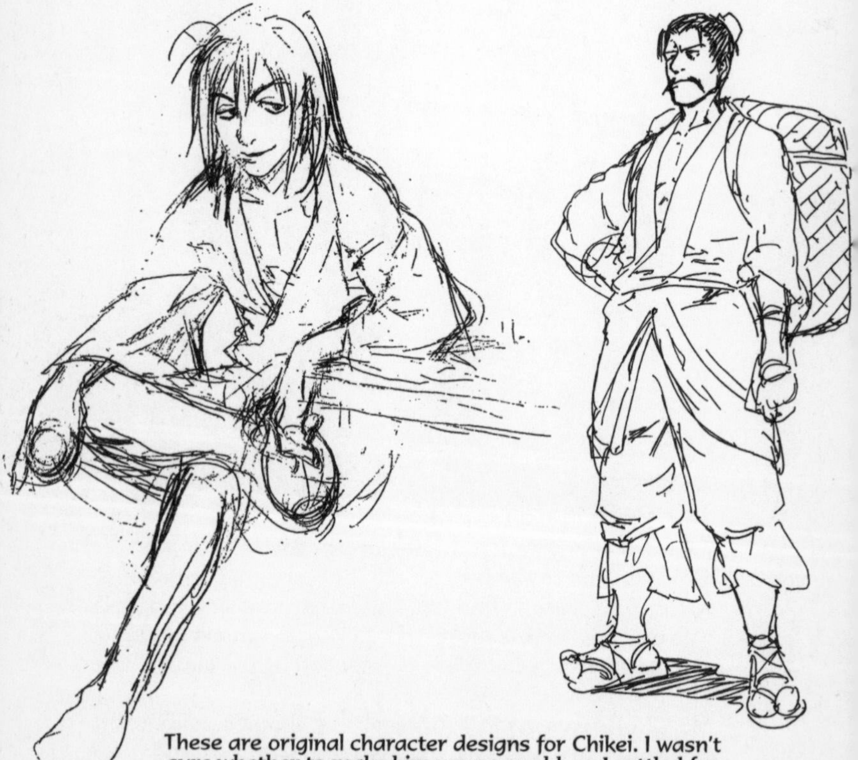

These are original character designs for Chikei. I wasn't sure whether to make him young or old, so I settled for something in between...

In the Third Chronicle of Qwan...

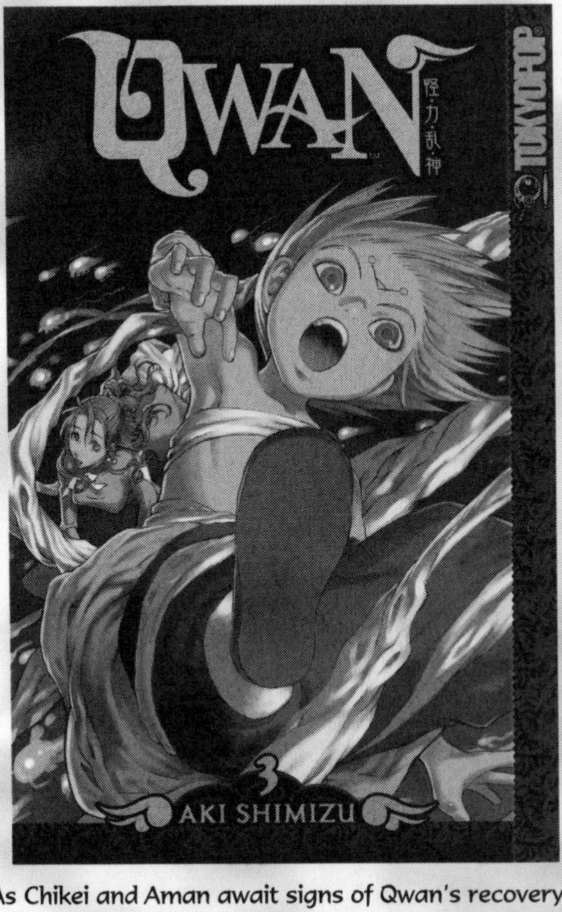
QWAN
怪・力・乱・神
TOKYOPOP
3
AKI SHIMIZU

As Chikei and Aman await signs of Qwan's recovery, Daki returns to the bug forest in an attempt to save it. Meanwhile, Yuushi finds that the aristocrat Jou Kai now possesses the Essential Arts of Peace. Who is Jou Kai really, and what is his connection to the scroll?

More surprises await as we learn of Shaga's connection to Qwan, journey to the land of Qwan's origin...and meet the author of the Essential Arts of Peace, who has the power to explain it all!

TOKYOPOP SHOP

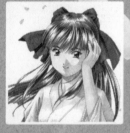
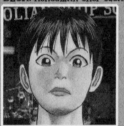

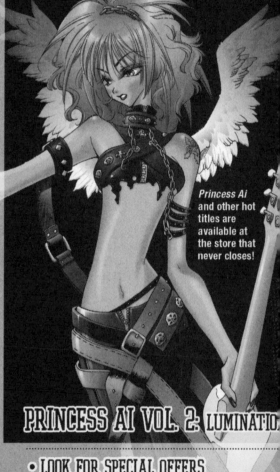

that I'm not like other people...

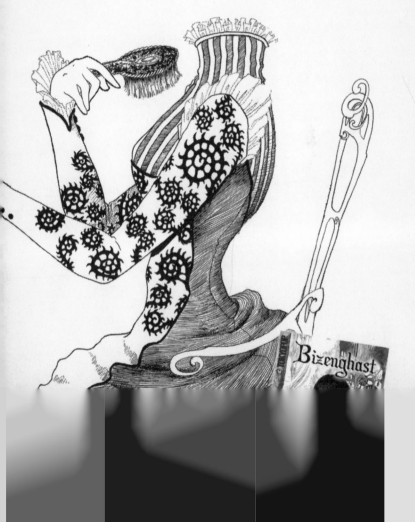

Bizenghast

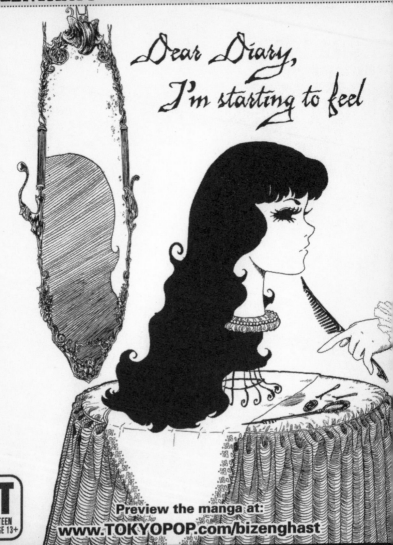

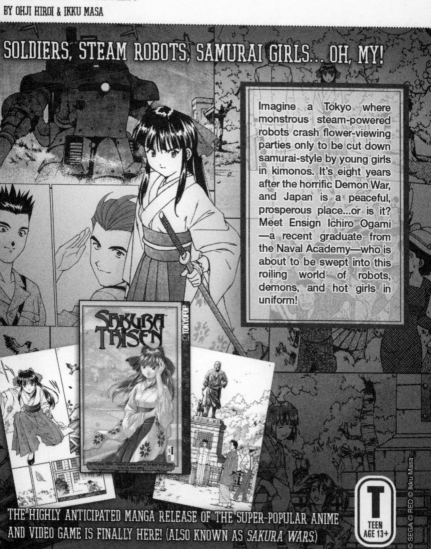

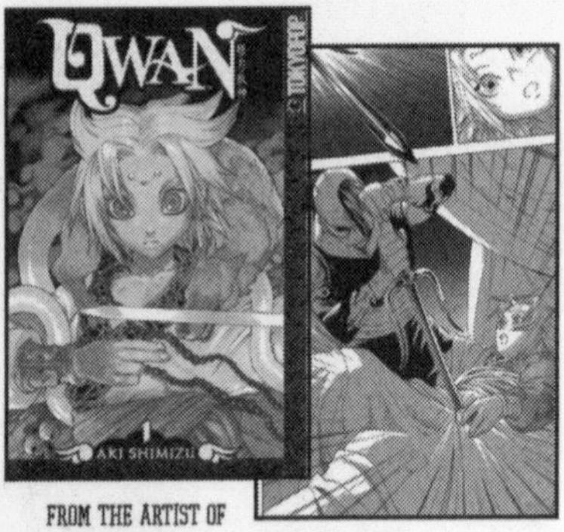
QWAN
1
AKI SHIMIZU
TOKYOPOP

FROM THE ARTIST OF SUIKODEN III

BY AKI SHIMIZU

QWAN

Qwan is a series that refuses to be pigeonholed. Aki Shimizu combines Chinese history, mythology, fantasy and humor to create a world that is familiar yet truly unique. Her creature designs are particularly brilliant—from mascots to monsters. And Qwan himself is great—fallen to Earth, he's like a little kid, complete with the loud questions, yet he eats demons for breakfast. In short, *Qwan* is a solid story with great character dynamics, amazing art and some kick-ass battle scenes. What's not to like?

~Carol Fox, Editor

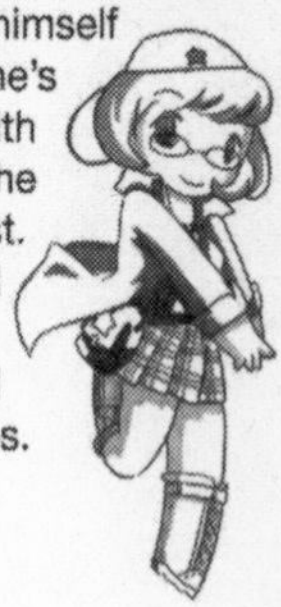

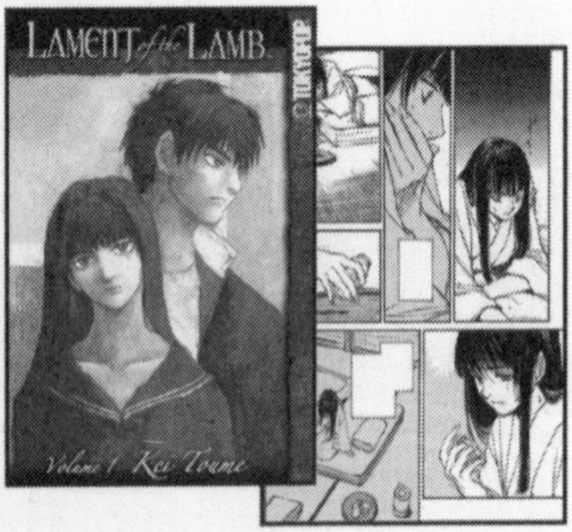
LAMENT of the LAMB
TOKYOPOP
Volume 1 Kei Toume

BY KEI TOUME

LAMENT OF THE LAMB

Kei Toume's *Lament of the Lamb* follows the physical and mental torment of Kazuna Takashiro, who discovers that he's cursed with a hereditary disease that makes him crave blood. *Lament* is psychological horror at its best—it's gloomy, foreboding and emotionally wrenching. Toume brilliantly treats the story's vampirism in a realistic, subdued way, and it becomes a metaphor for teenage alienation, twisted sexual desire and insanity. While reading each volume, I get goose bumps, I feel uneasy, and I become increasingly depressed. Quite a compliment for a horror series!

~Paul Morrissey, Editor

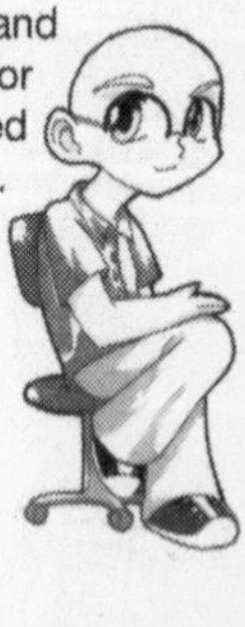

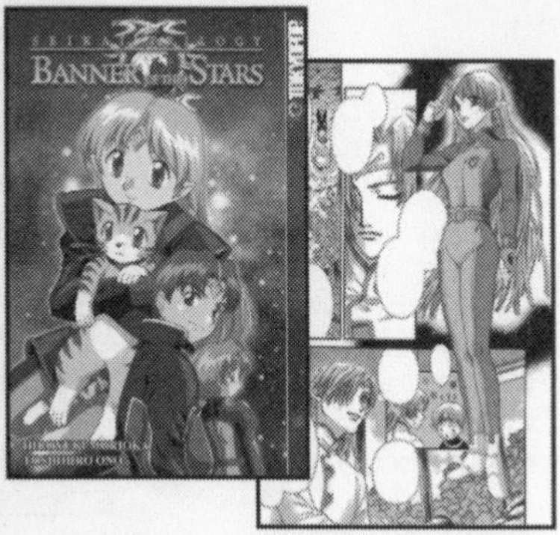
BANNER
STARS

THE SEIKAI TRILOGY

The Seikai Trilogy is one of TOKYOPOP's most underrated series. Although the trilogy gained popularity through the release of the anime, the manga brings a vitality to the characters that I feel the anime never did. The story is a heart-warming, exciting sci-fi adventure epic, the likes of which we haven't seen since *Star Wars. Banner of the Stars II*, the series' finale, is a real page-turner—a prison colony's security is compromised due to violent intergalactic politics. Each manga corresponds to the story from the novel…however, unless you read Japanese, the only way to enjoy the story thus far is through these faithful comic adaptations.

~Luis Reyes, Editor

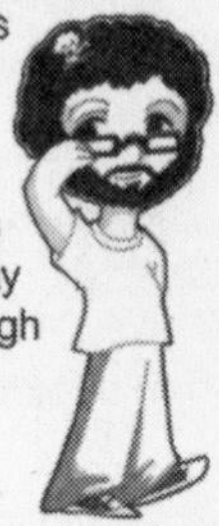

BY AYA YOSHINAGA, HIROYUKI MORIOKA, TOSHIHIRO ONO, AND WASOH MIYAKOSHI

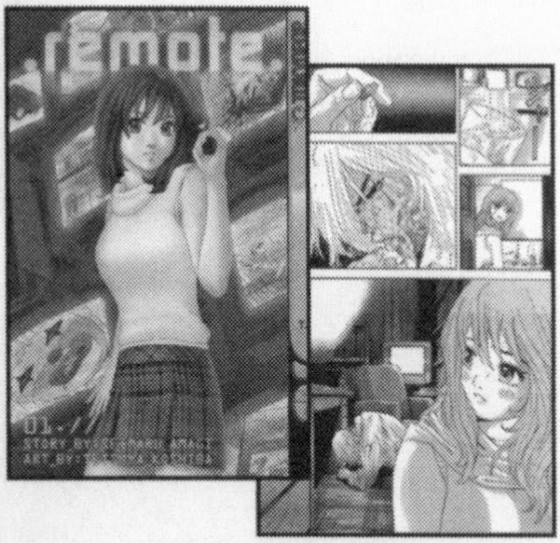
remote

REMOTE

Imagine Pam Anderson starring in *The Silence of the Lambs* and you've got a hint of what to expect from Seimaru Amagi and Tetsuya Koshiba's *Remote*. Completely out of her element, Officer Kurumi Ayaki brings down murderers, mad bombers and would-be assassins, all under the guidance of the reclusive Inspector Himuro. There's no shortage of fan-service and ultraviolence as Kurumi stumbles through her cases, but it's nicely balanced by the forensic police work of the brilliant Himuro, a man haunted by his past and struggling with suppressed emotions awakened by the adorable Kurumi.

~Bryce P. Coleman, Editor

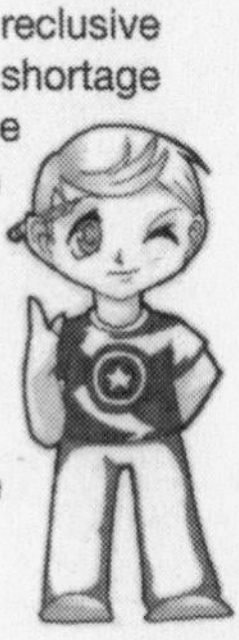

BY SEIMARU AMAGI AND TETSUYA KOSHIBA

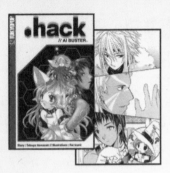

.HACK//AI BUSTER – NOVEL
BY TATSUYA HAMAZAKI

In the epic prequel to *.hack*, the avatar Albireo is a solo adventurer in The World, the most advanced online fantasy game ever created. When he comes across Lycoris, a strange little girl in a dungeon, he soon comes to realize that she may hold a very deadly secret—a secret that could unhinge everything in cyberspace... and beyond!

Discover the untold origins of the phenomenon known as *.hack*!

© Tatsuya Hamazaki © Rei Izumi

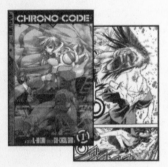

CHRONO CODE
BY EUI-CHEOL SHIN & IL-HO CHOI

Time flows like a river, without changing its course. This is an escape from the river's flow...

Three people must cross time and space to find each other and change their destinies. However, a powerful satellite, a secret code and the future police impede their progress, and their success hinges on an amnesiac who must first uncover the true nature of her past in order to discover who her friends are in the future.

T TEEN AGE 13+

© IL-HO CHOI & EUI-CHEOL SHIN, DAIWON C.I. Inc.

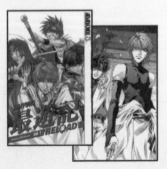

SAIYUKI RELOAD
BY KAZUYA MINEKURA

Join Sanzo, Gojyo, Hakkai, Goku and their updated wardrobe as they continue their journey west toward Shangri-La, encountering new challenges and new adventures along the way. But don't be fooled by their change in costume: The fearsome foursome is just as ferocious and focused as before...if not more so.

The hit manga that inspired the anime, and the sequel to TOKYOPOP's hugely popular *Saiyuki*!

OT OLDER TEEN AGE 16+

© Kazuya Minekura

STOP!

This is the back of the book.
You wouldn't want to spoil a great ending!

This book is printed "manga-style," in the authentic Japanese right-to-left format. Since none of the artwork has been flipped or altered, readers get to experience the story just as the creator intended. You've been asking for it, so TOKYOPOP® delivered: authentic, hot-off-the-press, and far more fun!

DIRECTIONS

If this is your first time reading manga-style, here's a quick guide to help you understand how it works.

It's easy... just start in the top right panel and follow the numbers. Have fun, and look for more 100% authentic manga from TOKYOPOP®!

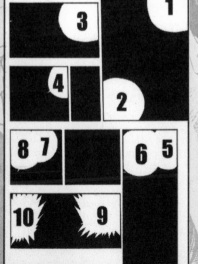

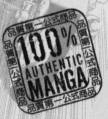

Wherein Qwan Is Attacked by Two Wasp Demons

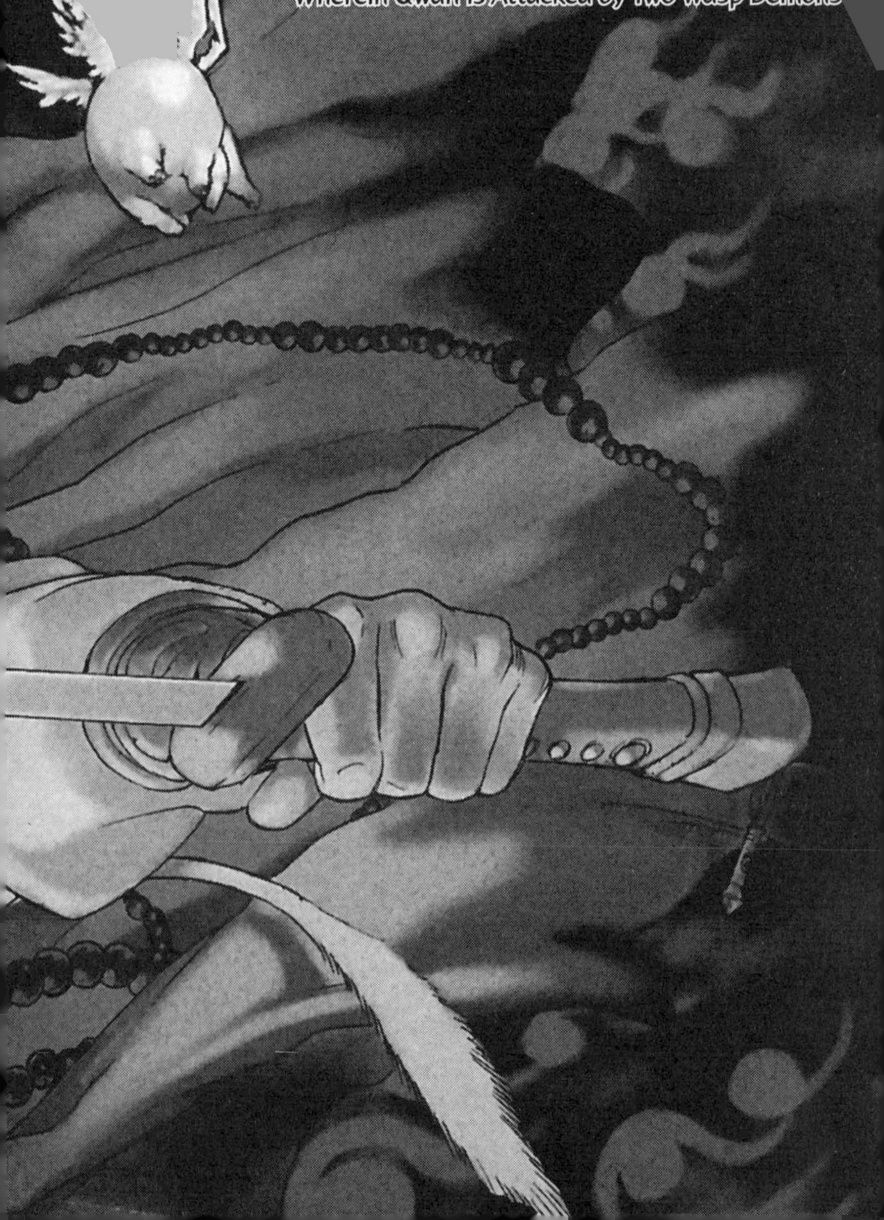